Lecture Notes in Computer Science 9182

Commenced Publication in 1973
Founding and Former Series Editors:
Gerhard Goos, Juris Hartmanis, and Jan van Leeuwen

More information about this series at http://www.springer.com/series/7409

Gabriele Meiselwitz (Ed.)

Social Computing and Social Media

7th International Conference, SCSM 2015
Held as Part of HCI International 2015
Los Angeles, CA, USA, August 2–7, 2015
Proceedings

 Springer

Editor
Gabriele Meiselwitz
Department of Computer
    and Information Sciences
Towson University
Towson, MD
USA

ISSN 0302-9743   ISSN 1611-3349 (electronic)
Lecture Notes in Computer Science
ISBN 978-3-319-20366-9   ISBN 978-3-319-20367-6 (eBook)
DOI 10.1007/978-3-319-20367-6

Library of Congress Control Number: 2015941127

LNCS Sublibrary: SL3 – Information Systems and Applications, incl. Internet/Web, and HCI

Printed on acid-free paper

Springer International Publishing AG Switzerland is part of Springer Science+Business Media
(www.springer.com)

Foreword

The 17th International Conference on Human-Computer Interaction, HCI International 2015, was held in Los Angeles, CA, USA, during 2–7 August 2015. The event incorporated the 15 conferences/thematic areas listed on the following page.

A total of 4843 individuals from academia, research institutes, industry, and governmental agencies from 73 countries submitted contributions, and 1462 papers and 246 posters have been included in the proceedings. These papers address the latest research and development efforts and highlight the human aspects of design and use of computing systems. The papers thoroughly cover the entire field of Human-Computer Interaction, addressing major advances in knowledge and effective use of computers in a variety of application areas. The volumes constituting the full 28-volume set of the conference proceedings are listed on pages VII and VIII.

I would like to thank the Program Board Chairs and the members of the Program Boards of all thematic areas and affiliated conferences for their contribution to the highest scientific quality and the overall success of the HCI International 2015 conference.

This conference could not have been possible without the continuous and unwavering support and advice of the founder, Conference General Chair Emeritus and Conference Scientific Advisor, Prof. Gavriel Salvendy. For their outstanding efforts, I would like to express my appreciation to the Communications Chair and Editor of HCI International News, Dr. Abbas Moallem, and the Student Volunteer Chair, Prof. Kim-Phuong L. Vu. Finally, for their dedicated contribution towards the smooth organization of HCI International 2015, I would like to express my gratitude to Maria Pitsoulaki and George Paparoulis, General Chair Assistants.

May 2015

Constantine Stephanidis
General Chair, HCI International 2015

HCI International 2015 Thematic Areas and Affiliated Conferences

Thematic areas:

- Human-Computer Interaction (HCI 2015)
- Human Interface and the Management of Information (HIMI 2015)

Affiliated conferences:

- 12th International Conference on Engineering Psychology and Cognitive Ergonomics (EPCE 2015)
- 9th International Conference on Universal Access in Human-Computer Interaction (UAHCI 2015)
- 7th International Conference on Virtual, Augmented and Mixed Reality (VAMR 2015)
- 7th International Conference on Cross-Cultural Design (CCD 2015)
- 7th International Conference on Social Computing and Social Media (SCSM 2015)
- 9th International Conference on Augmented Cognition (AC 2015)
- 6th International Conference on Digital Human Modeling and Applications in Health, Safety, Ergonomics and Risk Management (DHM 2015)
- 4th International Conference on Design, User Experience and Usability (DUXU 2015)
- 3rd International Conference on Distributed, Ambient and Pervasive Interactions (DAPI 2015)
- 3rd International Conference on Human Aspects of Information Security, Privacy and Trust (HAS 2015)
- 2nd International Conference on HCI in Business (HCIB 2015)
- 2nd International Conference on Learning and Collaboration Technologies (LCT 2015)
- 1st International Conference on Human Aspects of IT for the Aged Population (ITAP 2015)

Conference Proceedings Volumes Full List

Social Computing and Social Media

Program Board Chair: Gabriele Meiselwitz, USA

- Leonelo Almeida, Brazil
- Ania Bobrowicz, UK
- James Braman, USA
- Farzin Deravi, UK
- Carsten Kleiner, Germany
- Niki Lambropoulos, Greece
- Fernando Loizides, Cyprus
- Anthony Norcio, USA
- Darius Plikynas, Lithuania
- Portia Pusey, USA
- Elaine Raybourn, USA
- Stefan Stieglitz, Germany
- Giovanni Vincenti, USA
- Evgenios Vlachos, Denmark
- Yuanqiong (Kathy) Wang, USA
- June Wei, USA
- Brian Wentz, USA

The full list with the Program Board Chairs and the members of the Program Boards of all Thematic Areas and Affiliated Conferences is available online at:

http://www.hci.international/2015/

HCI International 2016

The 18th International Conference on Human-Computer Interaction, HCI International 2016, will be held jointly with the affiliated conferences in Toronto, Canada, at the Westin Harbour Castle Hotel, 17–22 July 2016. It will cover a broad spectrum of themes related to Human-Computer Interaction, including theoretical issues, methods, tools, processes, and case studies in HCI design, as well as novel interaction techniques, interfaces, and applications. The proceedings will be published by Springer. More information will be available on the conference website: http://2016.hci.international/.

General Chair
Prof. Constantine Stephanidis
University of Crete and ICS-FORTH
Heraklion, Crete, Greece
Email: general_chair@hcii2016.org

http://2016.hci.international/

Contents

Designing Social Media

Utilizing Virtual Worlds for Personalized Search: Developing the PAsSIVE Framework

James Braman[1(✉)] and Charles Dierbach[2]

[1] School of Applied and Information Technology, Community College of Baltimore County, 7201 Rossville Boulevard, Rosedale, MD, USA
jbraman@ccbcmd.edu
[2] Department of Computer and Information Sciences, Towson University, 8000 York Rd, Towson, MD, USA
cdierbach@towson.edu

Abstract. Search engine technology has greatly enhanced our ability to filter through the chaos of finding relevant information online. Despite the current capabilities, however, there is the promise of further improvement through the use of personalization and alternative interfaces. In this paper we examine one such alternative named PAsSIVE (Personalized Assisted Search in a Virtual Environment). PAsSIVE immerses the user in the virtual world of Second Life in which results are rendered. As part of this research, we investigate the design and development of a 3D search interface, and reflect on insights gained. This paper also discusses future work related to personalization and proactive search.

Keywords: Virtual worlds · Personalized search · Second life · PAsSIVE

1 Introduction

There have been a growing number of 3D environments that have emerged for a vast array of purposes and target age groups [14]. With a wide range of multi-user virtual environments (MUVEs) available today, social interactions and applications of all kinds are increasingly common place. Adding to these forms of interaction, there is the possibility of extensions and integration into other applications through scripting languages, allowing for additional features. From this added flexibility, some virtual worlds allow for the possibility of interacting with web data in a more realistic and natural way. Despite the diverse virtual worlds and features available, they all have some common characteristics, particularly with the user's representation, the avatar. An avatar is a personification of the user as an interactive artifact, with a level of habitation (which enhances realism of the space) and a representation or sense of space [17]. MUVEs can be used in a range of domains, including education, simulation, data visualization, business, and much more, with far reaching implications [1, 24, 25].

Due to its popularity, flexibility and applicability for research, Second Life was chosen as the virtual world to utilize for this project. Second Life is an Internet based three-dimensional virtual world, created by Linden Labs. Other similar virtual environments include Twinity, Active Worlds and There. Linden Lab encourages creativity among its user base, and allows for the protection of Intellectual Property of created

G. Meiselwitz (Ed.): SCSM 2015, LNCS 9182, pp. 3–11, 2015.
DOI: 10.1007/978-3-319-20367-6_1

elements in-world. Users interact within Second Life with objects and other users. One can customize the appearance of their avatar, transform their environment (by creating virtual objects), communicate, collaborate and cooperate [11]. The "residents" of Second Life create content and communicate via text chat or voice communication. Interactive objects are built by using a scripting language (Linden Script Language) that is designed to theoretically be simple enough for those with little previous programming experience.

In this project, the aim is to use the inherent visual display and immersive qualities of Second Life for the main interface of a search engine, while alsoimproving the results through personalization. Many researchers agree that in order for search engines to effectively personalize results, they must tailor their actions based on information from individual users and web content [10]. It follows, therefore, that search engines should incorporate (a) the individual user's general interests, (b) the individual user's current information need, and (c) information about the content searched. The search agent PAsSIVE (Personalized Assisted Search in a Virtual Environment) is designed to use a virtual world interface while incorporating these three points towards personalization. Another unique aspect of the personalized search agent is the ability to perform self-directed, proactive search of web content while the user is offline. This feature adds new content to the search index, which is more specific to the user's general interests, building a more custom tailored set of links. As the system learns more about the user, search results are ranked using amulti-layered approach making use of both content, page structure and user interests.

To address the problem of users needing to sift through the many links of a search query, the PAsSIVE system search results are presented as a 3D visualization within Second Life. The user's avatar is used to both perform a search and navigate through the search results. The goal of the visualization is to present the resulting information in a more intuitive form than simply as a list of links. The goal of this work is to demonstrate the potential for personalized, proactive search in a 3D environment. The overall long term research questions for this project are: (1). What demonstrated potential is gained through this type of search framework? and (2). Is there demonstrated potential in satisfying a user's information need by the use of a 3D visualization of search results? In this paper, we reflect on feedback gained from the design of the interface as we seek to investigate our overall research questions expanding on our previous research [3].

2   Virtual Environments as a Search Interface

Over the past several years there have been a growing number of data, text and web mining tools that utilize traditional statistical analyses to find trends. Many of these tools differentiate themselves through various visualization techniques [26]. This same trend can also be seen with mainstream search engines, as the search interface visualization is how people interact with the system and is how links are displayed, serving an important role [12, 16]. As virtual worlds like Second Life have potential beyond their intended scope, we foresee many new creative and innovative developments from these technologies in the future, specifically regarding visualization.

The role of the interface for a virtual environment is to provide a graphical representation of the environment in which the user is interacting. In our case we are extending the interface to mean, not simply the environment "window" itself, but the graphical representation of our 3D search interface and its display of search results. PAsSIVE uses the virtual world to show the search results in an immersive way while being an interactive component of the user's avatar. This idea allows for interactions that limit the breaking of the "Magic Circle" while also potentially maintaining immersion by allowing all interactions for search to happen in-world. Many Projects have used 3D environments for visual displays and Information Retrieval purposes. These projects have used 3D spaces in a limited way to project a representation of images or results to help the user view content [6, 19]. These experimental systems have included the display of shapes or colors to display document similarity or explored content, or by using spatial metaphors to assist with navigation [13]. There have been other initiatives aimed at visualizing web content by displaying traditional 2D lists into a 3D space [18] or by using other variations on treemaps [8]. Others aimed at creating virtual objects such as virtual interactive "books" that mimic a physical book where one can flip through "pages" of similar content [5]. In contrast, implementations using technologies such as VRML for 3D interface applications for use on the web has generally not caught on.

Several major industries have gained substantial benefits from using 3D representations such as in medical imagery, architecture, and computer aided design [20]. Advancements in display technology, including the Oculus Rift, have afforded new possibilities for visualizations [15]. As cited by Rohrer [18], there are several common approaches for visualizing hierarchal data: cone trees, treemaps and hyperbolic browsers. Objects that represent information can be displayed in a way to emphasize certain data by changing size, height or surface appearance [7]. Additionally, the VR-Net project of Cleary et al. [9] used a VRML based interface to visualize related search results in a virtual space. Pages are represented as basic objects (box, cone, cylinder, line and spheres) and displayed based on reaction to the query and other topics related to the topic.

There have been several attempts to visualize large quantities of information by researchers in the domain of information visualization. However, very limited research has been conducted using virtual worlds or online games for visualization. One example of an integrated application is the Sloodle browser, an open source Second Life tool in which avatars can collaboratively interact to view web content often associated with the Moodle Learning Management System [22]. Another example is Daden Limited's DataGlobe, a 3D interactive globe created for Second Life that can be clicked on specific areas to view information about an item or information on a nearby display screen [2]. DataGlobe was made interactive via LSL and linked data feeds and other outside information from the web. In a separate project by Daden, live air traffic data can be visualized in Second Life. Smallman et al. [23] have a similar display using a traditional 3D display of aircraft data. Virtual worlds in particular are very flexible simulations that can incorporate degrees of real and unreal elements. Due to the potential of interactivity, flexibility and the benefits of 3D search interfaces, coupled with the rise of popularity of virtual worlds, we have chosen to design PAsSIVE's interface as a virtual browsing object or component as described in the next section.

2.1   The Virtual Browsing Component (VBC)

Unique to the design of PAsSIVE is its interface. To our knowledge, no other personalized search engine currently uses an online game or virtual world as its primary interface. Since PAsSIVE is integrated into Second Life, users need a representation (avatar) in the environment. The user controls their avatar to interact within the world of Second Life, and specifically with the Virtual Browsing Component (VBC). It is through the avatar that the user is able to search and view results. The location of the virtual browsing component is at a fixed point within Second Life and requires approximately 1024 meters of simulated land.

To use the PAsSIVE system, one's avatar would walk within ten meters of the VBC and click the search object to activate it. This object looks like a magnifying glass. The user can then "speak" (via the default text chat channel #10) the search query they which to submit to the system. The query is then intercepted and tokenized by a script written in the Linden Scripting Language (LSL), and then passed to a PHP script running on a webserver that is listening for search requests. LSL is required in order to make objects in Second Life interactive or to connect to external programs outside of Second Life. LSL "follows the familiar syntax of a C/Java style language, with an implicit state machine for every script" [4]. The framework for PAsSIVE is implemented in the Python programming language, but connects to Second Life using LSL via the HTTP request library. Data from any user interaction including query terms are sent to the agent, processed, and then sent back to SL. Based on the search query, the Search Personalization Component (SPC) sends back to the VBC the top 10 URLs that it has calculated to be the best match to satisfy the user's information need. Each of the 10 URL's returned are sent to individual display units that display a given URL and various personalization values as part of the interface.

A key benefit of using a 3D virtual environment is having the ability to manipulate multiple camera views and the avatar's positioning, and the ability to change virtual objects. Users of virtual worlds have certain expectations of interaction. As with most displays of information "Users will want to filter, select and restructure their information rapidly and with minimum effort" [21]. The display of search results follows this idea, with the presentation of personalized links in a simple, filtered approach that can be viewed in different ways and angles. Once a data sphere receives the URL data it represents, it changes its color and position (and sometimes movement) to indicate to the user the strength of likelihood that it matches their search interests. Above each sphere, the webpage appears for its respective URL. If the user clicks on a sphere, the actual webpage is loaded into the main display area, where the user can use and interact with the site as normal. When a user clicks on a website, that information is sent back to the SPC.

3   Preliminary Survey Discussion

A preliminary survey was conducted to gain insight into three main aspects of user interactions with search engines. This included collecting information on 1. Typical user search habits and encountered problems; 2. Participant willingness to interact within a 3D search engine environment compared to a traditional web based applications; and 3. Preferences for using personalization features. In the paper, we are only reporting the main findings related to the interface.

The survey was administered to two classes at Towson University (the second author's institution) in the fall of 2011 and 2012. Both classes consisted of 30 Information Technology students (for a total of 60 students for both semesters) in a class titled "Emerging Internet Technologies". This is an elective course for junior and senior IT majors. Due to the specific course content, all students surveyed had previously used search engines and were also familiar with the concept of search personalization, the basics of search engine functionality, and the use of virtual worlds (specifically Second Life). From both classes, fifty-seven participants responded for a 95.0 % completion rate. The average age of the participants was 23.9 years old and consisted of forty-five males and twelve females. The feedback obtained from the preliminary survey was advantageous in gaining better insight into the general problems, interactions and desired features of search engines from advanced users.

We were also able to gain some insights for the design on the 3D PAsSIVE interface survey. In general, from the participants surveyed, we were able to substantiate that search engines are used frequently, and that despite their usefulness, there is still considerable room for improvement to meet the needs for users. Fifty-six percent of the participants surveyed noted that they do use additional features (Advanced Search) offered by search engines to enhance their searches. Many also noted that their primary search engine still provides irrelevant search results despite the fact that they felt they were provided mostly good search results. Often there was still a need to update their query or evaluate additional links in order to satisfy their information need. Regarding the display of search results returned to the users, most (71.9 %) reported that they did not feel there was a need for any visual changes to the interface. Only a small number believed that changing the display of the results would have a beneficial effect on search engine usability (17.5 %). From the summary of responses from the proposed interface changes, there was a wide variety of comments without a consensus on any particular change. However, sixteen participants from those suggesting general improvements (28.0 %) did note that providing better or more refined search results would be useful. Regarding personalization specifically, the majority of the survey participants (65.0 %) responded "yes" or "maybe" regarding their willingness to use of a more personalized search engine, but some expressed concerns about privacy and the potential for more biased results.

The final part of the survey focused on gaining feedback regarding their potential use of a 3D search engine. When the students were asked if they would use such a system if one were available, the results were generally mixed. Thirty-five percent noted that they would not use such a program, 40.4 % of the participants said "Yes", and 24.5 % said "Maybe". In this particular study, the participants were not provided a particular visual representation of a prototype for that question. Comments, however, about the possibility of a 3D search engine revealed that such a program could be useful and potentially allow for quicker reading of results, while also potentially more distracting and harder to use.

Lastly, the participants were shown three images of a 3D display of a search interface. These were based on a general Tree Structure, a Search "Room", and also a set of linking virtual spheres in Second Life. When asked which potential display they would prefer as a 3D search engine interface, the results were mixed. It is important to note that with this question there was no discussion on how these prototype designs would specifically function; users were simply provided the image. An equal number of the participants (21) reported that they preferred the Tree structure and Link sphere design, while the remaining 14 participants preferred the idea of a "Search room". From this question we wanted to investigate if the participants had a particular preference for one design over another. Since the majority of users noted the first and last design, we improved the PAsSIVE interface to include a better display of the results and changed how the results were displayed. With a tree based structure, the hierarchical nature of the result placement can provide insightful meaning of relationships. Using this idea, combined with the original idea of the link sphere structure, the PAsSive interface was updated to provide a combination of these features.

4 Interface Survey

A second survey designed to gain insights into the construction of the interface of PAsSIVE was administered in the fall of 2013 in a course at Towson University titled: "Virtual Worlds: Impacts of Online Interaction". The participants for this survey were all very knowledgeable of Second Life, and had experience scripting and using advanced features and controls. All participants also had experience using interactive objects in-world and had spent at least one full semester using SL. Additionally, all participants were experienced search engine users. For this survey there were a total of 21 participants, with all 21 responding to the survey, yielding a 100 % response rate. The survey was administered electronically.

The survey consisted of two open-ended questions. The first question asked participants to imagine the idea of using a virtual world to search and view information online in a 3D space through an avatar, and "If a 3D search engine existed in Second Life, how would you imagine the information would appear or be displayed"? Table 1 summarizes the main points outlined by the participants, including response frequency.

Table 1. Summary of proposed display interface interaction

Main feature	Frequency (n = 21)
Floating screen, webpage or holographic display	7
Information displayed around user or in environments	5
User can choose view or display type	5
Displayed as a normal webpage	4
Search room or space	3
Virtual computer or object to be used by the avatar	3
Virtual objects are associated with the search	2
Includes voice or other sound	1
Clickable objects that display page	1
Heads-up Display (HUD)	1

While most responses for this question varied in detail and length, the "main feature" description was used to delineate the response in constructing the table below. Participants could list multiple features in their responses.

The second question described a particular scenario, and also included an image of a preliminary design of PAsSIVE and asked participants to comment. The following statements were provided:

How would you feel about a 3D search engine interface as provided in the image? In this example, websites are displayed based on what an avatar is searching for. The top search results are displayed as web pages around the user. If the user likes a page, and wants more information about it, they are able to click on the colored sphere where the page would load in the web browser. Please explain how you feel about the display in detail.

The purpose of this open-ended question was to gain additional feedback on the PAsSIVE interface as a result of the adjustments from the first survey administered. The image and scenario presented to the participants was based on the actual implementation of the program. The responses to this question was greatly varied and difficult to summarize. However, several general themes emerged. Twenty participants (95.2 %) expressed a positive sentiment towards the presented design. (One participant felt that the information presented was forcing 2D content into a 3D space, and preferred to use a regular browser.) Four participants (19 %) commented on the colored spheres, noting that they were either too big, unnecessary, or out of place. Generally, the comments did not indicate the need for major changes. Several comments pointed out such things as the potential need to change camera angles, and moving the avatar to view information more clearly (or zoom into the web page display area).

5 Discussion

Many of the results of the first survey did correlate with our expectations and the findings in the literature about search and search interface problems. The interface survey in particular was essential as we are making changes to the program and updating the design before carrying out more experiments and in-depth user testing. As the participants of the second survey were very familiar with Second Life, we were able to better understand how potential users of the system would view such an application. As a result of this information, the following changes are being implemented to improve the design:

- Shrinking the overall area of the interface to a more manageable size.
- Making the size and location of the colored spheres less obtrusive.
- Providing more feedback through the sphere about web pages in relation to a user's query.
- Including a link to a video tutorial and detailed instructions in text on how to use the system (which can be accessible in-world).
- Changing the display of the web pages for easier viewing.

Feedback obtained from both surveys was helpful making improvements and justifying some features. We plan on conducting other surveys and testing which is discussed in the next section.

6 Conclusions and Future Work

This paper discusses some of the key ideas and results of the development of the PAsSIVE agent framework, in particular the interface. The framework provides personalized search using Second Life to render search results. Through one's avatar, the user is able to view web content, and search and manipulate results. As the project investigates the use of both personalization and user interaction within a 3D interface, this paper mainly focuses on the interface design. The survey results were very useful for the continued development and testing of the system. The resulting changes to the overall size, color and the angle of the in-world object, we believe will improve navigation. Eventually, we want to take advantage of the full range of motion and camera angle capabilities to truly make an immersive search object that is more integrated and natural than current 2D renderings. Although the first survey was limited and a pilot for later designs, common search problems and desired search features were identified. The second interface-focused survey was helpful in finding features expected of a 3D search interface, and reactions to the latest 3D design. In the near future we will be updating the overall design of the virtual interface, and implementing some of the changes needed for further personalization. Through this research, we aim to eventually demonstrate the effectiveness of search interfaces that incorporate the features of 3D visualization, personalization, and proactive search.

References

1. Balkin, J., Noveck, B.: The State of Play: Law, Games, and Virtual Worlds. University Press, New York (2006)
2. Boulos, M., Burden, D.: Web GIS in practice V: 3-D interactive and real-time mapping in Second Life. Int. J. Health Geogr. 6(51), 1–16 (2007)
3. Braman, J., Dierbach, C.: Using Second Life as an interface for personalized search. In: Proceedings of SLACTIONS Research Conference in the Second Life World (2010). http://slactions.org
4. Brashears, A., Meadows, A., Ondrejka, C., Soo, D.: Linden Scripting Language Guide. Linden Lab, San Francisco (2003)
5. Card, S.K., Robertson, G.G., York, W.: The web book and the web forager: an information workspace for the world-wide web. In: Proceedings of the SIGCHI conference on Human factors in computing systems, pp. 111-ff. ACM (1996)
6. Christmann, O., Carbonell, N., Richir, S.: Visual search in dynamic 3D visualizations of unstructured picture collections. Interact. Comput. 22(5), 399–416 (2010)
7. Chuah, M., Roth, S., Mattis, J., Kolojejchick, J.: SDM: malleable information graphics. In: Proceedings on Information Visualization (INFOVIS 1995), pp 36–42. IEEE Computer Science press, Los Alamitos (1995)

8. Clarkson, E., Desai, K., Foley, J.D.: Resultmaps: visualization for search interfaces. IEEE Trans. Visual Comput. Graphics **15**(6), 1057–1064 (2009)
9. Cleary, D., O'Donoghue, D.: Creating a semantic-wed interface with virtual reality. In: Proceedings of the SPIE – The International Society for Optical Engineering, vol. 4528 pp. 138–146 (2001)
10. Eirinaki, M., Vazirgiannis, M.: Web mining for web personalization. ACM Trans. Internet Technol. **3**(1), 1–27 (2003)
11. Fetscherin, M., Lattemann, C.: User acceptance of virtual worlds. J. Electron. Commer. Res. **9**(3), 231–242 (2008)
12. Hearst, M.: Search User Interfaces. Cambridge University Press, Cambridge (2009)
13. Hemmje, M.: Lyberworld: a 3D graphical user interface for fulltext retrieval. In: Proceedings of the ACM SIGCHI 1995, pp. 417–418 (1995)
14. KZero.: KZero Reports – Universe Charts (2014). http://www.kzero.co.uk/
15. Oculus VR.: Oculus Rift (2015). https://www.oculus.com/rift/
16. Morville, P., Callender, J.: Search Patterns. O'Reilly Media, Inc., Sebastopol (2010)
17. Pearce, C.: Communities of Play: Emergent Cultures in Multiplayer Games and Virtual Worlds. MIT Press, Cambridge (2009). ISBN 978-0-262-16257-9
18. Rohrer, R., Swing, E.: Web-based information visualization. Proc. IEEE Comput. Graph. Appl. **17**(4), 52–59 (1997)
19. Schoeffmann, K., Ahlstrom, D.: Using a 3D cylindrical interface for image browsing to improve visual search performance. In: IEEE 2012 13th International Workshop on Image Analysis for Multimedia Interactive Services (WIAMIS) (2012)
20. Shneiderman, B.: Why not make interfaces better than 3D reality. IEEE Computer Society **23**(6), 12–15 (2003)
21. Shneiderman, B., Plaisant, C.: Designing the User Interface: Strategies for Effective Human-Computer Interaction, 4th edn. Addison Wesely, Boston (2005). University of Maryland, College Park
22. Sloodle: Sloodle Browser (2010). http://www.sloodle.org/browser
23. Smallman, H., St. John, M., Oonk, H.: Information availability in 2D and 3D displays. IEEE Comput. Graphics Appl. **21**(5), 51–57 (2001)
24. Vincenti, G., Braman, J.: Teaching through Multi-User Virtual Environments: Applying Dynamic Elements to the Modern Classroom. Information Science Reference, Hershey (2010)
25. Vincenti, G., Braman, J.: Multi-User Virtual Environments for the Classroom: Practical Approaches to Teaching in Virtual Worlds. Information Science Reference, Hershey (2011)
26. Yang, Y., Akers, L., Klose, T., Yang, C.: Text mining and visualization tools- impressions of emerging capabilities. World Patent Inf. **30**(4), 280–293 (2008)

Enabling Continuous Emotional Status Display in Mobile Text Chat

Jackson Feijó Filho[✉], Wilson Prata, and Thiago Valle

Nokia Technology Institute, Av. Torquato Tapajós, 7200 - Col. Terra Nova,
Manaus, AM, Brazil
{jackson.feijo,wilson.prata,thiago.valle}@indt.org.br

Abstract. Nonverbal communication is essential to human interaction. All this information is absent in mobile text conversations. This work describes an effort to extend text chat in mobile devices by continuously displaying emotional status and inserting automatically detected facial expression responses, such as a smile, to conversations. Acknowledged related work, regarding the examination of nonverbal communication through text messaging are considered and distinguished from the present solution. The implementation of a mobile phone application with the debated feature is described and user studies are reported. Context of application, conclusions and future works are also discussed.

1 Introduction

Nonverbal communication has been intriguing researchers for very long. In early 1870 s, scientific literatures on nonverbal communication and comportment were published in Charles Darwin's book "The Expression of the Emotions in Man and Animals" [5]. Darwin claimed that all mammals, both humans and animals, presented emotion through facial expressions. Affirming questions such as: "Why do our facial expressions of emotions take the particular forms they do?" and "Why do we wrinkle our nose when we are disgusted and bare our teeth when we are enraged?" [6].

Humans depend on visual signals when interacting within a social setting, and in an online conversation scenario, the lack of eyesight due to physical remoteness hinders the quality of social interactions. Since essential nonverbal communication is comprised of facial gestures and expressions, text chat users are at a disadvantage when engaging in interpersonal communication.

2 Problem Scenario

Nonverbal indications carried in a conversation is often conclusive for disambiguation. In [8], long-distance relationships and video chat technology is well debated. In one of the interviews from this work, some subjects have described video as a way to see their partners' facial expressions and body language. In some cases, this helped avoid miscommunications.

G. Meiselwitz (Ed.): SCSM 2015, LNCS 9182, pp. 12–19, 2015.
DOI: 10.1007/978-3-319-20367-6_2

"I always apparently sound pretty harsh when I'm talking ...even when I'm joking it doesn't sound like I'm joking...I would sometimes upset her without even knowing I upset her and, of course, without intending..." – P3.

Moreover, from the work in [18] where emotional feedback is discreetly inserted to the conversation timeline, experiments and interviews have shown that an isolated insertion of an emotional response is not always suitable to represent the continuity of the nonverbal expression. That suggests that another form of continuous representation of emotions is still lacking in the interface proposed in [18].

3   Related Work

There has been substantial work on the recognition and conveying of emotions in computer-mediated communications.

3.1   Video Chat

As described in [9], the use of video chat successfully transmits consistent non-verbal elements in conversations. In this work, we will not consider video chat scenarios as related work, since we are trying to intervene in online text chat scenarios. This distinction is appropriate due to the fact that video chat typically requires higher performance systems with more expensive hardware, faster networks and more processing power (compared to lower-end platforms with minimum requirements to exchange text through a server). Not only structurally, video-chatting establishes a different social ritual [9]. In addition, video-chat may often convey extra imagery such as background rooms, make-up, clothing and hair style, as opposed to transmitting only processed facial expressions, e.g. smile.

3.2   Conveying Emotion in Text Chat

Numerous existing approaches have been trying to derive affect from written language on a semantic basis, making use of common sense knowledge [11]. The work in [10] is an example of approaches that automatically identify emotions in texts.

The work in [12] attempts to detect deceptive chat-based communication using typing behavior and message cues. It is an example of deriving nonverbal information in chat texts with a non-semantics approach. It postulates that deception impacts response time, word count, lexical diversity, and the number of times a chat message is edited. It focuses on detecting deception, unlike our work, which is attempting to convey emotions.

The works in [10] and [13] distinguish themselves from the others because they attempt to assimilate natural language and emotions by performing the recognition of these emotions based on physiological user input. They o at collecting additional information on the user's emotional state by recording and analyzing physiological feedback. Therefore, while interacting with the application, the user is monitored by means of bio sensors, measuring skin conductivity, heart rate, respiration and muscle activity [10].

Specifically in [13] modifications in the display of the text are used to communicate emotions (animated text). Our work differs from these because it relies solely on low-resolution mobile phones front cameras, not requiring extra hardware. Also, it restricts the recognition of emotions to processing images of faces through mobile phones.

The accessibility proposal in [5] approaches the present matter by implementing a computer vision system with facial recognition and expression algorithms to relay nonverbal messages to blind users. This project differs from our work by focusing on visually impaired audience. In addition, unlike our solution, robust processing power is required for demanding algorithms if compared to our software. Lastly it is pertinent to mention that it relies on extra hardware, for example, using a high speed IEEE-1394b camera.

4   Continuous Emotional Status Display in Mobile Text Chat

Our solution attempts to intervene in mobile online text chat by detecting users' emotional reactions during the conversations. Initially, we implemented the chat application to be integrated with the emotion detection feature.

4.1   Mobile Chat Application

The mobile chat application was developed for Windows Phone, using the XMPP protocol [14] (formerly and also known as Jabber) as not only it is defined in open standards but it is also widely positioned across the Internet.

This standard is used by very popular chat platforms like Google Talk, Messenger and Facebook Chat, which made it simpler for test subjects to use our solution using their own everyday accounts.

4.2   Mobile Emotion Detection Software

In [18], the detection of emotions is performed only when new messages have arrived, in order to increase the possibility of a facial expression to be a reaction to the most recent message and minimize server requests.

Experiments and interviews have shown that these isolated emotional feedback ignores the continuity of nonverbal cues. Furthermore, it disregards the paralleled nature of verbal and nonverbal communications. That suggests that another form of continuous representation of emotions is still lacking in the interface proposed in [18].

To address this continuity feature, the image capturing and emotion recognition attempts to be executed every 2 s, providing a more fluid perception of nonverbal status.

This has enabled the discrete structure of the system to be maintained, and the image processing can still be executed on the server side. This is important because lower-end devices, with low memory and low processing power can be used with good performance.

In [15], Krishna et al. uses a Principal Component Analysis (PCA) algorithm for facial recognition. For the work in [18], our system used a commercial solution (Rekognition;

Orbeus, Inc.) [16] for face and emotion detection. Presently, we have implemented a more simple web service that accepts requests containing face images, and returns a JSON with emotion information. We have used Intel's Perceptual SDK to develop this server side system.

System Structure. As shown in Fig. 1, the user chats from the mobile, using our application. As soon as a conversation starts, the face images start being collected, converted to base64, and sent via http to the server to be processed. The server sends back a JSON feed, which is parsed to retrieve emotions status. The emotions results range from 0 to 1, providing the detected level of "happy", "surprised" and "calm". If the level one of these emotions are above a pre-determined threshold, the software automatically adds "<name-of-user > smiles" or "<name-of-user > is surprised", to the conversation thread. In parallel, the client software on the phone compares the higher emotion feedback, to continually update the status.

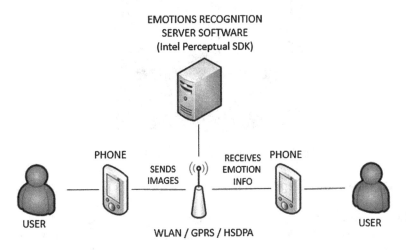

Fig. 1. System structure

4.3 Screenshot

Figure is a screenshot of the application, with an on-going dialogue. It is relevant to mention that no actual face images are exchanged. This consolidates the social ritual of the text dialoguing, when people are able to have conversations unmindful of make-up, hair and overall facial aesthetics status. There is also a clear demonstration of when the "emotions feature" is on or off (Figs. 2 and 3).

Fig. 2. Screenshot from the application in [18]

5 Interviews and Experiments

Firstly, we perceived that the test subjects were inclined to change their facial expressions for no reason, in order to check with their chat partners whether the emotion detection accurately worked. Because of that, we decided to implement a preliminary educational usability test phase, in order to get test subjects habituated with the software.

For the sake of productivity, we recruited test subjects, chat partners, who are used to talking to each other using mobile text chat.

We referred to some inquiries in the work by Wang [12] when developing the questionnaire. The subjects were asked to answer the questions after using both modes of chat. See Table 1.

6 Results and Discussion

We developed an approach to the integration of continuous nonverbal communication to mobile text chat. The motivation is to enrich mobile text chat by conveying frequently lost non-verbal communication. This benefits users by conveying information that is valuable to augment textual conversations.

Fig. 3. Screenshot of the application

Our solution differed from the related research for it did not attempt to extract affection from the semantics of the text and did not use any extra hardware to collect images or physiological signals. Finally, our work is devoted to relaying emotions on mobile text chat scenarios, relying on lower end devices with front cameras.

We implemented a mobile text chat application based on the XMPP protocol, easily connectable with popular chat platforms, with the feature of detecting users' emotions automatically and transmitting them to chat partners.

We have also implemented the server side software that processes that face images, returning a JSON feed with emotional feedback information.

During the experiments and interviews we found that people perceived their partners' reactions as an accomplishment or a reward to what they just posted.

This has included some sort of pressure in the commitment of the conversation, in comparison to plain text chat. In some cases, subjects have mentioned that their partners inserted more humor then usual to the dialogue, in order to receive the automatically detected smiles. During the preliminary trials, we found that people tended to try to foresee their chat partner's reactions, creating frustration when no smiles when detected or causing great sense of accomplishment when it did.

From the interviews, which were conducted individually and in groups, we were able to observe the rise of the sense of connection that chat partners experienced with one another, even more with the constant emotional status feedback.

Table 1. Comparison of the application with and without emotional feedback. Mean scores for questions about the interactive experience in chat systems with and without emotional feedback (EF and Non-EF). The possible responses ranged from 1 (disagree) to 5 (agree) (10 subjects).

Question	EF	Non-EF
I became very involved in the conversation	4.4	3.2
I enjoyed using the system	4.5	3.1
It was easy to understand my partner's emotions	4.8	2.9
I emulated some of my expressions	0.5	0
I felt more connected to my chat partner	4.7	2.1
I would use this application in my everyday chat conversations.	4.1	3.7

References

1. Argyle, M., Salter, U., Nicholson, H., Williams, M., Burgess, P.: The communication of inferior and superior attitudes by verbal and non-verbal signals. Br. J. Soc. Psychol. **9**, 222–231 (1970)
2. Intel Perceptual SDK. https://software.intel.com/en-us/perceptual-computing-sdk
3. Codes of professional ethics: Social Science Computing Review **10**(2), 453–469 (1992)
4. Liu, H., Lieberman, H., Selker, T.: A model of textual affect sensing using real-world knowledge. In: Johnson, W.L., Andre, E., Domingue, J. (eds.) International Conference on Intelligent User Interfaces, pp. 125–132. ACM, Florida (2003)
5. Astler, D., Chau, H.: Increased accessibility to nonverbal communication through facial and expression recognition technologies for blind/visually impaired subjects. In: ASSETS 2011 the Proceedings of the 13th International ACM SIGACCESS Conference on Computers and Accessibility, pp. 259–260. ACM, New York (2011)
6. Pease, B., Pease, A.: The Definitive Book of Body Language. Bantam Books, New York (2004)
7. Krauss, R.M., Chen, Y., Chawla, P.: Nonverbal behavior and nonverbal communication: what do conversational hand gestures tell us? Adv. Exp. Soc. Psychol. **1**(2), 389–450 (2000)
8. Power, M.R.: Chapter 11: Non-verbal communication Working Through Communication. Paper 12 (1998)
9. Neustaedter, C., Greenberg, S.: Intimacy in long-distance relationships over video chat. In: CHI 2012 Proceedings of the SIGCHI Conference on Human Factors in Computing Systems, pp. 753–762. ACM, New York (2012)
10. Bosma, W., Andre, E.: Exploiting emotions to disambiguate dialogue acts. In: IUI 2004 Proceedings of the 9th International Conference on Intelligent User Interfaces, pp. 85–92. ACM, New York (2004)
11. Barros, L., Rodríguez, P., Ortigosa, A.: Emotion recognition in texts for user model augmenting. In: INTERACCION 2012 Proceedings of the 13th International Conference on Interacción Persona-Ordenador, Article No. 45. ACM, New York (2012)

12. Detecting Deceptive Chat-Based Communication Using Typing Behavior and Message Cues. ACM Transactions on Management Information Systems (TMIS) TMIS. Homepage archive. 4 (2), Article No. 9. ACM, New York (2013)
13. Wang, H., Predinger, H., Igarashi, T.: Communicating emotions in online chat using physiological sensors and animated text. In: CHI EA 2004 CHI 2004 Extended Abstracts on Human Factors in Computing Systems, pp. 1171–1174. ACM, New York (2004)
14. XMPP Standards Foundation. http://www.xmpp.org
15. Little, G., Black, J., Panchanathan, S., Krishna, S.A.: Wearable face recognition system for individuals with visual impairments. In: 7th Annual ACM Conference on Assistive Technologies, pp. 106–113 (2005)
16. Rekognition APIs and SDK. https://rekognition.com
17. Marge, M., Joao Miranda, A.W.B., Rudnicky, A.I.: Towards improving the naturalness of social conversations with dialogue systems. In: Proceedings of the 11th Annual Meeting of the Special Interest Group on Discourse and Dialogue, pp. 91–94. Association for Computational Linguistics (2010)
18. Feijó Filho, J., Valle, T., Prata, W.: Non-verbal communications in mobile text chat: emotion-enhanced mobile chat. In: Proceedings of the 16th International Conference on Human-computer Interaction with Mobile Devices & Services. ACM (2014)

3D Virtual Worlds: An Ethnography of Key Artifacts and Processes

Nick V. Flor[(✉)]

Anderson School of Management, University of New Mexico,
Albuquerque, USA
nickflor@unm.edu

Abstract. The development of an educational 3D virtual world requires a complex skillset, which includes programming, modeling, texturing, animating, and quest/level designing. When these skills are distributed across multiple workers, the workers must negotiate a shared understanding of their intermediate work products, which ultimately culminate in the virtual world. This paper is an ethnography of the intermediate work products ("artifacts") and processes used in the development of Virtual Energy World—a 3D virtual world for instruction on sustainable energy issues. The resulting artifacts and processes have utility as a general development framework for both educational virtual worlds and video games.

1 Introduction

Educators usually have the most innovative ideas for using virtual worlds as part of their pedagogy. The problem is implementing those ideas. One option is to build over an existing virtual world like Second Life (SecondLife.com). However, building over existing virtual worlds introduces issues of student privacy, as well as issues of connectivity with other learning management systems. Flexibility is also an issue—one's ideas may be constrained by limitations in the existing virtual world's building rules and its scripting capabilities.

The most flexible solution is for the educator to develop a custom virtual world. Technology advancement combined with an abundance of free online video tutorials have made it possible for a single person to learn the skills needed to self-develop a virtual world, which include programming, modeling, and animation (Flor 2011). However, when there are time constraints and aesthetic concerns, it becomes necessary for the educator to enlist or hire specialists in each of the various skills.

This aim of this paper is provide educators a general framework for assembling a virtual world team and for organizing this team to build an instructional virtual world. The participant-observational study was carried out from January–December of 2014 in the University of New Mexico's Reality Augmented Virtual Environment (RAVE) laboratory, by the lab director and the senior members of the Virtual Energy World project team. The ethnography is based on the analysis of detailed project notes, team member reports, and work-in-progress submitted weekly and stored in a cloud repository.

© Springer International Publishing Switzerland 2015
G. Meiselwitz (Ed.): SCSM 2015, LNCS 9182, pp. 20–29, 2015.
DOI: 10.1007/978-3-319-20367-6_3

2   Overview: The Virtual Energy World

The Virtual Energy World (www.virtualenergyworld.com) is a 3D interactive visualization developed entirely by art, business, and engineering undergraduate and graduate
students as part of the National Science Foundation's Sustainable Energy Pathways
Through Education & Technology program (SEPTET 2012). The ultimate instructional
goal of the Virtual Energy World is to educate teenage students—middle-school through
college freshmen—on their renewable & sustainable energy options, as well as to
develop energy management & conservation skills (see Fig. 1).

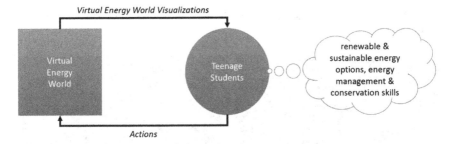

Fig. 1. Technology, Target Users, Learning Goal

2.1   The Basic Operation of the Virtual Energy World

Similar to other 3D virtual worlds, after a user selects an avatar, he or she can enter the
virtual world (see Fig. 2), and interact with objects in the environment.

Fig. 2. An avatar in a virtual world, depicting a neighborhood

The key object is the house. Users are assigned a house that they can enter by clicking
on the door of their house (see Fig. 3).

It is inside a user's home where an energy-themed virtual world starts to differ from
other virtual worlds. Specifically, appliances in non-energy-themed virtual worlds are
largely decorative and do not consume energy. In an energy-themed virtual world,

Fig. 3. A common interaction, clicking on a house's door brings the avatar inside the house

appliances have states (see Fig. 4), and when they are on they can consume variable amounts of energy.

Fig. 4. In an energy-themed virtual world, appliances have states. In this example, off is denoted by a red outline and on by a green outline.

2.2   Learning in the Virtual Energy World

The Virtual Energy World is designed to be a continually evolving platform for instructing users on renewable and sustainable energy management & conservation issues in a more immersive and interactive manner than current information sources. The instructional goal of the initial implementation is to help users understand the power requirements, or wattages, of various household appliances.

Users can learn about appliance power requirements in two modes. In free-form mode, users can wander around their homes, examine various appliance wattages, and switch appliances on and off. As each appliance is switched, the virtual world displays total power usage. In quest mode, the virtual world asks users to perform various actions on appliances, or to answer questions related to power requirements. In a classroom environment, teachers can create quests for their students either to instruct students on appliance power requirements or to test knowledge of appliance wattages.

Users switch appliances on and off by either clicking or tapping on their visual representations. Appliance on/off state is denoted by a colored border, with green indicating "on" and red indicating "off." Users can reveal the wattages of appliances by either hovering the mouse pointer over an appliance or tapping & holding an appliance. The virtual world will then superimpose the wattage over the appliance along with the total power used in the upper-right corner (see Fig. 5).

Fig. 5. The coffee maker is "on" as denoted by the green outline, and the number 900 superimposed over it indicates that it is consuming 900 w of power. The 3100 w in the upper-right corner is the total wattage of the coffee maker, stove, and dishwasher.

The current implementation of the Virtual Energy World provides a minimum feature set for learning about power issues at the household level, in an immersive and interactive manner. A future implementation, currently in testing, will allow teachers to create custom quests where students can learn the energy requirements of specific appliances, or the costs of running multiple appliances over time, or different ways of conserving energy.

3   Developing the Virtual World

While it is possible for a single skilled individual to create a virtual world, to create one with a high-level of aesthetically pleasing visuals, with entertaining gameplay, and with fast performance, requires hiring different kinds of specialists.

3.1   The Five Types of Specialists to Hire and the Actual Students Hired

It was the task of the Director of the Reality Augmented Virtual Environment (RAVE) lab, which sponsored the Virtual Energy World project, to hire the student specialists. Based on his experience self-developing virtual worlds, the Director determined that there were five different kinds of student specialists needed:

1. Artists—responsible for how the virtual energy world would look. Artists could be further categorized into concept artists, inorganic modelers, character modelers, and animators.
2. Designers—responsible for how users played the virtual world. Designers could be further categorized into level designers, and user-interface designers.
3. Programmers—responsible for coding and for all technology required by the virtual world.

4. Producers—responsible for managing the virtual world's schedule, as well as acquiring sound & music, testing, and marketing the virtual world.
5. Researchers—responsible for collecting data about the real world that is relevant to the virtual world.

This list is very similar to the specialists needed to develop video games (Co 2006), which is unsurprising given that virtual worlds can be conceived as a kind of videogame with educational goals. The Director hired a total of 9 student workers to develop the Virtual Energy World (refer to Fig. 6): four artists (orange); one designer (blue); one programmer (green); a single producer (yellow); a sound & music specialist (not shown); and one researcher (black rectangle).

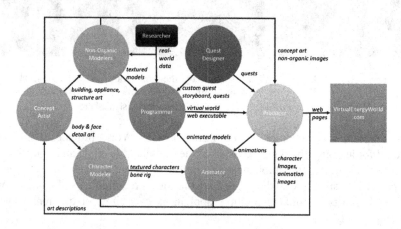

Fig. 6. General workflow process for the Virtual Energy World (Color figure online)

The particular students hired all had proven skills in videogame development and had worked together before both on a capstone videogame and on an award-winning indie videogame.

3.2 The Director's Instructions: Create a 3D Virtual World Using Scrum

The Lab Director instructed the student workers ("the team"), to create an initial version of a 3D virtual world that would increase a user's understanding of the energy requirements of typical home appliances. The only other instructions were to: (a) use *Streamline Moderne* as the artistic style; (b) use *Scrum* (Schwaber and Sutherland 2013)—an iterative method for the rapid prototyping of software; (c) to hold *weekly sprint meetings* to get feedback on work-in-progress; and finally to (d) *"check their egos at the door"* and be open to feedback from all team members regardless of specialty. All other hardware, software, design, implementation, and management details were left to the team to self-organize. The team had from January through December of 2014 to complete the Virtual Energy World.

3.3   Team Hardware and Software Decisions

For maximum access to the Virtual Energy World, the team decided that it would be implemented as a Web app running on the site VirtualEnergyWorld.com. The programmer chose Unity 3D as the game engine—an existing collection of code for displaying 3D objects & animations and for handling user interactions, which frees up the programmer to implement the gameplay and game logic. Other benefits of Unity 3D were that it was free, and that it could not only export the code as a web app but could also export the code as an iPhone, Android, or Windows phone app if the team decided that those mobile platforms were necessary in the future.

The key software used by the team included: Adobe Photoshop for creating concept art drawn on Wacom tablets; Autodesk Maya for 3D inorganic models and animations; ZBrush for 3D character models; Word Press for website content management; Trello for project management; Google Drive for sharing work-in-progress; and a private GitHub repository for sharing the code.

3.4   The Workflow that Evolved

Although neither discussed explicitly in its entirety, nor documented anywhere, the following workflow evolved (see Fig. 6).

We will focus on just the artists' work-in-progress.

Concept Artist → Non-Organic Modelers: Underspecified Detail & Team Feedback. Concept artists are crucial to the look and feel of the virtual world. They provide drawings known as "concept art" to the modelers—both non-organic and character—who then transform this art into the 3D models that are actually used inside the virtual world.

In the Virtual Energy World (refer to Fig. 7), almost all non-organic concept art consisted of a single angled view of an object. Although lacking in dimension and backside detail, this single drawing was all that the modeler needed to develop an initial 3D model. The initial model would then be subject to feedback from all team members during the weekly sprint meetings. Team feedback was key to the high quality of the final model. The modeler would get feedback from team, negotiate the changes to make, then revise and present the following week. This process would continue until the team agreed the model was finished. Thus, the final model was not often an exact copy of the concept art, but one that the artist, modeler, and team co-constructed with the aim of high quality. The team's concept of high quality was in comparison to similar art in commercial video games or in animated movies.

Concept Artist → Character Modeler: General & Focused Concept Art. Unlike non-organic objects such as buildings and appliances, where the concept artist could make a single angled drawing, a character requires the concept artist to create drawings with multiple angles (see Fig. 8) as well as close-up drawings for intricate body parts like the face (see Fig. 9). A character modeler has two options for creating a 3D character model based on concept art. He or she can either build the figure from scratch by doing a 3D papier-mâché (layering of polygons) over the drawing; or start from a base model

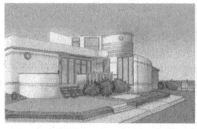

Fig. 7. Concept Art (left) and Final 3D Model (right)—note that it is not an exact copy of the concept art.

Fig. 8. Character Concept Art (left) and 3D Character Model without hair (right)

Fig. 9. Face Concept Art (left) and unfinished 3D Face (right)

—a featureless but proportioned 3D model—then digitally sculpt the based model to resemble the concept art.

In the Virtual Energy World, the character modeler used the base model approach. Similar to non-organic models, the model was subjected to feedback from all team members during the weekly sprint meetings, and the final model did not resemble the concept art exactly.

During one of the weekly sprint meetings, the character modeler requested more detailed drawings of the face. The concept artist responded with the face drawn from several angles (see Fig. 9, left). Like the body, the character modeler did not 3D papier-mâché the face, but sculpted a base model of the face to resemble the drawings (see Fig. 9, right).

Character Modelers → Animators: Using Prototypes to Allow Work-In-Parallel.
Animators add movement to the characters created by the character modeler. In order to add movement, an animator needs not only a model from the character modeler (see

Fig. 10. The Character Model (left) and its Underlying Skeleton (right, skin hidden)

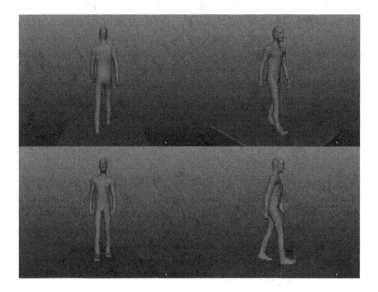

Fig. 11. Different Views of an Animated Walk

Fig. 10, left), but one that contains an underlying skeleton (see Fig. 10, right). This is known collectively as a rigged character.

From this rigged character, the animator rotates skeleton joints to simulate the angles and extensions of human movement such as walking (see Fig. 11).

The most detailed feedback during the weekly Virtual Energy World sprint meetings was reserved for the animations. The animator would create a looping video of an animation from different angles (see Fig. 11) and the team would critique many details such as the speed of limb motions, the bounce of the body, the stiffness of the torso, or under-/over- rotation of limbs. As with the models, the animator would revise and represent the work until the team felt the animation was of sufficient high-quality.

Note that the model used by the animator in Fig. 11 is a less detailed version of the final model in Fig. 8. So long as the underlying skeleton does not change, the animator could reuse his animations in the final character model. This less-detailed model was necessary because it allowed the animator to start working before the character model was completed, the latter of which took an entire semester. Without this less-detailed model, the animator would have been inactive for that semester.

4   Discussion: Virtual World as Distributed Cogntive System

A virtual world development team is a kind of distributed cognitive system (Hutchins 1995; Hollans et al. 2000). Like any distributed cognitive system, such as the brain, there are distinct modules, e.g., human vision, that specialize in transforming information into an interpretation that can serve as information for other modules. These modules are fault-tolerant—they can provide interpretations based on information that is either incomplete or underspecified.

In the case of the virtual world team described in previous sections, cognitive modules corresponded to the different student specialists. The tolerance for incomplete information can be seen in the interactions between the concept artist and the non-organic modeler, where the concept art's lack of details in terms of dimension or in terms of the backside of objects did not prevent the modeler from creating a model.

Modules upstream can give feedback to modules downstream, requesting additional information in order to complete the interpretation. This kind of feedback can be seen in the interactions between the concept artist and the character modeler, the latter of which requested additional concept art in order to complete the character's face.

There were two processes unique to the Virtual World development team qua distributed cognitive system, which are not found in neural-based distributed cognitive systems. The first was the character modeler giving the animator a prototype character so that the animator's work was not held up while the modeler finished. When the modeler did finish, the animations were simply applied to the final model. The second was the team feedback (see Fig. 12) that took place during the weekly sprint meetings, where each member regardless of specialty could critique work-in-progress. This team feedback, combined with the Scrum rapid-prototyping method were instrumental in the co-construction of high-quality models and animations.

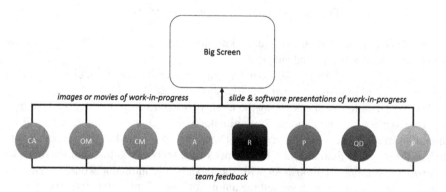

Fig. 12.   Diagram of the Weekly Sprint Feedback Meeting

5   Conclusion: Developing a Virtual World

To summarize, our study suggests that for an educator to lead the development of a custom virtual world, one approach is to:

1. Determine the main idea and the target user for the virtual world, e.g., teach users about appliance energy consumption.
2. Put together a team of specialists consisting of at least a concept artist, a modeler for non-organic objects and characters, an animator, a programmer, a producer, and a researcher.
3. Communicate the main idea to the team.
4. Organize a work flow similar to the diagram in Fig. 6.
5. Hold weekly team feedback meetings (see Fig. 12), as part of a rapid-prototyping method like Scrum, aimed both at improving the quality of the work products, and at continuously expanding the main idea.

Manage the team as a flexible distributed cognitive system—allowing the specialists to negotiate between themselves their works-in-progress. Where one specialist would be held back waiting for another's work, like the animator waiting for the character modeler, ask them to find prototypes that allow them to work in parallel and to reuse their final work.

The determined educator armed with knowledge of these processes and artifacts should be able to develop a custom virtual world and contribute to the growing science of the artificial (Simon 1969).

Acknowledgments. The author's work is supported by the National Science Foundation (NSF) under Division of Electrical, Communications and Cyber Systems (ECCS) - 1231046. Any opinions, findings, and conclusions or recommendations expressed in this material are those of the author and do not necessarily reflect the views of the NSF.

References

Co, P.: Level Design for Games, p. 5. New Riders, Berkeley (2006)

Flor, N.: Self-developing a MUVE for research and educational innovations. In: Vincenti, G., Braman, J. (eds.) Teaching Through Multi-user Virtual Environments, pp. 453–470 (2011)

Hollan, J., Hutchins, E., Kirsh, D.: Distributed cognition: toward a new foundation for human-computer interaction research. ACM Trans. Comput.-Hum. Interact. (TOCHI) **7**, 174–196 (2000)

Hutchins, E.: Cognition in the Wild, vol. 262082314. MIT press, Cambridge (1995)

SEPTET. Sustainable Energy Pathways Through Education and Technology (2012). http://nsf.gov/awardsearch/showAward?AWD_ID=1231046. Accessed 17 December 2014

Sutherland, J., Schwaber, K.: The Scrum Guide (2013). http://www.scrumguides.org/docs/scrumguide/v1/Scrum-Guide-US.pdf. Accessed 17 December 2014

Simon, H.A.: The Sciences of the Artificial, vol. 136. MIT press, Cambridge (1969)

Text-Mining of Hand-Over Notes for Care-Workers in Real Operation

Toward an Employee-Driven Innovation

Ken Fukuda[⊠], Kentaro Watanabe, Tomohiro Fukuhara, Masahiro Hamasaki,
Ryoji Fujii, Miharu Horita, and Takuichi Nishimura

AIST Center for Service Research, Tokyo, Japan
ken.fukuda@aist.go.jp

Abstract. Hand-over note in elderly care facilities is a very important media for the employees to share information about non-routine task procedures in the daily operation. Reviewing these memos regularly will help the facility find potential risk factors and inefficiency in routine protocols. However, hand-over notes are typically hand-written memos and conducting periodical review is not easy for an average employee with heavy workload. To capture this field community intelligence, we have conducted text-mining on hand-over text. This paper describes results of hand-over note text-mining cases that lead to employee driven re-design of service processes for better care service.

Keywords: Nursing-care service · Text-mining · Data-mining · Employee driven innovation

1 Introduction

The long-term care insurance cost in FY 2009 rose to 7.7 trillion yen, showing a continuously rising trend [1], which becomes more and more serious as a social burden. In addition, the Long-Term Care Insurance Act sets a low service unit price yielding to a low profitability of the care facility business. The profitability of many of these businesses is less than 5 %. Moreover, healthcare workers face huge amount of workloads. And thus, improving productivity while maintaining quality of service remains an urgent task.

The heavy workload in care facilities is widely known and a variety of supporting system with information technology such as PDA and RFID are proposed. Various points of care systems for nursing have been proposed and assessed [2, 3]. They are useful to record routine work as official evidence such as vital data.

However, the expertise of highly experienced care workers resides in how good one can response to a non-routine operation or an unexpected irregular incident. And this know-how is mostly recorded in hand-written hand-over notebooks and not captured in conventional information technology systems. The experience and intuition of care workers gathered over many years of their employment are extremely important to provide high quality service in care facilities. However, these experience and related

© Springer International Publishing Switzerland 2015
G. Meiselwitz (Ed.): SCSM 2015, LNCS 9182, pp. 30–38, 2015.
DOI: 10.1007/978-3-319-20367-6_4

know-how including implicit knowledge and intuition are subjective, making it difficult to share.

To curate this implicit field community intelligence, we have developed a hand-over support system called DANCE (Dynamic Action and kNowledge assistant for Collaborative sErvice fields) for elderly care facilities [6]. The System is now in a full-scale real operation in a care facility for more than a year [7] and has replaced the conventional hand-written notebook based hand-over protocol. Our proposed system utilizes mobile devices and is based on a point-of-care recording technology, which uses a database containing ActionLog [4] to record information at each point-of-care when a task is conducted, with Social Infobox [5] that provides related information from a collated knowledge base.

Every hand-over comment and operation is now logged in a machine-readable medium, which makes it easier for the employee to utilize for Employee-driven innovation (EDI) [8, 9].

In this paper the authors report a case study where the authors conducted text mining on the hand-over text to support EDI.

2   Hand-Over Text in Elderly Care Facilities

To cope with potential risk factors to prevent accidents and improve service quality, employees of elderly care facilities have to share various kinds of informal information, for example, requests from residents' family or resident's daily mood and condition. Notebook is commonly used to write down this information as a hand-over memo (Fig. 1).

Hand-over memos

Fig. 1. Hand-over memo written in a notebook

A typical hand written hand-over memo starts with a header line addressing the supposed receiver of the information followed by its body that describes how the author encountered an irregular incident or instructions for handling the abnormality.

3   Method

The DANCE system was installed in an elderly-care facility called Wakoen after a co-design project with several employees of the facility to develop a mobile communication system among employees for elderly-care services [6, 10].

Wakoen is a health institute for long-term and short-term care for elderly people. The facility has 3 floors with 150 beds for long-term care and 40 seating capacity for short-term care with 120 employees. About 10 to 20 employees work at the same time on each floor in daytime or night-time shift.

The system started to operate as the primary media for hand-over messages from February 1, 2014, followed by three months of test operation and replaced the conventional notebook based hand written hand-over message protocol.

The system runs separately in each floor. The biggest floor (Group A) for long-term care and a floor specialized for dementia (Group B) and another floor for short-time care (Group C).

To assess the impact of the system installation, the authors have compared the number and the length of messages before and after the system installation as shown in Figs. 2 and 3.

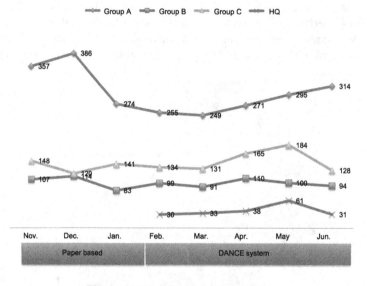

Fig. 2. Number of messages per month.

The total number of sent messages from February to June (5 months, 150 days) was 2813, on average, 18.8 per day, which breakdowns to 1384 for Group A, 494 for Group B and 742 for Group C. The head quarter also sent 193 messages. The total number of employees who sent at least one message was 133 (some employees belong to more than one floor).

With the system, 50.9 % of all messages had less than 50 characters and 93.8 % of the messages were less than 125 character long. Average length was 60.1 and the longest

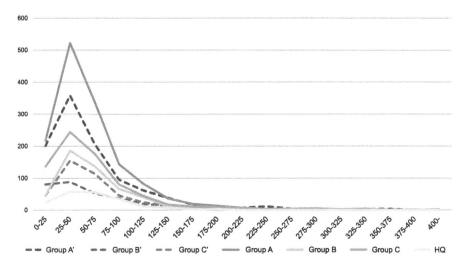

Fig. 3. Message length distribution (A', B', C' are paper based memo)

message had 434 characters. Before the system installation, 53.6 % of paper based messages had less than 50 characters and 94.9 % of the hand-written messages were less than 150 character long. The average length was 60.7 and the longest hand-written message had 362 characters.

There is a drop in the number of messages in January, which is before the system installation, in Group A, but the authors were not able to detect negative effects directly related to the system installation.

4   Results

Hand-over messages from February to March (8 weeks) were used for the text-mining. The authors held several workshops for the employees and explained general features of what text mining can do. Through this workshop, the employees made several requests on how they want to narrow down the data to abnormal incidents.

For each message in the DANCE system, employees can specify if the message is about certain residents or just a generous remainder. 1944 messages, which equals to 69.1 % of the whole, were about specific residents. As shown in Fig. 4, the number of messages per resident is not evenly distributed. Instead, most of the messages are about very small number of residents.

Based on the employees' discussion, the authors created co-occurrence networks of the top ten most referred residents of each floor. For example, if resident_A is a top ten resident, then the authors collected all the messages of resident_A and created a co-occurrence network from this set of messages. By showing these networks, several issues were suggested by the workshop participants. In the following sections, the authors report some examples where the text-mining results triggered discussions that actually lead to re-design of their daily operation.

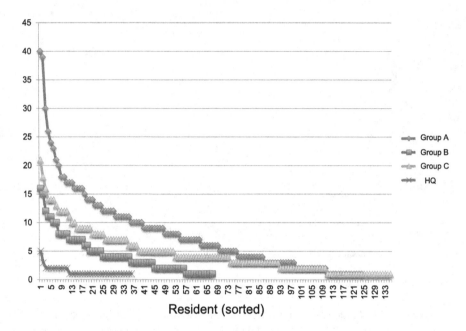

Fig. 4. Number of messages per residents

4.1 Case 1: Service Quality Improvement

In Fig. 5, the participants of the workshop noticed a sub-network of words such as 'visit,' 'husband,' 'eat' and 'become silent.' In general, one should be careful about family related terms because careful follow-up of family's request is very important to provide high quality elderly care service. These keywords helped them to back track to frequently sent messages such as "her husband provided food to her in the absence of care workers." This resident referred in Fig. 5 had difficulty in swallowing and needed assistance in eating by care staffs. However, her husband helped her eating in the absence of care staffs. This is a potential risk factor that may cause an incident.

After a discussion among employees of different roles, they decided to allow her husband to provide food to the resident but only at the dining room in the presence of care staffs so that they can adjust the posture of the resident before eating. This consensus was shared among every employee after the workshop. This employee driven re-design of a service process yield better customer satisfaction.

4.2 Case 2: Refinement and Standardization of Treatment

Network shown in Fig. 6 was closed up because 'bathing', 'assist equipment' 'transfer assistance' appeared frequently in the same sub-network.

By reviewing the hand-over messages of this resident, the participants found four conflicting messages: "From today, she only needs assistive equipment while bathing", "put the equipment on her at her room", "she does not need the equipment out of the tab", "put the equipment on her while assisting transfer from her bed to the stretcher.

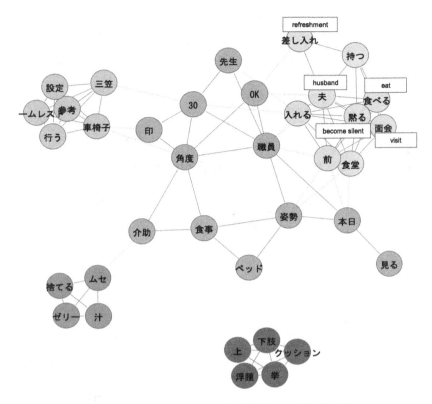

Fig. 5. Co-occurrence network with the term "husband".

Bath her with the equipment. Take the equipment off after supporting her getting out of the bath tab and wash her feet. After that, no assistive equipment is needed." Besides these conflicting messages, several employees answered to the workshop participants that care staffs were complaining that it was not clear to them which information was correct.

A meeting with care-staffs and nursing staffs were held after the workshop to understand what happened and to discuss effective measures. The situation was as follows: the resident complained that her leg hurts as an aftereffect of a fracture. But the doctor authorized the care staff that assistive equipments were not necessary because the fracture had healed. But because of the resident's complain, some care-staffs concluded that she needed the equipment during transfer. But the resident may lose her muscle if she rely too much on assistive equipments. After confirming the latest condition of the resident, the employees reached to a consensus that the resident does not need the equipment any more and a new hand-over message was shared saying "the resident's fracture healed and she does not complain pain any more. No assistive equipment required. But transfer from bed to wheel chair requires three staffs."

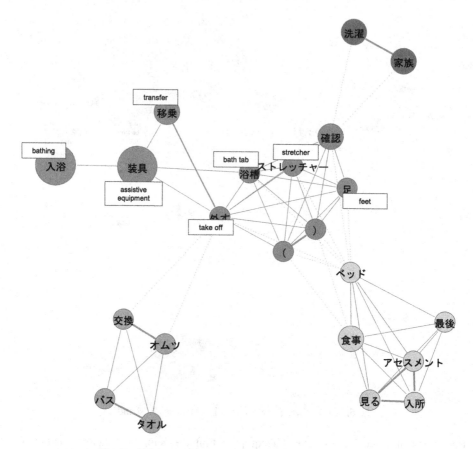

Fig. 6. Co-occurrence network about assistive equipments.

4.3   Case 3: Improvement of Operational Efficiency

Figure 7 has "juice", "fridge", "keep" as frequently occurring terms. There were 11 messages saying "juice from resident's family in the fridge. Give it to the resident when requested".

Because the resident had the ability to recognize that his family brought him some juice and that the care staffs were keeping them, it was sufficient to make a special space in the fridge for him and taking the juice out from the fridge per request. No hand-over messages concerning his juice were necessary after that.

5   Discussion

In this paper the authors report several use-cases of text-mining of hand-over messages where the employee actually designed a new service process based on the hand-over text-mining analysis. This shows that text-mining can be used to design better service

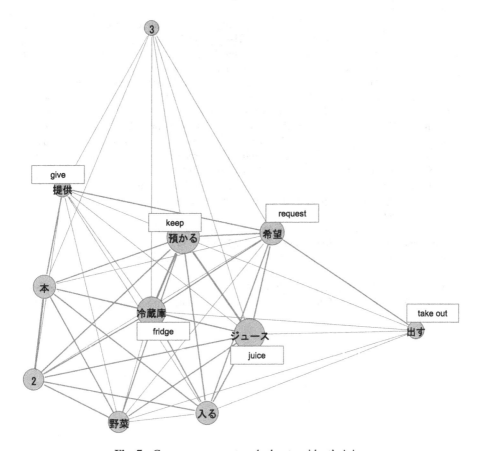

Fig. 7. Co-occurrence network about resident's juice.

based on evidence that was previously non-visible in conventional reports such as accident reports or near accident reports and can be used in employee driven innovation.

Acknowledgments. This work was supported by JSPS KAKENHI Grant Number 24500676 and 25730190. This study was conducted as a (service engineering research and development) project to promote new market creation through the fusion of IT and business services commissioned by the Ministry of Economy, Trade, and Industry FY 2011. The authors thank the Wakoen Long-Term Care Health Facility, the paid nursing home Super-court Hirano, and the Saga University Hospital for their cooperation in and support for this study.

References

1. Ministry of Health, Labour and Welfare (MHLW): Survey Results of Nursing-Care Service Facilities and Companies in 2009 (2011) (in Japanese)
2. Dennis, K.E., Sweeney, P.M., Macdonald, L.P., Morse, N.A.: Point of care technology: impact on people and paperwork. Nurs. Econ. **11**(4), 229–248 (1993)

3. Langowski, C.: The times they are a changing: effects of online nursing documentation systems. Qual. Manag. Health Care **14**(2), 121–125 (2005)
4. Numa, K., Uematsu, D., Hamasaki, M., Ohmukai, I., Takeda, H.: ActionLog: Real World Oriented Content Description Systems. Interaction, Interactive Session (2005)
5. Hamasaki, M., Goto, M., Takeda, H.: Social infobox: collaborative knowledge construction by social property tagging. In: Proceedings of ACM 2011 Conference on Computer Supported Cooperative Work (CSCW 2011), pp. 641–644 (2011)
6. Nishimura, T., Fukuhara, T., Yamada, C., Hamasaki, M., Nakajima, M., Miwa, H., Watanabe, K., Fukuda., K., Motomura, Y.: Proposal of handover system for care-workers using community intelligence. In: Proceedings of the 1st International Conference on Serviceology (ICServ2013), vol. 2013, no.10, pp. 34–41, October 2013
7. Fukuda, K., Hamasaki, M., Fukuhara, T., Fujii, R., Horita, H., Nishimura, T.: Findings on hand-over system for care-workers in real operation. In: Proceedings of ICServ2014, pp. 105–107, September 2014
8. Høyrup, S.: Employee-driven innovation and workplace learning: basic concepts, approaches and themes. Transf. Eur. Rev. Labour Res. **16**(2), 143–154 (2010)
9. Kesting, P., Ulhøi, J.P.: Employee-driven innovation: extending the license to foster innovation. Manag. Decis. **48**(1), 65–84 (2010)
10. Watanabe, K., Nishimura, T., Mochimaru, M.: A meta-methodology for service process design. In: Proceedings of the First International Conference on Serviceology (ICServ2013) (2013)

Talking Circles: Spiritual Aid for Teenagers Through Social Media

Markandeya Kunchi[1(✉)] and Shubhi Shrivastava[2]

[1] User Experience Designer, Make My Trip, Gurgaon, Haryana, India
kunchimarkandeya@hotmail.com
[2] User Experience Designer, Cognizant Technology Solutions,
Pune, Maharashtra, India
shrivastava.shubhi@gmail.com

Abstract. Social media has covered, conquered and affected almost all the aspects of our lives especially those of the teenagers and youngsters. There is still a space, which has not been affected by social media to a great extent and is yet to be explored. This paper reflects the deep study of integration of two entirely different worlds; social media of the 21th century and the evergreen and serene world of spirituality. It attempts to address the problems faced by teenagers and how they can be solved with the science, logic and approachability of spirituality with the help of social media acting as a mediator and catalyst to bridge the gap. At a conceptual level this paper defines, characterises and elaborates on a concept called "Talking Circles" where social media, spirituality and teenagers stand on a common stage and how each one can be modified, transformed and made adaptive to the current situation.

Keywords: Social media · Spirituality · Teenagers · Collaboration · Co-creation · Therapy · Guidance · Express · Journey · Problem solving

1 Introduction

Social media has knitted the whole world. We are all connected through this invisible thread of the web where we can reach to anyone anywhere. Chatting, video calling, sharing stuff online etc. Social media provides a platform that looks beyond the basic World Wide Web. Spirituality as a concept of being spiritual is contrary to the social media as it deals with the individual itself and its connection with the higher power. It is intended to bring together these two extremes to meet at a mean point where the amalgamation of both social media and spirituality starts a new chapter of how social media can effect and spread the concept of spirituality.

2 Literature Review

2.1 Spirituality

Spirituality is the process of personal transformation. As stated by the British author, physicist and meditation teacher Peter Russell the core of spirituality is the journey to

© Springer International Publishing Switzerland 2015
G. Meiselwitz (Ed.): SCSM 2015, LNCS 9182, pp. 39–47, 2015.
DOI: 10.1007/978-3-319-20367-6_5

discover our real self and be aware of our conscience. What we know about ourselves is a very meager part of who we actually are and spirituality brings us closer to our true self. It makes us realize that even though things around us are changing with the course of life, the 'I' in us is all pervasive and everlasting. Once we realize and know who we are, we are free from the burden of all the bondages of our life and the peace which transcends within us, fulfills our inner self. It's like when a boat lost on the trials and tribulations of the storms finally sees the shore and is able to reach there [1, 5]. Spiritual Healing has the potential to access disturbances on all levels of our being - emotional, mental, spiritual and physical.

2.2 Social Media

Social media is a group of communication channels which help people to create, share and exchange ideas and information. These channels can be virtual communities and networks. They introduce significant and widespread changes to communication between organizations, communities, and individuals facilitating interaction and collaboration. Social media helps us in sharing, co-creating, discussing, and modify user-generated content [2]. The different types of social media are Social Networks, Social News, Media Sharing, Micro blogging, Blog Comments and Forums.

2.3 Life of Teenagers

Adolescence is a time for rapid cognitive development. As stated by the developmental psychologist and philosopher Jean Piaget it is that stage of life when an individual's thoughts start transforming from being self centered to more intellectual which inculcates the ability of reasoning in them. Also at this age, innumerable and uncontrollable thoughts of confusion and curiosity are constantly hammering a teenager's mind, which leads to anger, exasperation and puzzlement [3, 6, 8]. Teenage as a midway between childhood and adulthood is a strange land of paradoxes and bewildering eloquence. It is hard to cope up with the do's and don'ts of the family and society without understanding the why's and how's around things. And this pressure arises the feelings of incompetence, inferiority and lack of acceptance in teenagers.

3 Theoretical Considerations

Literature review on different entities revealed that the subject needed a foundation for the concept to stand on. The theories considered for the forth coming practical study were ought to be human centric rather than data driven. The research methodology is based on the theories mentioned below which were taken in to consideration.

3.1 Behaviorism

Behaviorism is a concept of studying human reactions or arresting the stimuli of the humans to the given environment, conditions, and actions. As the theory evolved it captured the physical and emotional aspects of the reaction.

This paper ascertains to capture both these aspects as the research is taken place in the natural environment of all stakeholders. The viable features of behaviorism, which make it all but supportive of the subject is naturalistic, manipulative and reactive.

3.2   Qualitative Research

Most important features of the concept based on the literature review were qualitative and the sample size was predominantly random.

The persuasive emotions and psyche of the stakeholders (teenagers, spiritual gurus, psychologists, etc.) were important aspects in shaping the concept. The qualitative research approach is relevant than the empirical data keeping in mind the number of stakeholders. Qualitative research gives better portrayal of stakeholder behavior.

4   Research Methodology

Drawing an analogy between literature review and theoretical considerations, the research methodology was designed to meet the expectation and comfort of all stakeholders involved. All the field research was conducted at stakeholder's natural environment and no artificial set up was created during the research process.

The methods employed to capture qualitative data and behavior of stakeholders were:

Questionnaire
Interview
Observation

4.1   Questionnaire

The questionnaire was designed keeping in mind the persona of the stakeholders (Psychologists, Teenagers, Spiritual Gurus). All the questions were directed to understand life of teenagers in today's world, effects of social media on teenagers, counseling and spiritual aid methods. Some parts of the questionnaires were purposely designed to capture a little amount of quantitative data regarding various aspects like common problems and their frequency, total time spend on social media, etc.

4.2   Interview

Most of the research was on the field and around the natural environment of the stakeholders. The interview was more personal and most of questions and answers were accumulation of the personal journey around the three spheres of social media, spirituality and life of teenagers. The interview was directed to get a solution from the stakeholder hence capturing their mental models.

4.3   Observation

Behavior is one of the major entities that needed to be captured for better understanding of the entire scenario. Observation research methodology was employed because that would interfere the least with the actions and reaction of the stakeholders in their natural environment. All the interaction patterns of stakeholders with each other, their response to stimuli and reaction were carefully observed and noted.

5   Findings

According to the psychologists: It is important to listen to the teenagers and encourage them to share their daily activities including their problems. When they know someone is there to listen to them, it instills confidence and helps them see the positive side of life. Regarding teenagers who are addicted to substances, Psychologist suggest that it is important to build the level of trust with them so that one can reach to the root cause of their problems and then make suggestions. Sometimes psychologists even take group sessions with teenagers having similar kinds of problems. Usually when teenagers see that they are not the only ones with those kinds of problems and there are other people who are like them, they get a little consolation. Group sessions help them learn and understand things through each other's situation. Some forms of physical exercises are also found be to be effective.

According to spiritual institutions: A lot of teenagers are seeking guidance through spirituality remotely or directly at the spiritual institutions. The teachers at these spiritual institutions pointed out that teenagers are usually brought to these institutions by their parents seeking help for their wards to improve or develop concentration which will directly effect their decision making ability towards career choosing path. Meditation sessions are common activity in the spiritual institutions, which they conduct with teenagers as well. Meditation is nothing but an exercise to relax the mind, body and soul and induces a mode of consciousness in an individual. It helps develop positivity in teenagers, which fosters their general mental well-being and development of specific capacities such as calmness, clarity and concentration.

6   Talking Circles – Concept

The ubiquitous level of social media integration into the lives of teenagers speaks volumes about the paradigm shift in communication and community. On similar lines, Talking Circles is a structured concept used to bring teenagers together to better understand one another, build and strengthen bonds and solve their problems [7, 9]. The talking circle concept is a way of getting the complete picture of whatever issue is at hand to enable participants to move together in a good way and to build and maintain a healthy community and life. Through this process, they can share stories, learn about themselves and each other and gain a better understanding of their situation. The talking circle concept can be employed to achieve better solution for teenage related problems, community development, increasing social interaction and social conduct.etc. To be precise talking circles is a concept for helping teenagers by giving them a stage on which they can share and communicate their problems via proper and appropriate social media, and the problems are addressed and resolved through spiritual techniques.

In this concept, teenagers who are connected to any existing social media come, share and listen to a problem that they face and find a solution through spirituality. The various types of social media can be anything from social networking, social news, media sharing, micro blogging, blog comments and forums. The talking circle concept will be introduced and promoted through various social media activities only.

The talking circle concept will be a combination of social networking site, a micro blogging site and media sharing. There will be a spiritual Guru who will be connected to his students online. The teenager and no one else can make the choice of his/her Guru, but a teenager can seek advice in the forum for suggesting a Guru for his/her specific problem from peers. Each guru might form a group of teenagers with similar problem for group counseling and joining a group counseling session is solely teenager's choice. The sessions can be held via video calling, online chats, and virtual rooms. Students can share their problems and in return can get suggestions from the Gurus as well as the co-users (Figs. 1 and 2).

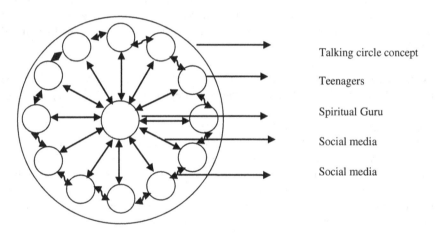

Fig. 1. Talking circle descriptive diagram

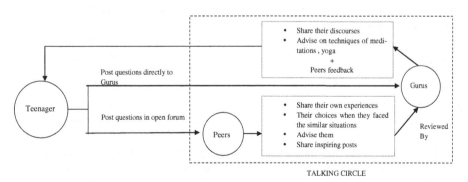

Fig. 2. How a problem is addressed in talking circle?

Features of talking circles:

Real time and easy connect to spiritual masters and like-minded people
Real time conferencing in such a way that people can share their problems with the
masters and other people.
Real time meditation classes
Online discourses for various masters
Students can download music, videos and discourses and also share them
Self-realization workshops
Music Therapy sessions

6.1   Scenario for Talking Circles

The talking circle concept can be explained with the help of an example.

For e.g.: One of the major problems teenagers face is while choosing their careers.
Lack of direction and sense of purpose affects their ability of decision making especially in this case. A spiritual platform can encourage teens to reveal their passion,
beauty and dreams, their fears, problems and insecurities that might hinder their ability
of decision making. The concept of talking circles allows the teenagers to put forth
their problems in a social space in the presence of their Guru and other likeminded
people and seek help.

A model can be created where once when the teenagers put forth their problems;
the Gurus have a technique of suggesting them solutions. It draws inference from the
concept of Monomyth or the Heroes Journey by Joseph Campbell [4, 10, 11]. The hero
in the monomyth lives his life in the ordinary world until he receives a call to venture
into the unknown world of eccentric powers and events. As the hero accepts the call to
seek for the unknown world, he undergoes several trials alone or with assistance. The
hero must survive this challenge and on survival he may achieve a 'boon'. The hero
must then decide to return to the ordinary world with this boon and on successful return
this boon may be used to improve the world. This structure is closely followed by the
stories of Prometheus, Moses, Gautama Buddha and Osiris. This ancient wisdom can
be applied to the current situation of the teenagers.

Campbell puts forth this concept in various stages:

Separation (or Departure): It deals with the hero's adventure prior to the quest.
Initiation: It deals with the hero's quests along the way.
Return: It deals with the hero's return home with knowledge and powers acquired on
   the journey.

On similar lines, the Gurus suggestions for the teenagers can fall under 3 stages.

Expression
The first and foremost thing to do when dealing with any problem or symptoms of a
problem is to say it or express it loud and clear. Most of the teenagers don't even know
if they have a problem, they might observe some symptoms but neglect. Talking circles
platform gives them this opportunity to express themselves, even on the slightest of the
symptoms of their problems in life. Many psychologist and spiritual Gurus believe that

most of the teenagers have no clue if there is something wrong in their life and to make it worse they don't discuss the symptoms with anyone. In recent years the developments in the social media and affinity of teenagers towards it is quite apparent. Leveraging on this, talking circles deal with employing different social media to give teenagers the opportunity to express themselves freely.

Expression Techniques: Some of the expression techniques through which one can express their problems in talking circles are:

Writing: Most of the psychologists advice their patients to maintain a dairy or express through words. Looking at the current lifestyle of teenagers and their engagement with texting, chatting, micro blogging, etc. It becomes very natural to them to express themselves through various social media in Taking Circle platform. Various technologies like text to voice and voice to text can come handy in helping them express freely and share it in the platform.

Voice Recording: There may be times when the teenagers might become too conscious about words and grammar during expressing through writing which might hamper the freedom of expressing oneself. Recording their voice and sharing is very helpful as user is less conscious about worrying about the technicality of his speech.

Video Sharing: With a mobile in every hand and a camera in every mobile, video recording has never been so easy. Teenagers can make a video expressing themselves and their problem and putting in talking circles. Using these technique teenagers can post their problems in talking circles, and these problems in different formats reach the spiritual Guru and other people in the group. Now looking at the problem, teenagers with similar problems can form groups and a Guru can then direct according to the problem either individually or in-group.

Initiation
After the initial expression of feelings and problem, the part, which is very important, is making the people associated with talking circle platform do something, which they never did before or were apprehensive in doing. Like the hero in monomyth the spiritual Guru takes teens to embark on some new activities, which are relevant to their problems.

As found out from research and insights from psychologists and spiritual Gurus, they always engage their clients in some sort of activity to take the mind off. This is where social media can play a big role with improvement in virtual world creation, gamification technique to every social media activity and apps development for every possible scenario and need. Teenagers can associate themselves to individual and group activities as directed by Guru with both in person and virtual presence. There can be certain self-esteem activities, which the Gurus can perform with the teenager's in-group or individually with each teenager, which are as follows:

Online Positive Focus Groups: Group exercises for building up self-confidence through affirmation can be performed. Teenagers are present online in the group along with the Guru. Each one has to say positive words about themselves and their family members one by one. Saying positive words out loud in a group has a positive effect on teenagers. Along with speaking, they can also share sketches or paintings related to the positive characteristic they are talking about. The activity challenges the participants in the following way.

Online Games: In the presence of the Guru, each member of the teenager's family is present along with the teenagers. There can be role-playing games online where each family member will be involved such that they have to together complete a particular task. When the family will work towards achieving a common goal together, this gives the teenagers the assurance that their family will be there always for them and this increases their trust on their family.

Online Meditation Groups: Meditation is one of the most important technique which helps teenagers to attain that state of thoughtlessness and freeness from their daily routine to look out for newer adventures in life which would help them have a broader perspective towards life. The Gurus can teach teenagers individually through video call, chat and also by sharing videos about the meditation technique. When seeing the Guru performing meditation right in front of them and the effect of the same, this might help the teenagers to learn the technique.

Illumination

Once the teenager has gone through the exercise for initiation, the teenager will have a much better sense of self-awareness which would provide him the zeal to live life to the fullest. We can call this stage as the stage of illumination. The teenagers now can share their stories and their struggles in their online meet up groups. There can be times when one individual is able to learn from the experiences of the other. One can also write something, record songs or movies retelling their stories and share them online.

7 Social Implications

The talking circles platform will play a major role in defining how teenagers cope with their problems through spirituality while being socially active and connected. The concept of sharing and solving will catch up and the major problem of teenagers of 'not sharing' can be solved. Since the platform does not use any new complicated system, concept or technology so it will be very easy for teenager through social media to learn and understand the technique of spirituality.

This could be a major step in community building where each one helps other to solve his/her problem without expecting anything. A building block for creating social awareness and social responsibility. A major step in making teenagers self reliable and mentally strong.

References

1. What is spirituality, 14 December 2014. http://www.peterrussell.com/Weaver/Weaver Spirituality.php

2. Social media, 14 December 2014. http://en.wikipedia.org/wiki/Social_media
3. Piaget's Stages of Cognitive Development, 14 December 2014. http://www.telacommuni cations.com/nutshell/stages.htm
4. Monomyth, 14 December 2014. http://en.wikipedia.org/w/index.php?title=Monomyth& redirect=no
5. Lopez, D.S.: Buddhism and Science. The University of Chicago Press, Chicago (2008)
6. Kimball, E.M.: Developing spirituality in adolescents: research-informed practice and practice –inspired research. In: Third North American Conference on Spirituality and Social Work, St. Paul, MN 55108 U.S.A (2008)
7. http://www.rogersparkywat.org/wpcontent/uploads/2011/09/Talking_Circle_Guidelines_ PSchaefer.pdf. Accessed 23 January 2014
8. http://www.icsahome.com/infoserv_articles/lutz_alison_teenagespiritualityandinternet.htm. Accessed 18 January 2014
9. http://www.designcouncil.org.uk/resources-and-events/designers/design-glossary/co-design. Accessed 20 January 2014
10. http://en.wikipedia.org/wiki/Monomyth
11. http://www.huffingtonpost.com/matt-ragland/the-heros-journey-using-a_b_4893165.html
12. http://images.shulcloud.com/111/uploads/drashot/Moshe-Buddha-and-Harry-Potter_-The-Unique-Power-of-Sefer-Shemot.pdf

Social Media Participation: A Narrative Way to Help Urban Planners

Erick López-Ornelas$^{(\boxtimes)}$ and Nora Morales Zaragoza

Information Technology Department and Theory
and Design Processes Department,
Universidad Autónoma Metropolitana – Cuajimalpa, Mexico City, Mexico
{elopez,nmorales}@correo.cua.uam.mx

Abstract. Social Media Participation can be very important when you have to make an important decision about a topic related to urban planning. Textual analysis to identify the sentiment about a topic or, a user analysis to identify the actors involved on a discussion, can be very important for the persons or institutions that have to take an important decision. In this paper we analyze the case study of the #nuevoaeropuerto in Mexico City to highlight the importance of conducting a study of this nature.

Keywords: Twitter · Social media participation · Urban planning · Sentiment analysis · Users analysis · Textual analysis

1 Introduction

Urban planning is a technical and political process concerned with the use of land and design of the urban environment, including air and water and infrastructure passing into and out of urban areas such as transportation and distribution networks. In the other hand urban planners are challenged to engage the public in meaningful ways to shape these planning processes [1].

In this paper we explore the idea of the use of social media participation, especially microblogs, such as, Twitter, in order to analyze the way the users interact with these urban topics, understanding who the actors are and how they can help urban planners taking their decisions.

Social Media participation represents one type of tool that can be used to support interaction between groups of people who share a common interest [2–4]. One of the features of many social networking tools is that they allow participants to microblog, the posting of short content, such as phrases, quick comments, images, or links to URLs, photos, audio, or video [5, 6]. According to [7], all this elements generates a small narrative bit (narb) that tells a tiny story about an individual.

All the digital social networking systems (Facebook, Twitter, Instagram, etc.) make an assumption that members would be interested in creating specific identity narratives about themselves. This is facilitated at the time of subscription when new members are requested to provide some basic information about them. All these users that complete their profile provide very important information that can be reused to categorize and classify them [8]. These are often considered 'demographic' information that could

© Springer International Publishing Switzerland 2015
G. Meiselwitz (Ed.): SCSM 2015, LNCS 9182, pp. 48–54, 2015.
DOI: 10.1007/978-3-319-20367-6_6

include basic attributes like gender and race. The participant is expected to truthfully indicate their specific attributes which are essential to become a member of the social network. The entire process of identity construction is based on information that is deliberately solicited by a digital social network system and disclosed by the one seeking membership in the network.

There are generally two mechanisms that are used to create these short stories. First, a member of any digital social network is asked to complete the basic demographic information at the time of joining the network. The members could also choose to disclose other information ranging from taste in music to political preferences. In combination, these self-disclosures create a "user profile" of the person that could remain relatively stable over long periods of time (Normally nobody change their personal information after their creation). Indeed, some components might never change such as the place where one was born or the date of birth of an individual. Secondly, the member is expected to continuously update specific events in one's life so that all those connected with the member would remain informed about the specific events in an individual's life, however banal or commonplace those events might be. Nevertheless, those constant updates could become the pieces that tell the story of a particular individual. These two strategies are shared by most social networking systems and together these strategies offer the opportunity to create a narrative within specific boundaries allowing participants to carefully pick and construct their selves.

Analyzing these narbs we can detect some relevant actors that interact in microblogs. This narb is a construction of an identity that depends on how well a person is able to tell a story about the self.

2 Microblogs and Twitter

If Twitter is a conduit for global stream of consciousness, it logically follows that the medium is a barometer for revealing everything, from occurrence of natural disasters to public perception of the city. In this paper we explore the potential awareness of this consciousness through the examination of Twitter and urban planning. Twitter can be understood as a new environment in which people gave their opinion about some problems in the cities.

Twitter is a popular social media service that allows people to share updates, news, and information (known at "tweets") with people in their Twitter network and beyond. In our approach we used tweets extracted from Twitter. A tweet is a little message of no more than 140 characters that users creates in order to communicate thoughts, feelings, or even participate in conversations. With over 200 million registered users [9] and 13 % of online Americans using Twitter [10], Twitter is one of the most popular social media available. Research has compared Twitter to earlier kinds of social media like blogs [11] and social network sites [12]. Recent analyses of microblogging suggest that the brevity and broadcastability of messages are important affordances of microblogging.

First, and perhaps most promisingly, we believe that microblogging data can offer city planners and developers better information that can be used to improve planning and quality of life in cities. This might include new kinds of metrics for understanding people's interactions in different parts of a city, new methods of pinpointing problems that people are facing, and new ways of identifying potential opportunities for improving things.

3 Text and User Analysis

In this article we will discuss the installation of the new airport in Mexico City as a case of study. This installation represents a major infrastructure project to be performed in the center of Mexico City. This project has some encouraging opinions and some strong criticism. In this article we are interested in discover what people say in Twitter and who are the important users that represent a sort of activists in social networks.

The role of social media during the announcement of installation of the new airport in Mexico City gained great importance because Twitter became the principal media for the youngest people. Our analysis is based on all the tweets collected during this announcement.

The tweet allows the communication of texts, videos or pictures by providing a link to it. Some words of the tweet are preceded by the pound sing # (hashtag). By using the hashtag, users can recover, reply (known as retweet) or follow conversations about a certain subject because this hashtag becomes automatically a hyperlink on Twitter. Everyone who clicks on a hashtag has the possibility to view the sear results of all other tweets that contains the same hashtag. In our case, we used the hashtag #nuevoaeropuerto, to recover all the conversations, ideas, phrases that were produced during the announcement of the installation of the new airport in Mexico City by the president Enrique Peña Nieto. The tweets that we recovered have different structures. For example:

- A simple phrase like: "La sustentabilidad y el desarrollo económico del aeropuerto deben ir de la mano para lograr el proyecto que tanto necesitamos." (In English "Sustainability and economic development of the airport should go hand in hand to achieve the project we need.")
- A phrase containing name(s) of the user(s). For example: "Obras del Aeropuerto de StaMta inician el 1 de febrero @carlosecaicedo @LINAPALMA @opinioncaribe @OpinaSantamarta @KARYMUCO @ELTIEMPO." (In English: "Works Airport StaMta initiate February @carlosecaicedo @LINAPALMA @opinioncaribe @OpinaSantamarta @KARYMUCO @ELTIEMPO")
- A phrase with links, for example: "Con el Nuevo Aeropuerto, no habrá problemas viales como se piensa http://t.co/cSnhHJYKZQ." (In English: "With the new airport, no traffic problems as you think http://t.co/cSnhHJYKZQ")
- A phrase with retweet RT. For example: "RT @pedestre: Plan de desarrollo urbano del aeropuerto es como Dios: dicen q existe, pero nadie lo ha visto." (In English: "RT @pedestre: Urban planning of the airport is like God, he exist, but no one has seen him")
- A phrase with hashtag(s), like: "Y hablando de #impunidad Primero era el problema #Tlatlaya, ahora es el #NuevoAeropuerto." (In English: "And speaking of #impunity #Tlatlaya was the first problem, now is the #Newairport")

For this test we used generated 1,400 tweets on September 2, 2014, the date on which the President of Mexico made the announcement of the installation of the new airport in Mexico City. The first reactions on Twitter showed a clear support for the installation of the airport. The following Table 1 shows an analysis of feelings generated tweets held in that period.

This sentiment analysis has been generated using the sentiment viz application developed by Healey and Ramaswamy [13] that is an application to estimate and visualize *sentiment* for short, incomplete text snippets. Sentiment is defined as "an attitude, thought, or judgment prompted by feeling." The specific goal is a visualization that presents basic emotional properties embodied in the text, together with a measure of the confidence. In the Fig. 1, we can detect that is a big concentration on opinions that are tense, active and alert, this is normally because is a new announcement of the government and all major actors are expecting the media reactions in order to have a real position of the announcement. In Fig. 2, we show the opinion of the same topic but two weeks later. We can see that almost all opinions are augmented and almost all passed of the status bored to the status active. Also, there are a large number of opinions that approve the project. This is due to the big media strategy generated by the government to manipulate the public opinion about the project. This analysis shows how opinion can change of one date to another in order to take a better decision about a topic.

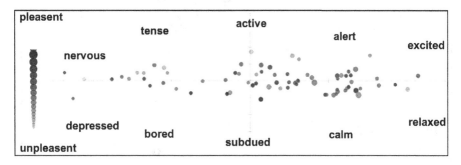

Fig. 1. Sentiment analysis related to the hashtag #nuevoaeropuerto, September 2, 2014.

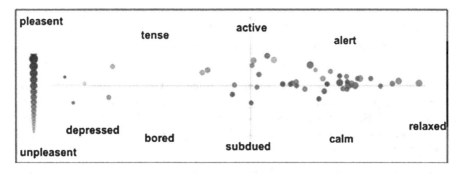

Fig. 2. Sentiment analysis related to the hashtag #nuevoaeropuerto, September 16, 2014.

The second major work in this paper is the identification of users who are participating in this discussion and how we might characterize them. Initially we map the most important actors in the discussion. Here we find several actors, for example : @cghunam, @ecoosfera, @atencofpdt, @galvanochoa, @mvsnoticias, @cgt, @lostejemedios, @elva_contra, @notipaco, @a_encinas_r, @padresolalinde, @monitordh, @omarel44, @article19mx, @kmiret, @jscesareo, @komanilel, @sme1914, @atilioboron. We can see all these actors in Fig. 3.

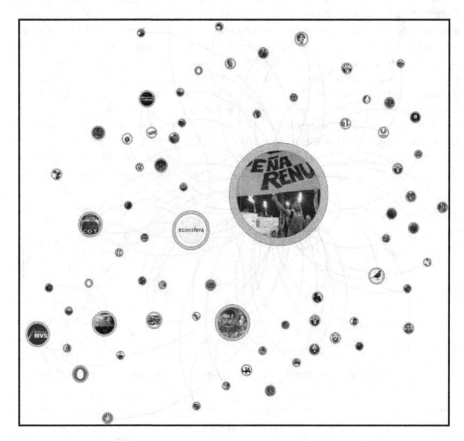

Fig. 3. Major actors associated to the hashtag #nuevoaeropuerto

Despite the fact that the online community being a relatively young phenomenon, some of attempts in classifying internet users have been undertaken. For example Brandtzæg and Heim [14] propose a study that can be well adapted to the urban planning activism developed in this article. According to Brandtzaeg and Haim we can identify 5 different users:

- *Sporadics* visit social network from time to time, mainly to check if somebody contacted them.

- *Lurkers* is the largest group, they do not create any content, but consume and spread the content created by other groups. They are also notable for a propensity to time-killing.
- *Socializers* use social networks to communicate and make interesting comments about a discussion. They need to be read and saw for a multiple users. For example: @galvanochoa, @mvsnoticias and @a_encinas_r.
- *Debaters* are a more mature and educated version of socializers. Besides communication, less shallow than in the previous case, they are interested in consumption and discussion of news and other information available in social networks. For example @padresolalinde, @ecoosfera, @kmiret, @jscesareo and @komanilel.
- *Actives* are engaged with all possible types of activity: communication, reading, creating, watching, and establishing groups. They have a strong criticism about a subject. Almost all users can are inside this category. For example @cghunam, @atencofpdt, @cgt, @lostejemedios, @elva_contra, @notipaco, @monitordh, @sme1914.

With this classification, decision makers may have better decision elements to analyze the behavior of the movement. With this analysis, we can detect who are the main actors or who is more important, even to know who is the leader who has a large number of followers, etc. All these elements define the strategy for the project and how to make better decisions for society.

4 Conclusions

The Social Media should be understood and taken as a medium that support the participatory process. In this paper we presented a review of advanced social media analysis method and tools, and an original methodology for textual analysis of Social Media Participation. Methodologies and analysis have been reviewed in order to discover potential suitable approaches for the integration of the Social Media Particpation in urban and regional planning.

In this article we sought to understand Twitter's role in activist movements that are related on urban planning by exploring the specific case of the installation of the new airport in Mexico City. Diverse opinions (favorable and unfavorable) were presented in order to evaluate the sentiment associated to an important decision in different time. Also a user analysis is explored in order to categorize the different actors involved on a discussion.

In this article we argue that having all this information (users and sentiment analysis) can be very important in urban planning, because the person or institution that take the decision could have a lot of information and take better decisions. Specially in urban planning because the people is directly involved in this decisions.

In order to use Social Media efficiently for planning practice, it is necessary to encourage inclusion of all groups, through the promotion of systems, rising public awareness, and enabling an access to modern technology; also to choose a right tool, or multiple tools, in addition to the traditional ones. Another important topic is carefully study users of the system in order to determine exactly which group it does represent.

In conclusion, the knowledge of Social Media Participation if proficiently elicited might be used to discover and expose the will of users and could be a valid support for design, analysis and decision-making in urban and regional planning. Further research is definitely needed and Social Media analysis methods and technology should be applied from within real-life urban and regional planning process to proof the full efficacy. Nevertheless, early results are promising and the research agenda challenging.

References

1. Borge, R., Colombo, C., Welp, Y.: Online and offline participation at the local level: a quantitative analysis of the Catalan Municipalities. Inf. Commun. Soc. **12**, 899–928 (2009)
2. Livingstone, S., Bober, M., Helsper, E.: Active participation or just more information? Inf. Commun. Soc. **8**, 287–314 (2005)
3. Christakis, N.A., Fowler, J.H.: Connected: The Surprising Power of Our Social Networks and How They Shape Our Lives. Little Brown and Company, New York (2009)
4. Sui, D., Goodchild, M.F.: The convergence of GIS and social media: challenges for GIScience. Int. J. Geogr. Inf. Sci. **25**(11), 1737–1748 (2011)
5. Rattenbury T., Good N., Naaman M.: Towards automatic extraction of event and place semantics from flickr tags. In: Proceeding of the 30th International ACM SIGIR Conference on Research and Development in Information Retrieval, New York, NY, USA, pp. 103–110 (2007)
6. Lewis, S., Pea, R., Rosen, J.: Beyond participation to co-creation of meaning: mobile social media in generative learning communities. Soc. Sci. Inf. **49**, 351–369 (2010)
7. Mitra, Ananda: Creating a presence on social networks via narbs. Glob. Media J. Am. Ed. **9**, 1–18 (2010)
8. Ramine, T., Carr, L., Hall, W., Bentwood, J.: Identifying communicator roles in twitter. In: Proceedings of the 21st International Conference Companion on World Wide Web (WWW 2012 Companion), pp. 1161–1168. ACM, New York (2012)
9. Halliday, J.: Guardian Activate 2011 Conference Live Blog. Guardian Activate 2011 Conference (2011). http://www.guardian.co.uk/media/pda/2011/apr/28/guardian-activate-2011-new-york. Accessed 2011
10. Smith, A.: Twitter Update 2011. Pew Internet & American Life, Washington DC (2011)
11. Java, A., Song, X., Finin, T., Tseng, B.: Why we twitter: understanding microblogging usage and communities. Paper presented at the Joint 9th WEBKDD and 1st SNA-KDD Workshop 2007, San Jose, CA (2007)
12. Gruzd, A., Takhteyev, Y., Wellman, B.: Imagining twitter as an imagined community. Am. Behav. Sci. **55**(10), 1294–1318 (2011)
13. Healey, C., Ramaswamy, S.: Visualizing Twitter Sentiment (2010). http://www.csc.ncsu.edu/faculty/healey/tweet_viz/
14. Brandtzæg, P.B., Heim, J.: A typology of social networking sites users. Int. J. Web Based Commun. **7**(1), 28–51 (2011)

Using Information Visualization Techniques to Improve the Perception of the Organizations' Image on Social Networks

Isabel H. Manssour, Milene S. Silveira, Caroline Q. Santos[✉],
Adolf J. Freitas, and Flávio T. Schirmer

Faculdade de Informática, Pontifícia Universidade Católica Do Rio Grande
Do Sul – PUCRS, Av. Ipiranga 6681, Porto Alegre, Brazil
{isabel.manssour,milene.silveira}@pucrs.br,
{caroline.queiroz,adolf.freitas,flavio.schirmer}@acad.pucrs.br

Abstract. Nowadays it is notorious the growth and the popularity of social networks such as Facebook, LinkedIn and Twitter, especially with the facilities provided by the use of mobile devices. Considering these social networks, Twitter has a different approach: a friendship connection doesn't need to exist and a person can follow another person or organization just to receive its tweets. So, this social network is often used as a way to get general or specific news and to express (dis)satisfaction about products, politics, organizations, etc. Considering this, the need for organizations to monitor what people are "saying" about them has arisen. Thus, the main goal of this work is to understand how information visualization techniques can support and improve the analysis of the perceived image of organizations on social networks. For this, we developed an application prototype to support sentiment analyses on Twitter and we conducted a study on how this prototype, called MentionStats, can contribute to the company's image analysis on Twitter. This study consisted on interviews with professionals about their perceptions of the MentionStats and its visualizations. Our main contribution are the presented possibilities of using information visualization techniques in order to help users to deepen the analysis of their organizations image on social networks, and also users' impressions about this.

Keywords: Data visualization · Social networks · Sentiment analysis

1 Introduction

The advent of Web 2.0 has changed the way people use the Internet. Nowadays it is notorious the growth and the popularity of social networks such as Facebook, LinkedIn and Twitter, especially with the facilities provided by the use of mobile devices. Social networks became one of the most important communication tools among people over the Internet. It allow users to find other users with similar interests, share with friends personal and professional information, data and

© Springer International Publishing Switzerland 2015
G. Meiselwitz (Ed.): SCSM 2015, LNCS 9182, pp. 55–66, 2015.
DOI: 10.1007/978-3-319-20367-6_7

applications, publish photos, engage on conversations, etc. [1]. Considering these social networks, Twitter has a different approach: a friendship connection doesn't need to exist. A person can follow another person or organization just to receive its tweets[1]. Thus, this social network is often used as a way to get general or specific news. It is also used to express (dis)satisfaction about products, politics, organizations, etc. Considering this, the need for organizations to monitor what people are "saying" about them has arisen [2].

According to Fan et al. [3], issues as "how to track social media return on investment", "how to identify and engage with the most influential social media users" and "what tactics to use to create an effective social media strategy" can be analyzed through social media analytical tools. In addition, at the same time that help to answer these questions, data analysis shall consider that social media transform the very nature of business. The large volume of data generated and stored by companies defies social media analytics about how companies can monitor and analyze social media conversations about them, their services or their products.

According to Zeng et al. [4], social media analytics aims derive information from social media in context-rich application, support decision-making process and provide architectural designs and solution frameworks for applications that can benefit from the "wisdom of crowds" through the Web. In other words, it involves developing and evaluating tools and frameworks to collect, monitor, analyze, summarize, and visualize social media data to facilitate conversations and interactions to extract intelligence [4].

In this context, the main goal of this work is to understand how information visualization techniques can support and improve the analysis of the perceived image of organizations on social networks (here organization's image is used with the same meaning as organization's reputation or company reputation). We choose to explore features as visualization of feelings and statistics about mentions in Twitter, whose data is public [5]. We defined the following guiding research questions: "Does the use of interaction techniques with information visualization help to deepen the social network data analysis?", "It is possible to have a dynamic analysis of a data set using information visualization techniques?", "Could the understanding of customer's perception assist the company in making decisions?".

Trying to answer these questions we developed an application prototype that allows us to visualize the mentions[2] about one specific user at Twitter. This application is aimed specifically at professionals working in the area of relationships and their needs, exploring features as visualization of feelings and statistics about mentions. Through interviews, we collected the users' opinions about the prototype and about how existing visualizations can aid the decision-making process in the company. Thus, as our main contribution, we presented

---

[1] Tweet is every message posted by a Twitter user. It can have a maximum of 140 characters and it can also be called "post".

[2] Mention is a way to talk to or reference someone on Twitter. For this, the tweet must contain the @username referenced in the message body.

possibilities of using interactive visualization techniques in order to help users to deepen the analysis of their organization's image on social networks, and also users impressions about this.

The remaining of this paper is organized as follows: next section presents the background of our work and it is followed by a section dedicated to related works. Section 4 presents the methodology adopted for this research. The MentionStats application prototype and its features are described in Section 5. Section 6 is dedicated to data analysis, where the preliminary user impressions are presented. Last section concludes the paper with final considerations and the future works.

2 Background

Mobile devices, social networks and spaces devoted to companies and products on Internet that make it easier to share information instantly, create a social media landscape that is quickly becoming part of the fabric of everyday business operations. With the growing number of users on social media sites, arises the need for businesses to monitor and use them to their advantage [3]. This has opened space for development of tools to support the analysis of social-media. In this section we present some fundamental concepts used in this research field.

2.1 Organizations and Social Networks

According to Fan et al. [3], social media has changed our conversations about products and services but not about the business activities behind them. Social media is more relevant to the design development and utilization stages in the product (or service) life cycle. In addition, the analysis of social media helps businesses to gather competitive intelligence and understand more completely their business environments, suppliers, and competitors. Trend analysis and other social media analytic tools help in the identification of any changes in behavior and sentiment affecting product design and development.

Customers' reactions can also help to change a marketing campaign or a product. Companies hope that social network interactions (retweets, reblogs, and social tagging) are positive, though it does not always mean they are. "Customers' on-line complaints about products and services are common, and real-time sentiment analysis, topic modeling, and other tools allow businesses to know how their customers feel about their products and services and respond quickly, before customer complaints become an on-line torrent" [3].

In spite of the growing interest of companies in this area, there is little understanding of the potential business applications of mining social networks. According to Bonchi et al. [6], while there is a large body of research on different problems and methods for mining social network, the potential business impact of these techniques is still largely unexplored.

2.2 Data Visualization

Data visualization is a growing research area that seeks to improve the presentation of data and its goal is to support users in the process of sensemaking, in which information is collected, organized, and analyzed to form new knowledge and inform further action [7]. In other words, it assists users to understand the data, store them and in the decision-making process [8,9].

According to Heer et al. [9], the goal of visualization is to aid the understanding of data by leveraging the human visual system ability to recognize patterns, spot trends, and identify outliers. If visual representations are well-designed, they "can replace intuitive cognitive calculations with simple perceptual inferences and improve comprehension, memory, and decision-making process". The challenge in visualization involves issues such as for any given data set, the number of visual encodings is extremely large. To improve this process, computer scientists, psychologists, and statisticians have studied how well different encodings facilitate the comprehension of data types such as numbers, categories, and networks [9]. Thus, we can consider the data visualization techniques a kind of big-dataset translator for a more easily understood language, using charts, tables, colors and other visual aids.

Another point to be considered is the fact that the human ability to perceive patterns and draw conclusions is a key factor [3], since it can vary from person to person. Because of this, visualization techniques shall also exploits an individual's visual perception to facilitate cognition [7–9].

2.3 Sentiment Analysis on Twitter

According to Fan et al. [3], opinion mining, or sentiment analysis, is the core technique behind many social media monitoring systems and trend-analysis applications. It leverages computational linguistics, natural language processing, and other methods of text analytics to automatically extract user sentiment or opinions from text sources at any level of granularity (words or phrases, up to entire documents). Such subjective information extracted about people, products, and services supports predicting the movement of stock markets, identifying market trends, analyzing product defects, and managing crises.

In this work we adopt the view of Pang et al. [10], to conceptualize the terms "opinion mining" and "sentiment analysis". The authors pointed that both terms denote the same field of study (which itself can be considered a sub-area of subjectivity analysis). The terms have multiple definitions that cover the subjective textual analysis of social media source.

As the audience of microblogging platforms - as Twitter - and services grows everyday, according to Pak et al. [11] data from these sources can be used in opinion mining and sentiment analysis tasks. For example, companies may be interested in questions such as: "What do people think about our product (service, company etc.)?", "How positive (or negative) are people about our product?" or "What would people prefer our product to be like?".

3   Related Works

Studies have been carried out aiming to analyze sentiments for popular topics on the Internet and social networks using visualization techniques. One of them [12] presents a framework with modules to collect, parse, analyze, estimate and visualize the estimated public sentiment from a Twitter corpus. A dictionary-based approach and a machine learning approach were implemented within the framework and compared using one case study: the royal birth of 2013. They found there is good correlation between the results produced by the popular dictionary-based approach and the machine learning approach when large volumes of tweets are analysed. However, to allow rapid analysis, faster methods need to be developed using big data techniques and parallel methods.

A similar work, SentiView [13], allows us to visualize the sentiment evolution of Web users along a timeline. It is an interactive visualization system that analyzes public sentiments for popular topics on the Internet. SentiView search and correlates frequent words in text data, mining and modelling the changes of the sentiment on public topics. The relationships of interest among different participants are presented in a relationship map. SentiView is adaptable for different social networking platforms, such as Twitter, blog and forum, and, through this work, the authors demonstrated the effectiveness of it in analyzing and visualizing sentiments.

Dong et al. [14] developed a prototype that automates the process of collecting and analyzing data from Twitter and offers a variety of simple visualizations to understand the public sentiment. According to the authors, during disasters, extracting useful information from pool of social media data can be useful in understanding the sentiment of the public, especially to improve decision-making process. They developed a prototype that automates the process of collecting and analyzing social media data from Twitter and then explore a variety of visualizations that can be generated by the tool in order to understand the public sentiment. The Hurricane Sandy disaster in 2012 was explored to generate a variety of visualizations. They performed a statistical analysis to explore the causality correlation between an approaching hurricane and the sentiment of the public.

In DeepTwitter [15], standard visualization techniques allow the understanding of how they can help in the analysis of users behavior in social networks. These techniques are used to see users connections and the frequency of tweets sent by one or a group of users, as well as ways to classify these tweets considering its content. Other tools available are tag cloud and the most popular users. Studies with users about the set of visualization techniques implemented in the DeepTwitter show different profiles of users are interested in different features (and in different visualization ways). Moreover we identified the trend of users to simultaneously use several small applications to monitor the use of social networks. Through the results of DeepTwitter users analysis arises the idea of focusing on specific market niches [2]. And, in this work, we focus on organizations needs.

On studies about the organization's image in social media, Fan et al. [3] presents the power of social media analytics. They present examples of companies that use social media and they discuss ways of "how to use, and influence, consumer social communications to improve business performance, reputation, and profit". Social media has opened several ways to assist in business visibility as well as provide real-time customer feedback. Data visualization tools (an social media analytics) have allowed companies to quantify, understand, and answer to customers questions about their corporate reputation and brands within social networks.

4   Methodology

To answer our guiding research questions, we divided our research work in three stages, as shown in Fig. 1 and following described:

- First stage: development of the MentionStats application prototype.
- Second stage: user study:
  - application of a pre-test questionnaire with seven questions about company profile and how it uses social networks.
  - presentation of the prototype for potential users of the tool for testing it.
  - realization of a semi-structured interview about this use, with ten open questions about users' perceptions from application use, its features and the implemented interactive visualizations.
- Third stage: qualitative analysis of the data collected during the process.

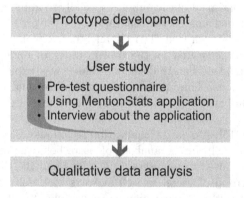

Fig. 1. Research steps.

5   MentionStats

MentionStats is an application prototype in which the user can monitor the mentions about a company, or individual, to get an overview of the perception that Twitter users have about it. The application was built for the operating system iOS, and works exclusively on the iPad platform (Apple). Its interface was planned and designed with custom items, based on iOS Human Interface Guidelines[3]. The user just need to login to start the visualization and have a perception of his (or the organization) image on social networks, according with the account used to login. The focus of the application is the visualization of polarity mentions on Twitter with the possibility to store the mentions for future query and analysis. It presents a navigation bar that appears on every screen, making easy the navigation between features (Timeline, Statistics, Dictionary, Filter) by the user.

MentionStats automatically analyzes each mention of the logged user and classifies them into three categories: Good, Neutral and Bad, based on predefined words that determine the message content. Also, it does a query of mentions according to day and time that the messages were sent and shows the mentions to the user through interactive graphics and a percentage meter in the statistics section. The list of mentions also offers a graphic marker in which each mention receives a small badge with a color that determines the message content, as shown in Fig. 2[4]. When the user profile is configured (by automatic integration between the MentionStats and the iOS), the application searches by keywords in all mentions that refer to any emotional charge, being positive, negative or neutral, assigning to each one its respective color.

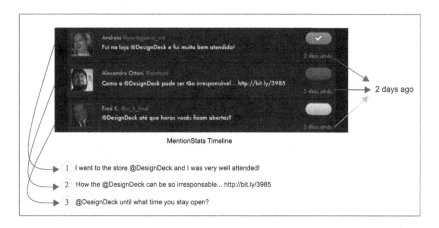

Fig. 2. Classification of the mentions (Color figure online).

When the application is searching by keywords, if an expression that refers to something positive is found, the system classifies such mention as positive. Besides the green check mark that appears next to the mention (Fig. 2), this information is included into the statistics (Fig. 3). The process is done in an

---

[3] http://goo.gl/WtDJx4.

[4] MentionStats application is in Portuguese Language. In the images used in this paper, translations will be presented when necessary.

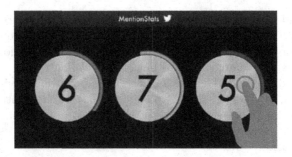

Fig. 3. Statistics of the total mentions (Color figure online).

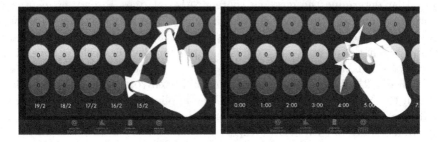

Fig. 4. Mentions presented per day or per hour (Color figure online).

analogous manner to negative words, but then the mentions are presented with a red mark. When the mention is not registered in the database as positive or negative, it is classified as neutral (yellow).

The statistics are shown in a panel divided into two parts: one static and other interactive. The first part allows the visualization of the percentages of mentions classified and the total number of positive, negative or neutral mentions (Fig. 3). The second part shows the total mentions per day or hour according to its classification. In this case, the visualization presents a circle for each polarity color (green, red and yellow), which contains the number of mentions (Fig. 4). The last thirty days are displayed and the user can change the granularity of the displayed timeline through pinch-out and pinch-in movement on the selected item, in this case, one day. Then, it is possible to see the mentions of one selected day classified per hour. The 24 hours of the selected day are presented.

The words used to classify the mentions are stored in a library that can be customized. So, the user can view, add and remove words in each category (positive, neutral or negative) for further classification of the mentions. It is also possible to use a lexicon of feelings such as Opinion Lexicon [16] for inclusion in this library to get better results of polarity classification. After making any changes in the library, user must update the list to save the changes and review their terms as the new indications.

6   Preliminary User Impressions

In this research, we have done a qualitative analysis of MentionStats through interviews with three professionals who are responsible for company's accounts in social networks (which is possibly our target audience). The three individuals were male with the mean age of 36 (34 to 40). The interviews were conducted in a private room in the University, lasting about 1 hour each one.

During the interviews, first, the participants answered a questionnaire about the company profile. After, a brief description of the application prototype were done and the participants were asked about their understanding of the tool and the purpose of MentionStats. In general, they replied that the application helps to monitor Twitter to detect opinion good or bad about their user profile. Finally, they used the application.

The interviewees reported that the companies have accounts on Twitter and Facebook to disseminate information about the company, its products and services, and do not have accounts on other social networks (or are little used). The use of Facebook is more intense than Twitter, and the company is interested to have a closer relationship with its customers and monitor conversations about their products and services in social networks. In general, companies maintains a professional dedicated in monitoring the mentions of their account on social networks. These companies access and use social networks every day and do not have a strategy or the company's disclosure plan on social networks. The relationship between companies and customers on social networks is more characterized by the dissemination of information and news, and little interaction. One interviewee reported that the company uses other means of communication with customers (telephone and on-line discussion lists), which more interaction than social networks.

Regarding to MentionStats, they said that the implemented techniques help to improve (and accelerate) not only the analysis of the organization image (*"with this [statistics] it is possible to get a general overview about positive, negative and neutral mentions (...) rapidly respond to the client in cases of negative mentions and give feedback to employees of the company, in case of positive mentions"*), but also in the decision-making process (*"you can quickly get a feedback from tweets posted by the organization (...) contributing in an agile decision-making process"*). The possibilities of personalization with the insertion of words related to the organization domain was also highlighted. According to one participant, *"viewing the timeline helps in finding relevant information about your organization's image. Not only in the organization's image but also in relation to the feedback from its own tweets. You can perform a quickly reading at the "image" of the company on social networks, each tweet that mentions the company is shown with its classification (good, neutral or bad)"*.

Other positive points mentioned: the visuals and colors are pleasant, the presentation of the list of tweets with photos of users (important to recognize people) and statistics are interesting. On the other hand they said that *"the library was considered nice but it could have a more "intelligent" way to associate words with their radical or verb tense"*.

The interaction with the application was considered non intuitive to one of the participants (Android mobile device user). In his opinion, to toggle between the visualization the number of mentions per hour and per day, user needs to know the fingers movements proper, and it was not easy to deduce.

As improvements, a participant pointed that the timeline update is not automatic - he could not drag the finger on the screen to update automatically (common feature in mobile applications) and he thinks this is an important functionality. In statistics, he would like to be able to separate also weekly or monthly. It would also be nice if an user could select a word in the timeline and set it as good or bad from that to be automatically incorporated into the words library. Another important point is to allow a synchronization with Twitter to enable answer users tweets directly from MentionStats.

Although the participants have suggested improvements, they were interested in employing these interactive visualization techniques.

7   Conclusion and Future Works

In this work it was possible to verify how interactive visualization techniques can facilitate and improve the analysis of the perceived image of organizations on social networks. We implemented MentionStats, an application prototype that provides interactive visualization techniques to support mentions analysis on Twitter. Through this prototype we conducted a user study in order to analyse the user impressions about it.

The presented related works contains some examples of the use of visualization techniques with social media data. They illustrate how the research in this area is evolving and the importance to combine several computational techniques to reach effective results. Some of them compare approaches for better data gathering and processing, such as machine learning and natural language processing, with little exploration of data visualization. Our work is similar to them in the aspect of sentiment analysis in social networks. On the other hand, our focus are in the design of interactive visualization techniques and not in the data gathering and processing, in order to help sentiment analysis on Twitter. We implemented an application prototype for mobile platforms and focused on the perception of the organizations image on social networks.

From the analysis carried out, we can see that companies are interested to know customers' opinion about their image, services or products, and also to give them a quickly feedback. As mentioned by the interviewees, these information could help in the decision-making process, which answers positively two of our guiding research question: "It is possible to have a dynamic analysis of a data set using information visualization techniques?" and "Could the understanding of customer's perception assist the company in making decisions?".

Although the participants suggested some improvements to be implemented, they made a good evaluation of the MentionStats, saying that they would adopt it and recommend it for monitoring mentions on social networks, because it support the analysis of opinion on Twitter and can be applied to the company's image monitoring. This demonstrates that we have a positive answer for our other guiding research question: "Does the use of interaction techniques with information visualization help to deepen the social network data analysis?".

Now we are improving the application prototype considering the users suggestions. As future work, we will deepen the user studies and we will continue to study and develop tools to support the sentiment analysis on large volumes of data, including data processing and visual mining. At now, we are using a database of tweets gathered during the World Cup 2014 and the Brazil presidential elections in 2014.

Acknowledgments. This work was partially supported by PUCRS (Edital 07/2012 - Programa de Apoio a Integração Entre Áreas/ PRAIAS).

References

1. Mohammad, A., Mohiuddin, K., Irfan, M., Moizuddin, M.: Cloud the mainstay: growth of social networks in mobile environment. In: 2013 International Conference on Cloud Ubiquitous Computing Emerging Technologies (CUBE), pp. 14–19, November 2013
2. Rotta, G.C., de Lemos, V.S., da Cunha, A.L.M., Manssour, I.H., Silveira, M.S., Pase, A.F.: Exploring twitter interactions through visualization techniques: users impressions and new possibilities. In: Kotzé, P., Marsden, G., Lindgaard, G., Wesson, J., Winckler, M. (eds.) INTERACT 2013, Part III. LNCS, vol. 8119, pp. 700–707. Springer, Heidelberg (2013)
3. Fan, W., Gordon, M.D.: The power of social media analytics. Commun. ACM **57**(6), 74–81 (2014)
4. Zeng, D., Chen, H., Lusch, R., Li, S.H.: Social media analytics and intelligence. IEEE Intell. Syst. **25**(6), 13–16 (2010)
5. Morstatter, F., Pfeffer, J., Liu, H., Carley, K.M.: Is the sample good enough? comparing data from twitter's streaming api with twitter's firehose. In: ICWSM (2013)
6. Bonchi, F., Castillo, C., Gionis, A., Jaimes, A.: Social network analysis and mining for business applications. ACM Trans. Intell. Syst. Technol. **2**(3), 22:1–22:37 (2011)
7. Card, S.K., Mackinlay, J.D., Shneiderman, B.: Readings in Information Visualization: Using Vision to Think. Morgan Kaufmann, San Francisco (1999)
8. Heer, J., Viégas, F.B., Wattenberg, M.: Voyagers and voyeurs: supporting asynchronous collaborative information visualization. In: Proceedings of the SIGCHI Conference on Human Factors in Computing Systems. CHI 2007, pp. 1029–1038. ACM, New York (2007)
9. Heer, J., Bostock, M., Ogievetsky, V.: A tour through the visualization zoo. Queue **8**(5), 20:20–20:30 (2010)
10. Pang, B., Lee, L.: Opinion mining and sentiment analysis. Found. trends inf. retrieval **2**(1–2), 1–135 (2008)
11. Pak, A., Paroubek, P.: Twitter as a corpus for sentiment analysis and opinion mining. LREC. **10**, 1320–1326 (2010)
12. Nguyen, V.D., Varghese, B., Barker, A.: The royal birth of 2013: Analysing and visualising public sentiment in the uk using twitter. In: 2013 IEEE International Conference on Big Data, pp. 46–54. IEEE (2013)

13. Wang, C., Xiao, Z., Liu, Y., Xu, Y., Zhou, A., Zhang, K.: Sentiview: sentiment analysis and visualization for internet popular topics. IEEE Trans. Human-Machine Syst. **43**(6), 620–630 (2013)
14. Dong, H., Halem, M., Zhou, S.: Social media data analytics applied to hurricane sandy. In: 2013 International Conference on Social Computing (SocialCom), pp. 963–966. IEEE (2013)
15. Rotta, G., Lemos, V., Lammel, F., Manssour, I., Silveira, M., Pase, A.: Visualization techniques for the analysis of twitter users behavior. In: Seventh International AAAI Conference on Weblogs and Social Media. (2013)
16. Souza, M., Vieira, R., Busetti, D., Chishman, R., Alves, I.M.: Construction of a portuguese opinion lexicon from multiple resources. In: 8th Brazilian Symposium in Information and Human Language Technology, pp. 59–66, Porto Alegre (2011)

Designing a Social Mobile Platform for Diabetes Self-management: A Theory-Driven Perspective

Hoang D. Nguyen[✉], Xinyi Jiang, and Danny Chiang Choon Poo

Department of Information Systems, National University of Singapore, Singapore, Singapore
{hoangnguyen,xinyi,dpoo}@comp.nus.edu.sg

Abstract. Diabetes mellitus (DM) is increasingly being accepted as a lifelong public health problem with profound consequences on the worldwide healthcare system. Self-management, therefore, has been long suggested as an integral solution of diabetes treatment [1] which requires patients to adopt strained lifestyle modifications (e.g., balancing diets and frequent monitoring of blood glucose) [2, 3]. With the proliferation of smart devices, this study proposes a theoretical framework as an important guideline for designing and prototyping a life-changing mobile platform for a next-generation diabetes self-management. It revolutionises the interaction between patients and their smart phone with a high degree of media richness and social connectivity for better health management success.

Keywords: Diabetes mellitus · Self-management · mHealth · Social support · Social presence

1 Introduction

The prevalence of diabetes mellitus (DM) has been growing rapidly on a global scale in recent decades. The International Diabetes Federation estimates a tremendous rise in cases diagnosed with diabetes to 592 million by 2035 [4] which suggests a huge economic burden of DM. In order to meet the public expectations on healthcare services within resource constraints, self-management, therefore, has been long regarded as an integral part of clinical treatment of DM [1]. It involves a considerable amount of strained tasks for patients, such as balancing diets, increasing physical activity, frequent monitoring of health status, and obtaining diabetes knowledge as well as adherence to treatment regimen and advice [1, 2].

Mobile applications (mobile apps) have been studied as viable tools for diabetes self-management [5–9] which empower patients with great advantages of usability and mobility [10, 11]. Moreover, the ubiquitous mobile technology promisingly brings patients closer to their friends and family members for social support thus creating persuasion power and generating sufficient motivation for patients to comply with their diabetes treatment protocols [12]. Nevertheless, it was unclear whether existing mobile apps in the market were designed based on behavioural science theory capable of modifying self-care behaviours [13]; hence, this research aims to fill the existing gaps in

© Springer International Publishing Switzerland 2015
G. Meiselwitz (Ed.): SCSM 2015, LNCS 9182, pp. 67–77, 2015.
DOI: 10.1007/978-3-319-20367-6_8

literature and practice to propose a theoretical framework for designing and prototyping a life-changing mobile platform for a next-generation diabetes management.

In this research, we have conducted systematic searches using the keywords: "Diabetes" and "Glucose" across different app stores, such as Apple AppStore, Google Play, and Windows Store; and there are over 2,000 mobile apps related to diabetes management. Similar to the findings from Holtz & Lauckner [6], and El-Gayar et al. [13], the majority of the apps offer health tracking capabilities including blood glucose, insulin treatment, and dietary intakes. However, there are only a handful of apps with family support features which are limited to the use of social blogs, forums or e-mails for disseminating patients' health status to their supporters.

In this study, the design of a social mobile platform for diabetes self-management brings social support to the next level of mobile social presence through the innovative use of loved ones' voice messages which will stimulate patients to self-manage their conditions. It also provides an effective mean of using social networking sites (SNS) for family members and friends to help patients with distributed inputs which will reduce the burden of manually entering data and will enhance the experience and accuracy of tedious self-care tasks like dietary tracking. Based on a strong theoretical foundation, it is capable of reshaping the interaction between patients and their smart phone with a high degree of media richness and social connectivity for effective diabetes management.

The structure of our paper is as follows. In the following section, we review the relevant literature background of diabetes self-management, behavioural theories, and mobile apps. Section 3 discusses our theoretical framework and the design of our social mobile platform. The last section concludes the paper with our direction of forthcoming research.

2   Literature Background

2.1   Diabetes Self-management

Diabetes is a chronic disease resulted from insulin deficiency (Type I Diabetes), insulin resistance (Type II Diabetes), insulin receptor problem in pregnancy (Gestational Diabetes Mellitus), or genetic defects (other specific types of diabetes) so that the plasma glucose level is above the normal range [14]. Self-management has been recognised as an important part of clinical treatment, which requires patients to adopt lifestyle modifications [1, 15]. According to the most recent Standards of Medical Care in Diabetes [16], patient self-monitoring of blood glucose level (SMBG) plus medication, nutrition therapy, and physical activity are the key elements required for both type I and type II diabetes patients. In addition, studies have shown that while many patients require 6-8 times of testing per day, SMBG frequency and timing should be adjusted by individual and proper SMBG correlates with a lower glucose level [17, 18]. While physical exercise and diet control also help to improve glycaemia and cardiovascular risk factors [19], individually tailored interventions are required in order to make a change towards healthy, low-fat eating [20]. The success of self-management, as social cognitive theory describes [21], is strongly influenced by various personal factors and environmental factors, in which the behavioural change theory plays a critical role [22, 23].

2.2 Behavioural Change Theory for Diabetes Self-management

As diabetes self-management requires changes in individuals' self-care behaviours (e.g., blood glucose testing, dietary management) [3], the effect of self-management is strongly understood by the behavioural change theory. This section reviews previous literature and summarizes relevant theories for self-management of diabetes.

Self-efficacy. Self-efficacy, defined as the strength of one's ability to carry out a behaviour to reach a desired goal, is fundamental to behavioural change interventions in social cognitive theory [23]. Self-management interventions need to attach importance to developing self-efficacy [22]. In addition, Bandura's behavioural change study [24] postulates that individuals' past performance accomplishments harden their belief leading to improvements in health-related behaviours. In terms of diabetes glucose control, which requires habitual diet and glucose tracking, the process of goal setting increases patients' self-efficacy [25]. More specifically to SMBG, which offers day-to-day information of glucose level in response to diet, exercise and medical treatment, outcome expectation also helps to improve the efficacy of diabetes self-management [25–27].

Social Support. The success of diabetes self-management essentially involves ongoing collaborative efforts of family members and friends [16, 28]. Social support empowers patients' self-care behaviours, such as adherence to the treatment regimen and acts as a protection layer against impact of stressful events [29]. Furthermore, studies on social support of diabetes care indicated the evidence of informal social support in improving health outcome, and diabetes care teams should encourage informal support from family members before the formal clinical support interventions [2, 30], especially in dietary management, which is vulnerable to social influences [3].

Social Presence. Social presence theory indicated that communication is more effective through the medium with higher social presence, such as motional, audio and visual, comparing to text-based medium [31]. In the newly published book, Social Media and Mobile Technologies for Healthcare [32], it was pointed out that there had been very few models integrating social network elements into mHealth, although mobile social presence has been newly discussed as an extension of virtual social presence with collaborative technologies like transmitting photos, videos, and local-based statuses [33]. According to Cialdini & Goldstein [12], higher mobile social presence strengthens the effect of social support by generating sufficient motivation for patients and their supporters to accomplish diabetes management tasks thus leading to increased levels of health related outcomes.

2.3 Mobile Apps for Diabetes Self-management

With the advancements in mobile technology, attempts of mobile diabetes support as well as related publications have increased rapidly since the early 2000s [5, 34]. Early efforts were mainly about giving lifestyle interventions through mobile text messages, so that patients' awareness, knowledge, and control of disease could be improved [35, 36]. With the increasing storage capacity as well as Wi-Fi accessibility, the majority of mobile apps nowadays offer health tracking capabilities of one or more areas in glucose, diet, exercise and medication [7–9, 13, 37, 38]. Personalisation and decision support are also heated topics in the existing market and research [11, 39, 40]. The mobile capabilities of communication and self-management education have been studied to show positive impacts on various health outcomes [13, 41, 42]; nevertheless, there are only a handful of apps with family support features and explorations in social media support are also limited [6, 13].

3   Social Mobile Platform for Diabetes Self-management

3.1   Theoretical Framework

We propose the following theoretical framework (Fig. 1) as an overarching design guideline of our social mobile platform for effective diabetes self-management.

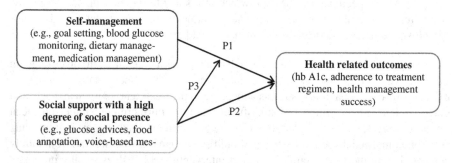

Fig. 1. The theoretical framework for self-management mobile app designing

Self-management interventions attach importance to developing self-efficacy [22, 23], which postulates that individuals' past performance accomplishments harden their belief leading to improvements in health-related behaviours [24]. The process of goal setting increases patients' self-efficacy [25]; which promotes their sense of responsibility and accountability in managing their own health thereby improving their health related outcomes. We propose Proposition 1 as enabling factors of a diabetes self-management mobile app, such as goal setting, blood glucose management and physical activity tracking.

Proposition 1. Individuals can achieve higher levels of health management success thus resulting in improvements of health and medical status progress by facilitating their self-management activities, such as goal setting of diabetes management, and management of blood glucose levels, dietary, physical activities, and medications.

The success of diabetes self-management essentially involves an ongoing supporting role of family members and friends [28]. According to the social support theory, it influences patients' self-care behaviours, such as adherence to the treatment regimen and acts as a protection layer against impact of stressful events [29]. With mobile technologies, mobile social presence [31, 33] has been newly discussed as an extension of virtual social presence with collaborative capabilities like transmitting voices, photos and videos, and local-based services, which strengthen the effect of social support by generating sufficient motivation for patients and their supporters to accomplish diabetes management tasks thus leading to increased levels of health related outcomes [12]. We, therefore, posit a direct effect of social support in Proposition 2 and an interaction effect between self-management and social support in Proposition 3 which in turn allow us to design a comprehensive feature set of our mobile app in the Table 1.

Table 1. The theory-driven feature set

Theory	Feature
Self-care [6, 15, 20]	• Glucose monitoring
	• Dietary tracking
	• Physical activity and medication management
Self-efficacy [23–26]	• Goal setting
	• Reporting and advice
Social support [2, 3, 27, 30, 36]	• Social glucose monitoring
	• Social dietary tracking
Social presence [31, 33]	• Voice-based reminders

Proposition 2. Individuals can achieve improved health management success thus resulting in increased levels of health and medical status progress by facilitating social support for them and their supporters to access diabetes management activities and to engage in a high degree of social presence.

Proposition 3. By facilitating both self-management and social support for individuals and their supporters to access diabetes management activities and reports, they can achieve improved health management success thus resulting in increased levels of health and medical status progress.

3.2 User Interface Design

This study aims to design a patient-centric minimalistic mobile platform for diabetes self-management. The following sections describe the comprehensive set of theory-driven features in great details.

Glucose Monitoring. Our design offers an important function of glucose self-monitoring at patients' convenience (Fig. 2 - the left screen). A patient can set the blood glucose level using a scrollbar of the input circle after taking fingerstick blood tests. The date and time of record will be automatically captured, and, further edit is allowed by scrolling the time picker. The target range of blood glucose for different people before and after meals are different. Hence, the design allows users to have a personalized target range for both before meal glucose level and after meal glucose level.

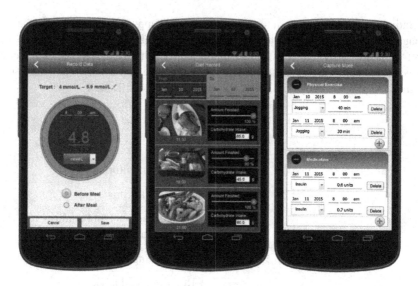

Fig. 2. Self-care features

Dietary Tracking. A patient simply needs a few steps to log their diet (Fig. 2 – the middle screen). The first step is to take a photo of the meal by clicking "Capture Meal" in the home page. The second step is to enter the type of food which allows the app to know the carbohydrate count for diabetes management. The last step is to indicate the amount of finished food. These steps can even be shorter with the use of Social Support Features. Patients could also select the time frame of the diet record that he or she would like to review. Both the starting date and end date could be edited through scrolling the date picker at the top part of "Diet Record" screen.

Physical Activity and Medication Management. Other than glucose monitoring and diet tracking, physical activity and medication are two other important aspects of diabetes self-management. Our design caters for a minimalistic way of capturing users' inputs on physical activities and medication like jogging and insulin treatment (Fig. 2 – the right screen). It facilities the selection of different types of activity or treatment therapy together with the amount of work done or treatment dosages. Integration with fitness devices and location-based services are yet to be explored.

Goal Setting. This features the process of goal setting which breaks major target into concrete and manageable objectives within a desired timeframe (Fig. 3). For instance, a goal of glucose monitoring can be "from Jan 10, 2015 to Jan 24, 2015, having a minimum glucose level of 4 mmol/L". Once the user accesses this feature, the fulfilment ratio will be updated based on glucose input, diet log, physical exercise log, and medication records within the time range indicated at the top of the screen. This design provides users with useful feedback about their efficacy of achieving goals.

Reporting and Advice. For reporting purposes, the user could select the time range they want to view data logs as shown in Fig. 4. The functionality displays the period

Fig. 3. Goal setting

average as well as each day's test results in the bar form. The daily average is shown as an orange line, and each meal's intake time and carbohydrate exchange amount are indicated as orange triangles. The design is capable of motivating users by displaying friendly status related to their health-related outcomes.

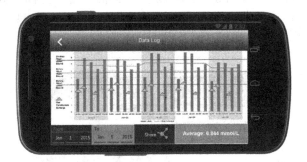

Fig. 4. Reporting and advice

Social Glucose Monitoring. Our design allows the ability to connect with family and friends based on the Facebook's friend list (Fig. 5 – the left screen). Once connected, various reports of the patients will be sent to their supporters for information exchange and advices including glucose charts and health-related status messages. The app also reports the adverse events, such as hyperglycemia and hypoglycemia to supporters who can act in time to prevent life-threatening consequences. The interactions between users and the mobile app, therefore, are enhanced for frequent usage and healthier lifestyle.

Fig. 5. Social support features

Social Dietary Tracking. The design further simplifies the tediousness of food tracking by sending requests to connected family members and friends for distributed inputs as shown in Fig. 5. When a patient takes a photo of their food, it will be sent automatically to their loved ones on Facebook. And it is important to guide the supporters through a series of steps to tag the food based our calories count database. Two hours later, the mobile app will prompt the patients to complete their dietary tracking tasks based on the collected inputs.

Fig. 6. Voice-based reminders

Voice-Based Reminders. Rather than using the traditional notification or alarms, the design implements voice-base reminders with a family member or a friend's photo shown in Fig. 6. This aims to facilitate effective interventions for lifestyle changes, as well as long term efforts in self-management because the reminders will be based on physical exercise schedules, glucose testing schedules, medication schedules, etc. Family members and friends can record their voices based on certain event triggers. After the setup, the mobile phone will start to notify patients through the voice selected for the reminder, and the screen will show the profile photo of the voice's owner at the same time.

4   Conclusion

Our study has established forceful contributions to the literature and practice of mobile diabetes management in two folds. First, based on the behavioural science theory, our research proposed the theoretical framework capable of reshaping the current generation of diabetes management towards a more active and supportive direction. Second, we designed and prototyped a next-generation mobile app for diabetes self-management through the use of voice-based reminders and collaborative features. It provides a solid mean to promote the practice of self-management amongst patients and their social networks which is exceptionally valuable for healthcare professionals to impart necessary interventions to patients with diabetes.

The paper is not an end; but rather a beginning of forthcoming research. In the future, we are looking into ways of further simplifying our mobile app by interfacing with devices, such as glucose meters, fitness devices, and insulin pumps. Furthermore, we are in the process of conducting an experimental design study to assess the impact of the mobile app on apprising and predicting the user behaviour and on understanding how contextualized social support should be given to increase the likelihood of behaviour change and improvements in health status.

References

1. Funnell, M.M., Anderson, R.M., Arnold, M.S., Barr, P.A., Donnelly, M., Johnson, P.D., Taylor-Moon, D., White, N.H.: Empowerment: an idea whose time has come in diabetes education. Diabetes Educ. **17**, 37–41 (1991)
2. Stopford, R., Winkley, K., Ismail, K.: Social support and glycemic control in type 2 diabetes: a systematic review of observational studies. Patient Educ. Couns. **93**, 549–558 (2013)
3. Gallant, M.P.: The influence of social support on chronic illness self-management: a review and directions for research. Health Educ. Behav. **30**, 170–195 (2003)
4. International Diabetes Federation: Diabetes Atlas 6th edn (2013)
5. Eng, D.S., Lee, J.M.: The promise and peril of mobile health applications for diabetes and endocrinology. Pediatr. Diabetes. **14**, 231–238 (2013)
6. Holtz, B., Lauckner, C.: Diabetes management via mobile phones: a systematic review. Telemed. J. e-Health **18**, 175–184 (2012)

7. Faridi, Z., Liberti, L., Shuval, K., Northrup, V., Ali, A., Katz, D.L.: Evaluating the impact of mobile telephone technology on type 2 diabetic patients' self-management: the NICHE pilot study. J. Eval. Clin. Pract. **14**, 465–469 (2008)

8. Carroll, A.E., Marrero, D.G., Downs, S.M.: The HealthPia GlucoPack Diabetes phone: a usability study. Diabetes Technol. Ther. **9**, 158–164 (2007)

9. Istepanian, R.S.H., Zitouni, K., Harry, D., Moutosammy, N., Sungoor, A., Tang, B., Earle, K.A.: Evaluation of a mobile phone telemonitoring system for glycaemic control in patients with diabetes. J. Telemed. Telecare **15**, 125–128 (2009)

10. Kollmann, A., Riedl, M., Kastner, P., Schreier, G., Ludvik, B.: Feasibility of a mobile phone-based data service for functional insulin treatment of type 1 diabetes mellitus patients. J. Med. Internet Res. **9**, e36 (2007)

11. Quinn, C.C., Shardell, M.D., Terrin, M.L., Barr, E.A., Ballew, S.H., Gruber-Baldini, A.L.: Cluster-randomized trial of a mobile phone personalized behavioral intervention for blood glucose control. Diabetes Care **34**, 1934–1942 (2011)

12. Cialdini, R.B., Goldstein, N.J.: Social influence: compliance and conformity. Annu. Rev. Psychol. **55**, 591–621 (2004)

13. El-Gayar, O., Timsina, P., Nawar, N., Eid, W.: Mobile applications for diabetes self-management: status and potential. J. Diabetes Sci. Technol. **7**, 247–262 (2013)

14. National Diabetes Data Group: Classification and diagnosis of diabetes mellitus and other categories of glucose intolerance. Diabetes **28**, 1039–1057 (1979)

15. Clark, N.M., Becker, M.H., Janz, N.K., Lorig, K., Rakowski, W., Anderson, L.: Self-management of chronic disease by older adults: a review and questions for research. J. Aging Health **3**, 3–27 (1991)

16. American Diabetes Association: Standards of medical care in diabetes–2014. Diabetes Care **37**, 514–580 (2014)

17. Miller, K.M., Beck, R.W., Bergenstal, R.M., Goland, R.S., Haller, M.J., McGill, J.B., Rodriguez, H., Simmons, J.H., Hirsch, I.B.: Evidence of a strong association between frequency of self-monitoring of blood glucose and hemoglobin A1c levels in T1D exchange clinic registry participants. Diabetes Care **36**, 2009–2014 (2013)

18. Ziegler, R., Heidtmann, B., Hilgard, D., Hofer, S., Rosenbauer, J., Holl, R.: Frequency of SMBG correlates with HbA1c and acute complications in children and adolescents with type 1 diabetes. Pediatr. Diabetes. **12**, 11–17 (2011)

19. Goldhaber-Fiebert, J.D., Goldhaber-Fiebert, S.N., Tristan, M.L., Nathan, D.M.: Randomized controlled community-based nutrition and exercise intervention improves glycemia and cardiovascular risk factors in type 2 diabetic patients in rural Costa Rica. Diabetes Care **26**, 24–29 (2003)

20. Vallis, M., Ruggiero, L., Greene, G., Jones, H., Zinman, B., Rossi, S., Edwards, L., Rossi, J.S., Prochaska, J.O.: Stages of change for healthy eating in diabetes: relation to demographic, eating-related, health care utilization, and psychosocial factors. Diabetes Care **26**, 1468–1474 (2003)

21. Bandura, A.: Social Foundations Of Thought And Action. Prentice-Hall, Englewood Cliffs, NJ (1986)

22. Lorig, K., Holman, H.: Arthritis self-management studies: a twelve-year review. Health Educ. Q. **20**, 17–28 (1993)

23. Clark, N.M., Dodge, J.A.: Exploring self-efficacy as a predictor of disease management. Health Educ. Behav. **26**, 72–89 (1999)

24. Bandura, A.: Self-efficacy: toward a unifying theory of behavioral change. Psychol. Rev. **84**, 191–215 (1977)

25. Langford, A.T., Sawyer, D.R., Gioimo, S., Brownson, C.A., O'Toole, M.L.: Patient-centered goal setting as a tool to improve diabetes self-management. Diabetes Educ. **33**(Suppl 6), 139S–144S (2007)
26. Gross, T.M., Mastrototaro, J.J.: Efficacy and reliability of the continuous glucose monitoring system. Diabetes Technol. Ther. **2**(Suppl 1), S19–S26 (2000)
27. Chlebowy, D.O., Garvin, B.J.: Social support, self-efficacy, and outcome expectations: impact on self-care behaviors and glycemic control in Caucasian and African American adults with type 2 diabetes. Diabetes Educ. **32**, 777–786 (2006)
28. Prohaska, T.R., Glasser, M.: Patients' views of family involvement in medical care decisions and encounters. Res. Aging. **18**, 52–69 (1996)
29. Cohen, S., Wills, T.A.: Stress, social support, and the buffering hypothesis. Psychol. Bull. **98**, 310–357 (1985)
30. Van Dam, H.A., van der Horst, F.G., Knoops, L., Ryckman, R.M., Crebolder, H.F.J.M., van den Borne, B.H.W.: Social support in diabetes: a systematic review of controlled intervention studies. Patient Educ. Couns. **59**, 1–12 (2005)
31. Bentley, F., Metcalf, C.J.: The use of mobile social presence. IEEE Pervasive Comput. **8**, 35–41 (2009)
32. Cummings, E., Borycki, E.: Soc. Media Mob. Technol. Healthcare **2011**, 2012–2014 (2014)
33. Tu, C.-H., McIsaac, M., Sujo-Montes, L., Armfield, S.: Is there a mobile social presence? EMI. Educ. Media Int. **49**, 247–261 (2012)
34. Tatara, N., Årsand, E., Nilsena, H., Hartvigsen, G.: A review of mobile terminal-based applications for self-management of patients with diabetes. In: Proceedings of International Conference on eHealth, Telemedicine, and Social Medicine, eTELEMED 2009, pp. 166–175 (2009)
35. Wangberg, S.C., Arsand, E., Andersson, N.: Diabetes education via mobile text messaging. J. Telemed. Telecare **12**(Suppl 1), 55–56 (2006)
36. Hanauer, D.A., Wentzell, K., Laffel, N., Laffel, L.M.: Computerized automated reminder diabetes system (CARDS): e-mail and SMS cell phone text messaging reminders to support diabetes management. Diabetes Technol. Ther. **11**, 99–106 (2009)
37. Arsand, E., Tatara, N., Ostengen, G., Hartvigsen, G.: Mobile phone-based self-management tools for type 2 diabetes: the few touch application. J. Diabetes Sci. Technol. **4**, 328–336 (2010)
38. Chomutare, T., Fernandez-Luque, L., Arsand, E., Hartvigsen, G.: Features of mobile diabetes applications: review of the literature and analysis of current applications compared against evidence-based guidelines. J. Med. Internet Res. **13**, e65 (2011)
39. Chen, Y.: Take it personally: accounting for individual difference in designing diabetes management systems. In: Methodology, pp. 252–261 (2010)
40. Garcia-Saez, G., Rigla, M., Martinez-Sarriegui, I., Shalom, E., Peleg, M., Broens, T., Pons, B., Caballero-Ruiz, E., Gomez, E.J., Hernando, M.E.: Patient-oriented computerized clinical guidelines for mobile decision support in gestational diabetes. J Diabetes Sci Technol. **8**, 238–246 (2014)
41. Ciemins, E., Coon, P., Sorli, C.: An analysis of data management tools for diabetes self-management: can smart phone technology keep up? J. Diabetes Sci. Technol. **4**, 958–960 (2010)
42. Funnell, M.M., Brown, T.L., Childs, B.P., Haas, L.B., Hosey, G.M., Jensen, B., Maryniuk, M., Peyrot, M., Piette, J.D., Reader, D., Siminerio, L.M., Weinger, K., Weiss, M.A.: National standards for diabetes self-management education. Diabetes Care **34**(Suppl 1), S89–S96 (2011)

Providing ICT Support to Promote Communities' Emotional Balance

Rener Baffa da Silva$^{(\boxtimes)}$ and Junia Coutinho Anacleto

Advanced Interaction Laboratory, Federal University of São Carlos,
Rodovia Washington Luís, Km 235 – SP-310, São Carlos
SP CEP 13565-905, Brazil
{rener.silva, junia}@dc.ufscar.br

Abstract. This paper presents a study on how hierarchical communities can emotionally balance themselves and how this process happens. For that we've created Emotifeed, an ICT tool to provide sttaf decision made information, allowing them to give emotional feedback. The communication inside organizations and communities are quicly changing for a more organic and flexible structure and emotions play an important role in this scenario. However the knowledge about the emotional world of communities and organizations is still very short. Aiming to contribute in this scenario, we developed EmotiFeed using a public display to support the communication in a community and collect emotional feedback. The footage analysis showed that the EmotiFeed promoted the emotional balance in the community and showed that the tendency is it runs in the direction of the "Neutral" emotion.

Keywords: Organizations · Emotifeed · Emotional feedback · Emotional balance · Responsiveness

1 Introduction

The communication inside organizations and communities are changing over the time and becoming more responsive to their members desires, need and emotions [3]. Meanwhile it is not clear how this responsiveness is present in this communication scenario.

As known, emotions play an important role in the development of intelligence, perception, learning and mainly in the communication and relationship either person to person or person to technology application/device which indicates that responsiveness occurs also in the emotional level [4, 10, 17, 19, 30].

The emotional responsiveness is a critical component of social interaction and competence once individuals who don't respond appropriately to reactions came from other or don't understand it are unable to satisfying relationships and probably will have troubles in their social live and in the workplace [24, 28].

Individuals work toward a state of emotional balance, which consists of tacitly experiencing emotions. Once the individual becomes emotionally unbalanced in the social situation and experiences an emotion, he/she will work toward rebalancing his/her emotion(s) once the need for emotional balance is a vital component of the individual's broader need for ontological security [6].

© Springer International Publishing Switzerland 2015
G. Meiselwitz (Ed.): SCSM 2015, LNCS 9182, pp. 78–88, 2015.
DOI: 10.1007/978-3-319-20367-6_9

Although the knowledge of the emotional world of communities and organizations is very short as there are not so much studies in this field. Some questions concerning this subject are still not answered, such as: How comfortable people feel to express themselves emotionally? What kind of emotions does the community express? How does the organization change over time? How well people understand others? How does the community balance itself? [22, 31].

Most communities and organizations are organized hierarchically according to the members post inside of it [12]. In those communities, the communication tends to happen only from members of high posts to low posts [18]. Some examples of communities hierarchically organized are universities, corporations, hotels and hospitals.

In order to contribute for a better understand of the emotional world of communities this work aims to study if hierarchical communities balance themselves emotionally and if the usage of technology can help with that.

The next section presents the background on emotions highlighting what is an emotion and how it happens. The Sect. 3 presents the related works discussing how they are related with the present work. Section 4 describes the EmotiFeed the ICT system created to collect and analyze data. The results are shown in the Sect. 5 followed by the conclusions on the data analysis in the Sect. 6 and the future works in the Sect. 7.

2   Background on Emotions

The scientifically researches on emotions started in the 19 century when William James [11] and Charles Darwin [4] proposed their theories. More than 90 definitions on emotions were proposed along the 20th century [20], some of them can be found in [13]. It means that there isn't a consensus of what is an emotion [8].

For the present work the Schachter-Singer model [26] is adopted. The authors indicate that emotion is the individual response according to a stimulus, contextualized for each individual experience.

The stimulus may have an internal origin – stemmed from memories, thoughts or physiological sensations – or external origin – as an event, conversation or action. This stimulus triggers a series of physiological reactions in the human being's body in the same time that cerebral cortex (cognitive process) evaluates what is happening to his/her body together with all elements of the context in which the stimulus occurred (such as memories, skills, experience etc.). This contextual evaluation is unconscious and innate. In the end of this process a corresponding emotion is generated and experimented, as shown in the Fig. 1.

3   Related Works

We found only few works that analyze some emotional aspects of online communities in the literature.

Yu [31] studied the emotional status of online health community members according to the members' role (patient or caregivers). Laniado et al. [14] examined

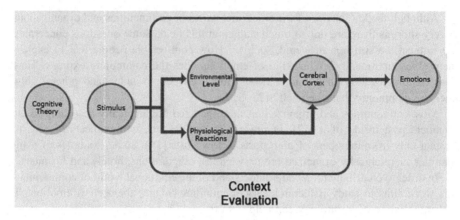

Fig. 1. Schachter-Singer theory (adapted from [15])

what emotions were presents in the communication between editor of Wikipedia pages content considering the users gender as well as their role in the page edition. Both works analyzed the emotions related to messages in order to understand how people behave and express themselves emotionally but they do not consider the emotional balance of the studied community which is the purpose of this work.

Preece's work [21] aims to understand how empathy occurs highlighting the importance of empathy in communication and social relationship between members of an online community to support people and athletes with knee ligament problems.

Behrens [1] created a platform with only two buttons: Like and Dislike. Through these buttons the community could give their opinion about the event and the talks that they participated. This work aimed to augment virtual communication with location based narratives and real time sharing of opinions. It is not directly related with emotions itself but only with like and dislike.

The authors [25] created an ICT system that attempts to avoid, reduce or resolve incivility in workplace, called MACS (M-s Affective Conditioning System), by monitoring and controlling individuals' behavior in this workplace.

As shown none of the related works analyzed the emotional balance on the community they were experimented and the applications/systems created do not have the focus to provide a tool to allow that emotional balance. Thus in order to achieve the objective of this work, an Information and Communications Technology (ICT) system called EmotiFeed was created. The EmotiFeed will be described in details in the next section.

4   EmotiFeed

With the technology advance, it is becoming easier to provide some ways to allow the communication for people from both high and low posts in communities [3, 7].

This fact meets the third HCI paradigm, defined by [2, 9]. They say that in the third HCI paradigm the designer's challenge is to give user the chance to experiment ICT solutions to support their desires, needs and emotions.

Following the third HCI paradigm and aiming the objective of this work, an ICT system called EmotiFeed was created. The EmotiFeed allow people from a community to express themselves emotionally based on an announcement came from member of high post of that community.

4.1 Collecting Emotional Expression

As mentioned in previous sections the Schachter-Singer model of what is an emotion was adopted. However this model does not deal with the emotion classification or what emotions an individual can experience. Instead this model explains what an emotion is and how it is experienced.

For this purpose it was adopted the Russell classification of emotions [23] since it can be measured and computed as well as Nguyen et al. [16] pointed out. Russell's model shows a set of emotions organized in a circle where the opposite emotions are place in the opposite position in that circle.

The total amount of emotions covered by this model is 28 emotions. As it is not known yet what kind of emotions the community wants to express it is used only the scale between happy and sad because those were the most common emotions found in the literature on emotions and also they are considered innate. To represent the scale between Happy and Sad emotions we used 5-points Likert Scale [29].

The emotions can be expressed in different ways, such as through the facial recognition, body language, speech recognition, physiological signals and self-report. Some works [5, 27] pointed out that the emotional feedback should be quick and nonverbal to describe an emotion so that emoticons appear to be an appropriate way to communicate emotions.

Thus the approach used to collect the emotional data by the EmotiFeed is the self-report [7, 10] based on voting where people choose an option provided by the system that better represent their emotion.

In the EmotiFeed case the emoticons were developed according to observations on how emotions can be represented based on facial expression [4]. The 5-points Likert scale of emoticons can be found in Fig. 2.

Fig. 2. Emoticons arranging according to likert scale: from happy to sad

4.2 System Architecture

EmotiFeed was designed as a web based system to obviate the need to install any software for the user and to facilitate the access to it. The EmotiFeed architecture and its web pages can be seen in the Fig. 3.

EmotiFeed was created using the new technology called Meteor[1] which is an open source platform to build transparent reactive web apps. Meteor uses MongoDB as its database and NodeJS in its structure. Moreover, Meteor allows the developers to use either JavaScript or CoffeScript as the programming language.

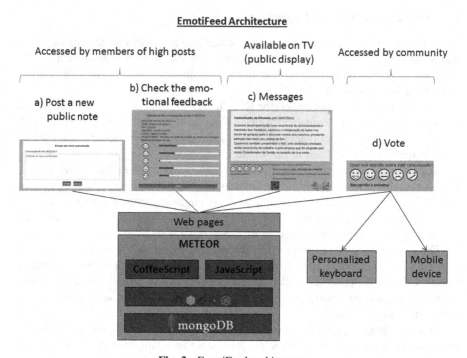

Fig. 3. EmotiFeed architecture

As can be seen in the Fig. 3, the EmotiFeed is composed by 4 web pages:

1. The first one is the interface for the members of high posts to publish a new message in the system. This interface can only be accessed by the members of high posts inside the community as it is organized hierarchically. It has an input text area where the user can type the desired message and a button to publish the message.
2. The second one is the interface to check out the emotional feedback for each published message. This interface can only be accessed by the members of high posts inside the community also and it shows the published message content and a visual graph with the emotional feedback provided by the community.
3. The third one is the interface that makes the last message published visible for all community. Taking advantage of a public display, we installed a TV in a place for socialization that all the members of that community attend to. This public display

---

[1] Meteor Preview 0.9.3 – https://www.meteor.com.

exhibits the last published message so that people can read it and eventually discuss about it and it also shows an instructional message that teaches how to interact with the EmotiFeed and express the emotions.

4. The last one is the page to collect emotions expressed by the community's members. Every member connected in the community's network has access to this page and can express their emotions. This page can be accessed either by devices or by a personalized keyboard developed to reproduce the same voting options that the web page (see Fig. 4). The keyboard was installed right below the public display.

Fig. 4. Personalized keyboard to express emotions in the EmotiFeed

4.3   Interaction Flow

The high posts members prepare a message to publish for all members of the community. Then this message is published in the EmotiFeed that will be visible in the public display for everybody from the community.

This message will act as the ignition to generate the emotion in the community members that read the message. The emotion experienced will differ from one another according to their experiences, desires, memories and abilities (context evaluation) and at this moment the corresponding emotion is generated. Therefore the emotional feedback is expressed in the EmotiFeed in compliance with the process of experience emotions defined by the Schachter-Singer model, described in the Sect. 2.

This emotional feedback can be accessed for high posts members. The interaction flow is described in the Fig. 5.

5   Results

We installed an instance of EmotiFeed in a psychiatric hospital during 9 weeks to collect data for analysis and improve the communication among the staff. The hospital is a chronic mental care hospital with approximately 400 professionals and 300 patients located in the city of Lins, Brazil.

During the experiment period 18 messages were posted by the directors of the hospital, an average of one new message every 3.5 days. A total amount of 2644

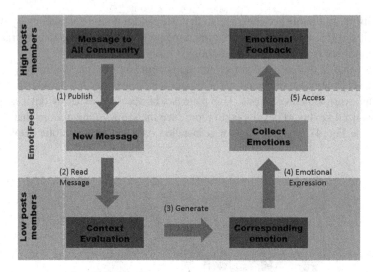

Fig. 5. EmotiFeed interaction flow

emotions were expressed by the hospital employees, an average of one emotion every 34 min approximated. Figure 6 presents a summary of what emotions were expressed in the EmotiFeed during the experiment, showing that the most expressed were the "Very Sad" and the least expressed were the "Happy".

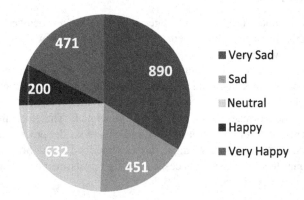

Fig. 6. Total emotions expressed in the EmotiFeed

As each message has a predominating emotion – most expressed – it was possible to emotionally classify them according to that predominant emotion related to them.

Shows all the messages exhibiting all emotions expressed for them by the community and highlighting their predominant emotion. This table shows that the most recurrent emotion was the "Very Sad" as well as the most expressed, appearing 6 times while the least recurrent emotion was the "Sad" (Table 1).

Table 1. Predominant emotion for each message

Message	Feedback					Predominant Emotion
	Very Sad	Sad	Neutral	Happy	Very Happy	
1	4	12	34	17	63	Very Happy
2	0	0	7	17	0	Happy
3	1	3	4	1	1	Neutral
4	2	2	3	5	4	Happy
5	382	141	152	34	122	Very Sad
6	1	9	4	5	3	Sad
7	30	12	15	14	5	Very Sad
8	1	0	3	5	0	Happy
9	28	75	37	23	58	Sad
10	42	53	20	12	84	Very Happy
11	63	17	45	25	25	Very Sad
12	20	18	89	7	6	Neutral
13	168	48	108	6	68	Very Sad
14	4	9	28	2	3	Neutral
15	0	2	5	8	3	Happy
16	49	25	31	9	14	Very Sad
17	95	24	45	6	11	Very Sad
18	0	1	2	4	1	Happy
Total	890	451	632	200	471	2644

6 Conclusion

Aiming to verify if the emotional balance occurs in fact and how it happens, it was compared the current message with the previous message in order to check how they change their classification. For this, the Fig. 7 shows the emotional occurrence chronologically organized, represented by the blue line.

It is possible to observe that the next message's emotion compared with the current message's emotion tends to follow the direction to the center of the graph where the "Neutral" emotions is located as shown by the black line which shows for where the emotions tend to be driven.

In this way we conclude that there is evidence that the community does balance itself emotionally and that the tendency is to run in the direction neutrality.

Also it is possible to see that in only one case the emotional classification remained the same (Message 16 and 17) while in all other cases the emotional classification changed compared with the previous message. Furthermore we observed that 6 of the 18 messages were reposted by the hospital directors changing their content in aiming to convey other emotions.

Thus we conclude that the EmotiFeed promoted the emotional balance of the community once it gives the opportunity to people change their minds, thoughts or behaviors and change the emotions related to people, improving the communication among them. We identified that in the fact that members of high posts to evaluate the emotional feedback of each message and then respond to that, adjusting the content resend it to get another feedback from community. Those are the steps *a* and *b* in the Fig. 8 that represents the new interaction flow identified.

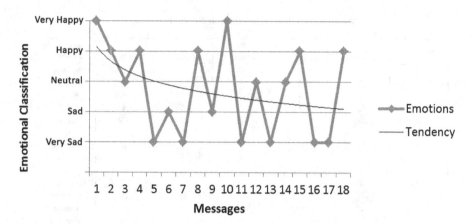

Fig. 7. Emotional occurrence chronologically organized

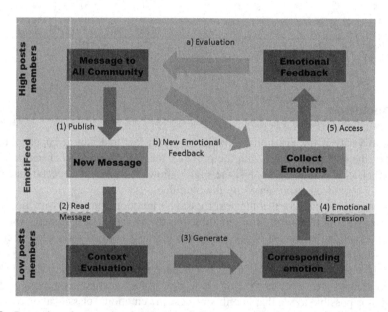

Fig. 8. Promoting the emotional balance of the community by the new interaction flow identified

7 Future Works

It is needed to verify if the tendency found in that specific community can be applied to other communities in order to find a behavioral pattern on them if it really exists of if it is a particular characteristic of each community.

We do not know if the feedback of the next message is according to the expectation of the directors that evaluated and re-posted it for all the community. When they evaluated the emotional feedback of a message he/she posted they have an expectation on what might be the next emotional feedback for the next message. That would be an interesting future work.

It is possible to change the focus of the study and analyze the collected data with the directors' perspective verifying how the emotion expressed for them through the posted message change and is related to the emotional feedback provided.

Acknowledgements. We would like to thank all CAIS Clemente Ferreira, the hospital, for the partnership. We also would like to thank Capes, Fapesp, Microsoft and Boeing for the financial support.

References

1. Behrens, M.: Swipe 'I like': location based digital narrative through embedding the 'Like' button in the real world. In: Presented at 5th International Conference on Communities and Technologies - Digital Cities 7 (2011)
2. Bødker, S.: When second wave HCI meets third wave challenges. In: Proceedings of the 4th Nordic Conference on Human-Computer Interaction: Changing Roles, Oslo, Norway (2006)
3. Cheney, G., Christensen, L.T., Zom, T.E., Ganesh, S.: Organizational Communication in an Age of Globalization: Issues, Reflections, Practices, 2nd edn. Waveland Press Incorporation, Long Grove (2010)
4. Darwin, C.R.: A expressão das emoções no homem e nos animais. Companhia das Letras, São Paulo, SP (2009)
5. Derk, D., Arjan, E.R., Jasper, C.G.: Emoticons in computer-mediated communication: social motives and social context. Cyber Psychol. Behav. **11**, 99–101 (2008)
6. Gata, M.L.: Juggling Food and Feelings: Emotional Balance in the Workplace. Lexington Books, Maryland (2002)
7. Goldhaber, G.M., Porter, D.T., Yates, M.P., Lesniak, R.: Organizational communication: 1978. Hum. Commun. Res. **5**, 76–96 (1978)
8. Goleman, D.: Inteligência emocional: a teoria revolucionária que redefine o que é ser inteligente. 39.edn. Rio de Janeiro: Objetiva (1995)
9. Harrison, S., Sengers, P., Tatar, D.: The Three Paradigms of HCI. In: CHI. San Jose (2007)
10. Jacob, H., Kreifelts, B., Brück, C., Erb, M., Hösl, F., Wildgruber, D.: Cerebral integration of verbal and nonverbal emotional cues: impact of individual nonverbal dominance. NeuroImage **61**(3), 738–747 (2012)
11. James, W.: What is an emotion? Mind **9**, 188–205 (1884)
12. Kennedy, W.S., Morgenstern, J., Wilfong, G., Zhang, L.: Hierarchical community decomposition via oblivious routing techniques. In: First ACM conference on Online Social Networks (COSN 2013). ACM, New York (2013)
13. Kleinginna Jr., P.R., Kleinginna, A.M.: A categorized list of emotion definitions, with suggestions for a consensual definition. Motiv. Emot. **5**(4), 345–379 (1981)
14. Laniado, D., Kaltenbrunner, A., Castillo, C., Morell, M.F.: Emotions and dialogue in peer-production community: the case of Wikipedia. In: Proceedings of 8th Annual International Symposium on Wikis and Open Collaboration (WikiSym 2012). Article 9, p. 10 (2012)
15. Morris, C.G., Maisto, A.A.: Understanding Psychology. Prentice Hall College Division, Englewood Cliffs (2000). ISBN 10: 0130189340/ISBN 13: 9780130189349
16. Nguyen, T., Phung, D., Adams, B., Tran, T., Venkatesh, S.: Classification and pattern discovery of mood in weblogs. In: Zaki, M.J., Yu, J.X., Ravindran, B., Pudi, V. (eds.) PAKDD 2010. LNCS, vol. 6119, pp. 283–290. Springer, Heidelberg (2010)

17. Norman, D.A.: Emotional Design: Why We Love (or Hate) Everyday Things. Basic Books, New York (2004)
18. Pereira, R., Baranauskas, M.C.C., da Silva, S.R.P.: Social software building blocks: revisiting the honeycomb framework. In: International Conference on Information Society (i-Society), pp 253–258 (2010)
19. Picard, R.W.: Affective Computing, 1st edn. The MIT Press, Cambridge (2010)
20. Plutchik, R.: The nature of emotions. Am. Sci. Res. Soc. **89**, 344–350 (2001)
21. Preece, J.: Empathic communities: balancing emotional and factual communication. Interact. comput. **12**, 63–77 (1999)
22. Rogers, Y.: The changing face of human-computer interaction in the age of ubiquitous computing. In: Proceedings of the 5th Symposium of the Workgroup Human-Computer Interaction and Usability Engineering of the Austrian Computer Society on HCI and Usability for eInclusion (USAB 2009), pp. 1–19 (2009)
23. Russell, J.A.: A circumplex model of affect. J. Pers. Soc. Psychol. **39**(6), 1161–1178 (1980)
24. Santos, M.S., Pitt, J.V.: Affective conditioning, social cohesion and the office experience. In: CHI 2010 Workshop on Designing and Evaluating Affective Aspects of Sociable Media to Support Social Connectedness (2010)
25. Santos, M.S., Pitt, J.: Emotions and norms in shared spaces. In: Balke, T., Dignum, F., van Riemsdijk, M., Chopra, A.K. (eds.) COIN 2013. LNCS, vol. 8386, pp. 157–176. Springer, Heidelberg (2014)
26. Schachter, S., Singer, J.E.: Cognitive, social and physiological determinants of emotional states. Psychol. Rev. **69**, 379–399 (1962)
27. Schleicher, R., Shirazi, A.S., Rohs, M., Schmidt, A.: WorldCupinion: experiences with an android app for real-time opinion sharing during soccer world cup games. Int. J. Mob. Hum. Comput. Interact. (IJMHCI) **3**, 4 (2011)
28. Sigman, M., Ruskin, E.: Chapter I.V. social and emotional responsiveness. Monogr. Soc. Res. Child Dev. **64**, 54–65 (1999)
29. Wikipedia Contributors.: "Likert Scale". Wikipedia, The Free Encyclopedia [Online]. http://en.wikipedia.org/wiki/Likert_scale. [Access in 20 September 2014]
30. Willis, M.J., Jones, C.M.: Emotishare: supporting emotion communication through ubiquitous technologies. In: OZCHI 2012, Melbourne, Australia (2012)
31. Yu, B.: The emotional world of health online communities. In: Proceedings of the 2011 iConference (iConference 2011), p. 2 (2011)

User Modeling on Social Media for Art Museums and Galleries

Kingkarn Sookhanaphibarn[1]([✉]), Utaiwan Chatuporn[2],
and Kodchakorn Na Nakornphanom[3]

[1] Multimedia Intelligent Technology Laboratory, School of Science and Technology,
Bangkok University, City Campus, Bangkok 10110, Thailand
kingkarn.s@bu.ac.th
http://mit.science.bu.ac.th
[2] Southeast Asian Ceramics Museum, Bangkok University, Rangsit Campus,
Pathum-thani 10120, Thailand
utaiwan.c@bu.ac.th
[3] School of Science and Technology, Sukhothai Thammathirat
Open University (STOU), Nonthaburi 11120, Thailand
kodchakorn.nan@stou.ac.th

Abstract. This paper shows the results of studying relevant factors for expanding an experience of museum visitors by using social media technology. The constructed questionnaire was used as a tool to elicit the opinion of members in the Facebook fan page of Southeast Asian Ceramics Museum, Bangkok University, Thailand. In this study, there were 222 respondents whose occupations were related to either arts and cultures (42.79 %), and not related to (57.21 %). The results indicated that the perceived usefulness of technology factors and perceived ease of use to technology were related to the expansion of museum visitors experience with social media applications at statistically significant level of 0.01.

Keywords: Technology Acceptance Model (TAM) · Adoption computer technology · Digital museum · User experience · Facebook

1 Introduction

In the past decade, the role of art museums and galleries has been changing from static storehouses of artifacts to active learning environment for visitors [3]. The museums then must look both inward to their collections and outward to their audiences. Therefore, their role has changed from object collection to communication with people. The raised questions are how, with what, and to whom the museums should make links.

With the advanced technologies in Web and Internet, museums have been easily approach to their audiences via websites. There are two types of websites as follows: websites for general information of museums, and websites as a digital place where users can find information of the collections of their artifacts [7]. The latter one can provide some knowledge about the artifacts without traveling to the real place.

© Springer International Publishing Switzerland 2015
G. Meiselwitz (Ed.): SCSM 2015, LNCS 9182, pp. 89–95, 2015.
DOI: 10.1007/978-3-319-20367-6_10

In this paper, we are interested in a use of Facebook (social media) as a communication tool between a museum and its audience. This communication must meet the audience needs such as new information, entertainment, and social activities, which is so-call "visitors' experience [2]." The objective of this paper is to develop a user model to expand the visitor experience via the Facebook fanpage and the Facebook application (as shown in Figs. 1 and 2) for Southeast Asian Ceramics Museum, Bangkok University, Thailand, where is a sort of art museums.

Fig. 1. The Facebook fanpage of Southeast Asian Ceramics Museum, Bangkok University, Thailand

Fig. 2. The Facebook application of Southeast Asian Ceramics Museum, Bangkok University, Thailand

2   Experiences of Museum Visitors

2.1   Type of Experience

As addressed by Falk and Dierking [2], combination among individual, group of people, places can develop the experience of each museum visit. Three dimensions are the personal context, the social context and the physical context.

The interaction of these three dimensions constitutes the way in which a museum visit is perceived by every individual museum visitor as shown in Fig. 3.

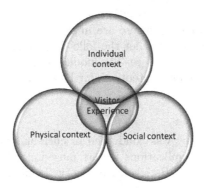

Fig. 3. Factors of the museum's visitor experiences

From the aforementioned dimensions, the other experience types will be developed inside the visitors (as illustrated in Fig. 3), but the formulation is depend on the intensity of each dimension. For example, the level of interaction among visitors that can develop a social network of special interest group for a particular museum. Increasing the degree of interaction will extend the size of social network. This is one of museum goals because the more shared knowledge and interest, the more experience will be perceived. Therefore, the online social media is the most suitable alternative to convey the visitor experience on these three dimensions.

While the visitors explore the exhibitions, the visitors' experiences surrounding with three contexts can be listed in the followings [4]:

1. Recreation: Visitors enjoy of free, relaxed, unstructured time and activity playful and diversionary activity. They can try out interactive devices, sit down for a meal, shopping in a gift shop, etc.
2. Sociability: Visitors meet with or participating with others, look at and spend time together with others, take part in shared, public activity.
3. Learning Experience: Visitors gather and acquire information, perceive new things and new patterns, exercise curiosity and a sense of discovery.
4. Aesthetic Experience: Visitors engage in sensory perceptions, especially visual and tactile, see objects with a view toward their beauty, rather than what is moral or useful, compare things and find patterns.
5. Celebrative Experience: Visitors observe and honor a leader, event, group, or organization, share in historical achievements.
6. Enchanting Experience: Visitors encounter things that uplift the mind, imagination, and spirit, find magic, delight, fascination, and rapture in things and places.

3   Methodology

3.1   Conceptual Framework

Our proposed user model is mainly adopted from Technology Acceptance Model (TAM) proposed by Davis [1], where are important theoretical bases in information system field [8]. We consider the following three two factors: perceived usefulness, and perceived ease of use. The model will present how the two factors are influence on the behavioral intentions for Facebook applications.

3.2   Research Method

Questionnaire-based survey was conducted in current study. Since we focused on the use of Facebook applications for art museums, the Facebook members of Asian Ceramics Museum, Bangkok University, Thailand were selected as the sample frame.

Facebook Application: The Facebook application [6] has important features such as an virtual gallery of museum objects with their description, an virtual souvenir shop, the visualization to illustrate the visitors' comments having links to the objects and the visitors. For the virtual gallery, the photographs of museum objects, which were taken by a museum expert, are displayed in six views (top, bottom, and 4-side views) and all the series of photographs can be zoomed in (as shown in Fig. 4). The description, which were written by experts and curators, will be pop-up when holding a mouse over a particular object.

Fig. 4. Zoom on an museum object

Questionnaire: The questionnaires with a 5-point Likert scale were constructed based on the definitions of three variables [1, 5] as shown in Table 1. The independent variable "behavioral intentions" in this research emphasized the Facebook application in order to expand the visitors' experience in the following dimensions: from immersive to integrative and active participation to passive participation. There are six areas in the dimensions as follows: learning experience, aesthetic experience, celebrative experience, sociability, issue-oriented experience, and recreation [4].

Table 1. Definitions of considering variables

Dependent variables	Perceived usefulness	The degree to which an individual believes that using a particular system would enhance his or her knowledge.
	Perceived ease of use	The degree to which an individual believes that using a particular system would be free of physical and mental effort.
Independent variables	Behavioral intentions	The degree to which an individual intend to use a particular system

Subjects: After the contact with the Facebook members of the museum, five hundred questionnaires were distributed to them who agreed to participate in our research. Because the sample size determined by using Taro Yamane's formula [9] is 222, we collected the first 222 responses who returned the questionnaires.

4   Results and Conclusion

4.1   Demographic Information

Among the two hundred twenty two respondents, most (59.46) of respondents were aged above 35, and they (56.76) hold the master degree or higher. Detailed descriptive statistics relating to the respondent's characteristics are shown in Table 2.

4.2   User Modeling

We construct the user model with the linear regression on the two dependent variables influencing on each area of visitors' experience as shown in Fig. 5. We found that only the perceived usefulness influenced on the overall areas of experience with the following Eq. (1). The averages of the expectation to gain experiences are shown in Fig. 6.

$$Visitors'Experience = 0.781 * PerceivedUsefulness \qquad (1)$$

Table 2. Demographic information of the respondents

Demographics		Frequency (%)
Gender	Male	112 (50.45)
	Female	110 (49.55)
Age	Under 26	13 (5.86)
	26-35	77 (34.68)
	36-45	82 (36.94)
	Above 46	50 (22.52)
Education Level	Below senior high school	24 (10.81)
	University/College	72 (32.43)
	Graduate school	126 (56.76)
Professional field	Relating to museums and galleries, arts and cultures	95 (42.79)
	Others	127 (57.21)

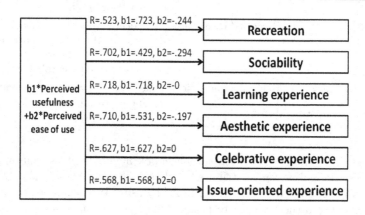

Fig. 5. User model of social media for art museums and galleries

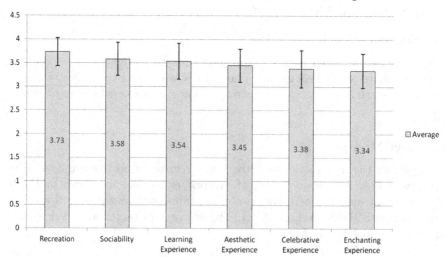

Fig. 6. Average of the expectation to gain six experiences (SD represented by error bars)

4.3   Conclusion

The propose of this research was to investigate a model of TAM to understand the determinants of users' intention to use the Facebook application of art museums and galleries. The perceived usefulness was found to be more influential than perceived ease of use in developing usage behavioral intention.

References

1. Davis, F.D., Bagozzi, R.P., Warshaw, P.R.: User acceptance of computer technology: a comparison of two theoretical models. Manage. sci. **35**(8), 982–1003 (1989)
2. Falk, J.H., Dierking, L.D.: The Museum Experience. Whalesback books, Washington (1992)
3. Hooper-Greenhill, E.: Museums and their Visitors. Routledge, New York (2013)
4. Kotler, N.G., Kotler, P., Kotler, W.I.: Museum Marketing and Strategy: Designing Missions, Building Audiences, Generating Revenue and Resources. John Wiley & Sons, San Francisco (2008)
5. Pu, P., Chen, L., Hu, R.: A user-centric evaluation framework for recommender systems. In: Proceedings of the fifth ACM conference on Recommender systems, pp. 157–164. ACM (2011)
6. Sookhanaphibarn, K., Chatuporn, U.: Expanding the experience of museum visitors with a social application on facebook. In: ICDS 2013, The Seventh International Conference on Digital Society, pp. 74–80 (2013)
7. Sookhanaphibarn, K., Thawonmas, R.: Digital Museums in 3D Virtual Environment. Handbook of Research on Methods and Techniques for Studying Virtual Communities: Paradigms and Phenomena. IGI Global, Hershey (2011)
8. Venkatesh, V., Davis, F.D.: A theoretical extension of the technology acceptance model: four longitudinal field studies. Manage. Sci. **46**(2), 186–204 (2000)
9. Yamane, T.: Statistics: An Introductory Analysis. Harper and Row, New York (1967)

Social Media and Higher Education: A Literature Review

Yuanqiong Wang[✉] and Gabriele Meiselwitz

Towson University, Annapolis, MD, USA
{ywang,gmeiselwitz}@towson.edu

Abstract. This paper presents a literature review of empirical research related to the use and effects of social media in higher education settings. The adoption of social media has been steadily increasing. However, a majority of the research reported focuses on students' perception on the effects of social media in learning. The research on the effects of social media on student learning and faculty perspectives are still limited. This literature review focused on the empirical studies that involved the use of social media in higher education in the computing field. Recommendations for future research directions were presented as the result of this literature review.

Keywords: Social media · Higher education · Student learning · Faculty

1 Introduction

The popularity of social media sites has been steadily increasing over the last few years, and over 70 % of online adults are now using a social networking site of some kind. Many users of social networking sites have more than one account, and check these accounts several times daily [6]. But even as social media has been widely adopted by many users, its use for higher education has also been questioned by educators. Although faculty in higher education often utilizes social networking sites in a professional context, many are reluctant to use social networking sites for teaching and learning. Moreover, even though computing faculty members may have more experience with the technology, their adoption of social media for teaching purpose has been at a lower rate comparing to faculty in other fields such as Humanities and Arts, Professions and Applied Sciences, and Social Sciences [6, 20].

Web 2.0 (often referred to as the "social web"), with its many benefits such as social networking and user-generated content, has drawn much attention for teaching and learning [2]. Learning paradigms have shifted over the last decades from a traditional classroom setting to include online learning, e-learning, collaborative learning, and many hybrid forms. This shift indicates a move from instructor-led and instructor-centered learning environments to learner-centered environments, which focus on knowledge creation and building rather than knowledge transmission [3, 5]. At first glance, Web 2.0 applications such as social networks, wikis, blogging, and micro blogging seem to be well suited for learner-centered environments, but a closer look reveals that the adoption of Web 2.0 technologies and applications in higher education learning is lagging behind the adoption of Web 2.0 technologies overall. Although roughly 90 %

© Springer International Publishing Switzerland 2015
G. Meiselwitz (Ed.): SCSM 2015, LNCS 9182, pp. 96–104, 2015.
DOI: 10.1007/978-3-319-20367-6_11

of young adults (18-29 years old) use some social network site, many faculty members also see limitations and potential problems with the use of online and interactive technologies in higher education [6, 20]. In a survey, 56 % of faculty members stated that they see online and mobile technologies as more distracting than helpful to students for academic work [20].

Several studies have investigated the use of social media in higher education, many concentrating on the use of Facebook in their courses. Facebook still dominates the social media landscape, and is popular across a diverse mix of demographic profiles, but other sites have gained popularity and many users now participate in multiple networks [20]. However, the popularity of Facebook has prompted many educators to integrate some elements into their learning environments.

Some studies point out that it is an obligation to prepare students for what they will encounter once they graduate from college and enter the workplace [1, 5]. Other studies examine the connection between social networking and informal and formal learning. Learning in a constructivist environment focuses on the individual learner and the situational context in which learning occurs, and the variety of options and tools that are available through social networking could support this type of situational learning. Students with different backgrounds, learning styles, and preferences can choose which tools they prefer for their individual learning process [19]. In addition, these technologies may create a higher level of student engagement that will build and support a community of scholars [9, 12, 23].

The majority of studies are experimental studies investigating specific social networking tools (e.g. MySpace, Facebook, Twitter) in specific settings (Business education, communication, medical school), and several studies focusing on pedagogy, learning outcomes, or teaching styles are emerging [19]. There is little discussion to date about some practical concerns for educators when integrating this technology into the higher education learning process. The fast pace in which technology changes, privacy and security concerns, intellectual property, accessibility for students with disabilities, or the increased workload for instructors have not received much attention [19, 20]. Many educators are concerned about the short lifespan of certain applications. MySpace, for example, once the top site for young adults, is practically non-existent in the list of social networks used by this age group [6]. Moreover, it recently resorted to mass-mailing its former users to convince them to reactivate their still existing accounts [25]. Many young adults also have moved on from Facebook to other social networking sites, are participating in several sites, and check only their preferred site frequently [6].

The purpose of this paper is to review existing literature related to the use of social media in computing education at higher education level, the effects of social media on learning, and the concerns of adopting social media in learning. Empirical studies that focused on the use of social media for computer education in colleges, the effects of social media on student learning, and potential barriers of the social media adoption are presented in this paper. This literature review attempts to answer the following research questions:

RQ1: Does social media lead to any improvement in higher education for learning computing related subjects?

RQ2: What are the general objective benefits associated to the use of social media in higher education for learning computing related subjects?

RQ3: What are the perceived benefits associated to the use of social media in higher education for learning computing related subjects?

RQ4: What are the barriers or concerns that computer faculties have toward the use of social media in higher education for learning computing related subjects?

2   Method

Literature focusing on the use of social media in higher education for computing subjects was collected and reviewed. The following online databases were utilized for the literature search: EBSCO, IEEE, ACM digital library.

The focus of the search was to gather full-text articles presenting empirical studies which involve the use of social media in higher education setting, especially the ones used for computing related subjects. To manage the scope and the comprehensiveness of the study, the following criteria were used to determine the inclusion of the paper for the review:

1. The study involved social media tools.
2. The study investigated the effects of the social media to students' learning perform-ance and behavior, the effects of the social media to students' perception of learning process, the perception of the faculty members related to the use of social media.
3. The study focused on higher education preferably in computing related field. There-fore, studies conducted at K-12 level were excluded from this review.
4. The study must include a clear discussion on the research method utilized.
5. The study must be published between 2010 and 2014.
6. The paper must be written in English.

3   Findings

This section discusses the findings of this literature research. The findings are organized based on the key perspectives of the study.

3.1   Student Perspectives

Majority of the studies reviewed are focused on students' perspectives of the social media use for instructional purpose, using various social media tools, such as Facebook, Blog, Wiki, and in-house social network tools, etc. Facebook has been the most frequently used site for the studies. This is consistent with the findings reported by Pearson's social media for teaching and learning survey [20]. Based on a survey to 191 students in the use of Facebook for a closed group discussion, Gonzalez-Ramirez, Gasco, and Taverner [7] reported that students' perceived weaknesses of Facebook in teaching included privacy issues, time required, and technological deficit; while the potential strengths that students predict include performance, communication, participation, and motivation. Students' perceived usefulness of the tool and students' learning achievements were the most frequently studied factors.

Student Perceived Learning Experience. In order to study the impact of social media in higher education setting, many researchers conducted explorative studies to investigate the students' perceived learning experience [4, 7, 12, 17, 21–23]. Veletsianos and Navarrete [24] conducted a case study utilizing Elgg as the online social network in an online course, and investigated students' perceived learning experience. The students reported to have overall enjoyed the experience. When being asked to compare the experience of using social network site (SNS) for class purpose to their previous experience of using traditional learning management systems (LMS), most students preferred SNS over LMS. However, when investigating further in terms of how students were using the tool, they noticed that there was limited participation to course related and graded activities, and little use for social networking and sharing purpose. In addition, students requested more support in managing the amount of information offered in SNS showing the potential of information overload by using SNS. While SNS provide more ways of communication and have the potential of accessing more resources, some students reported to have lacked the ability to effectively find and categorize content for future retrieval. However, all the findings from their study was based on students' self-reported usage and perception. No investigation in terms of students' actual usage of the site was done.

Li, Ganeshan and Xu [12] conducted an online survey to 300 students and a follow-up interview with nine of the respondents to investigate students' preference of the communication tools and social networking sites. They reported that the students preferred Facebook in general. However, when it is time to discuss course related topics, Facebook is much less preferred than email. Some of the factors that affected the use of SNS for learning purpose included network speed, security and privacy.

Ozmen and Atici [17] conducted semi-structured interviews with 15 students in the use of LMS supported by SNS. They've incorporated Ning to support a Blackboard site. When being asked the overall perception of their learning experience, students responded that although Ning may have the potential to enhance the communication by using the chat tool, the overuse of chat actually lead to more distraction than to help them learn. Therefore, it is suggested that more pedagogical considerations need to be taken when incorporating SNS to the class environment. Finding the appropriate level of integration with the existing LMS and identify the appropriate activities may be the key to improve perceived learning experience.

In addition to general learning experience and preferences, several studies focused on the specific elements that may have the potential of affecting students learning by incorporating SNS to their classes. One of the common studied effect was the social support provided by SNS. For example, DeAndrea, Ellison, LaRose, Steinfield, and Fiore [4] presented an experiment they conducted that involved first year college students utilizing SpartanConnect, a social media site they designed, to study the effect of SNS in enhancing students' perceptions of social support. Students were asked to create an account on the site before the semester started. The researchers then distributed pre-test survey after the first two weeks of classes to all first year students, and a post-test survey after using the site for the semester. Out of 1616 first year students who completed post-test survey, 265 students filled out both surveys. Higher level of perceived social support was reported after the use of the site.

Thoms, Eryilmaz and Gerbino [22] conducted a quasi-experiment in which students were asked to use an in-house online social network (OSN) to receive peer support recommendation. They also found that the use of OSN has improved students' perceived level of course interaction and peer support, which in turn may lead to better learning.

Taylor [21] conducted a case study that investigated the possible effect of SNS on students' retention rate in lower level computing class. The author reported to have seen an increased retention rate after the use of Facebook in CS1 class.

Unfortunately, although much previous research [21, 22] reported improvements in students' perceived learning experience and social support, there are also negative impacts reported. For example, Junco [9] conducted a survey to investigate the relationship between the use of Facebook and students' engagement in learning. A negative relationship was reported between the self-reported frequency of Facebook use and students' engagement. Based on the self-reported data, it shows a negative relationship between the frequency of engaging in Facebook chat and time spent preparing for class as well. This finding seems to be consistent with the study reported by Ozmen and Atici [17] that overuse of chat can become a distraction for learning since chat takes away the time that initially should have been allocated for study.

Student Learning Achievements. Unlike the studies of the impact on students' perceived learning experience, the actual learning achievements were not investigated as heavily. Laru, Naykki, Jarvela [11] conducted a case study that involved 21 students work in groups of four to five for 12 weeks to complete a wiki project. A number of social media tools were introduced to the students, such as ShoZu, Flickr, Google Reader Mobile, Wordpress.com, Wikispaces, FeedBlendr, and FeedBurner RSS. Data was captured by using video recordings, social software usage activity and pre-and post-tests of students' conceptual understanding of the materials. The comparison between the pre- and post- conceptual knowledge test showed an improvement in test scores received. Looking into more detail in terms of the relationship between the actual activities and the learning outcome, the researchers reported that the higher level of wiki-related activities was an indicator for determining the students improved scores.

Hernandez et al. [8] conducted an experiment to investigate the impact of different tools supporting students' learning and perception of interaction. The students were assigned into groups that used Facebook with wiki-style document creation and wall/comment feature, Google Docs, or LMS discussion forum. After comparing the level of activities in each group setting and their final product, it was reported that the number of messages posted was higher in SNS compared to those using traditional LMS forum, time between messages posted was shorter in Facebook compared to other groups, and groups using Facebook also reported higher level of perceived interaction. However, the final result was the same among all groups. No effect in the learning outcome was reported when comparing groups using different tools for group communication.

Instead of an objective measure of the students' learning achievement while SNS was used, many studies either overlooked the impact of SNS for learning outcomes or used only students' self-reported data for this purpose [9, 11]. More research is needed to look into the impact of SNS on student learning in addition to the impact on student learning experience.

Student SNS Usage Pattern. In addition to the potential impact of SNS for learning, the patterns of the posts in different tools were also investigated. Maleko et al. [13] reported their findings based on a case study conducted that compares Facebook and Blackboard usage by the students. They reported that posts in Facebook were unique in that they were concentrated in the expression of dissatisfaction, course admin, encouragement, discussions outside programming, and general advice; while the posts in Blackboard tend to be more for the purpose of community building and question to the lecturer. In addition, students reported to have preferred the use of Facebook for learning support where no authoritative figure was present.

Kear et al. [10] conducted a survey after students were asked to use an in-house wiki to co-edit a document after completing an online tutorial of how the wiki can be used. They collected data about students' use of wiki over time. The authors reported decreased use overtime although students learned how to use wiki. After further investigation through the survey instrument, they found that the students were unhappy about editing other students' work. When being asked to compare wiki and traditional discussion forum for this kind of collaborative activities, students preferred forum over wiki.

3.2 Faculty Perspectives

Unlike the studies focused on students' perspectives, only a handful of studies that we investigated looked into the SNS use from faculty members' perspectives.

Faculty Perception. Faculty perception of the SNS use for learning purpose has been mixed comparing to students perception. The survey conducted by Pearson [20] indicated that one of the reasons for faculty members not incorporating SNS in their teaching was because they consider the use of SNS as a distraction. Roblyer et al. [18] reported different perceptions of the faculty members compared to students. They found that students are more open to use Facebook when comparing to email for the communication purpose. Faculty members were more prone to traditional technologies, such as email. Brown also did a survey and a follow-up more in depth interview with the faculty members regarding the use of Web 2.0 technologies for learning purposes. The responses received from the faculty members indicated that promoting active student participation, enhancing distribution of and access to tutor-selected or generated learning content are the potential benefits indicated.

Faculty Concerns. The hesitance of faculty members regarding the use of SNS in classrooms may be explained by the concerns identified by previous studies. For example, Brown [2] reported that misalignments between the increasing amount of collaborative group work expected and continuing individual assessment, no "added value" to teaching, and too many constraints (because of the university policy) are the major concerns from faculty members. Kear et al. [10] reported that, in addition to the above mentioned concerns, performance of the SNS used, the difficulties in marking and monitoring students' work, workload issues are also among the concerns raised by the teaching staff members.

4   Discussion

The literature review has shown some empirical findings that this paper attempted to investigate. In terms of the question regarding whether social media lead to any improvement in higher education for learning computing related subjects, the literature shows some evidence of improvement. Although the empirical study is extremely limited in gathering objective performance data to showcase the improvement of learning, the student self-reported data shows promising potential of the effectiveness of SNS use in higher education. In addition, literature indicated that careful pedagogical consideration needs to be made in order to ensure the effective use of SNS. However, more investigation is definitely needed.

The general objective benefits associated to the use of social media in higher education for learning computing related subjects has been identified by case studies and survey data. The identified benefits included improved social support, improved retention rate through peer support, and improved perceived interaction. However, the empirical study also showed that there can be negative impact of the use of SNS to the students' engagement in learning.

When answering the perceived benefits associated with the use of social media in higher education for learning computing related subjects, the answers from students and faculty members are similar. Students tend to enjoy the activities using SNS considering it to help improve the interaction, and motivation to learning. In addition to the benefits identified by students, faculty members value the possibility of enhancing distribution of and access to tutor-selected or generated learning content through the use of SNS.

The specific concerns from computer faculty members were not identified from the literature review. However, the investigation of the literature shows that there is a list of potential concerns that are common for most of the faculty members. In general, faculty members share similar concerns as the students which include security, privacy and performance of the site/tool being used. In addition, faculty members are also concerned about the work load issue, the difficulty of performance evaluation and monitoring, and need for careful pedagogical design when it comes to the use of SNS for learning. Faculty members in computing field may be more concerned about the potential distraction of SNS and its security issues because of their familiarity of the technology. However, this was not identified in the literature and further investigation is definitely needed.

5   Recommendations and Future Research

Even though the literature review shows potential of social media usage for learning purpose, the use of the technology is still limited and not many controlled evaluations and in-depth studies in higher education settings have been conducted. First, more empirical study is needed to investigate the actual "added" benefits of SNS comparing to the use of traditional LMS. One of the major limitations of current literature is that most of the studies focused on self-report data to study the effect of the technology. Therefore, the actual usage and learning outcome should be addressed and investigated in more depth.

Although computing faculty members may know the technology better than faculty members in other field, their adoption of SNS is lagging behind. Is there any specific reason? Is it because of the nature of the topic that is sometimes hard to describe in texts? Is it because of the higher security concern from the faculty members? More investigation is needed to address this issue.

References

1. Alexander, B.: Web 2.0: A new wave of innovation for teaching and learning? Educause review 41.2 (2006)
2. Brown, S.: Seeing Web 2.0 in context: A study of academic perceptions. Internet High. Educ. 15(1), 50–57 (2012)
3. Brownson, S.: Embedding social media tools in online learning courses. J. Res. Innovative Teach. 7(1), 112–118 (2014)
4. DeAndrea, D.: Serious social media: on the use of social media for improving students adjustment to college. Internet High. Educ. 15(1), 15–23 (2012)
5. Duffy, P., Bruns A.: The use of blogs, wikis and RSS in education: In: A conversation of possibilities, pp. 31–38 (2006)
6. Duggan, M., Smith, A.: Social media update 2013. Pew Internet and American Life Project (2013)
7. González-Ramírez, R., Gascó, J., Taverner, J.: Facebook in teaching: strengths and weaknesses. Int. J. Inf. Learn. Technol. 32(1), 65–78 (2015)
8. Hernández, R. et al.: Facebook for CSCL, Latin-American experience for professors. In: Proceedings of the IEEE 12th International Conference on Advanced Learning Technologies (ICALT), IEEE (2012)
9. Junco, R.: The relationship between frequency of Facebook use, participation in Facebook activities, and student engagement. Comput. Educ. 58(1), 162–171 (2012)
10. Kear, K., et al.: From forums to wikis: perspectives on tools for collaboration. Internet High. Educ. 13(4), 218–225 (2010)
11. Laru, J., Näykki, P., Järvelä, S.: Supporting small-group learning using multiple Web 2.0 tools: a case study in the higher education context. Internet High. Educ. 15(1), 29–38 (2012)
12. Li, X., Ganeshan, K., Xu, G.: The role of social networking sites in e-learning, In: Proceedings of the FIE 2012 Conference on 42nd ASEE/IEEE Frontiers in Education (2012)
13. Maleko, M., et al.: Facebook versus Blackboard for supporting the learning of programming in a fully online course: the changing face of computing education. In: Proceedings of the Learning and Teaching in Computing and Engineering (LaTiCE), IEEE (2013)
14. Mamaqi, X.: The efficiency of different ways of informal learning on firm performance: A comparison between, classroom, web 2 and workplace training. Computers in Human Behavior (2015)
15. Moran, M., Seaman, J., Tinti-Kane, H.: Teaching, Learning, and Sharing: How Today's Higher Education Faculty Use Social Media. Babson Survey Research Group, UK (2011)

16. O'Keeffe, G., Clarke-Pearson, K.: The impact of social media on children, adolescents, and families. Pediatrics **127**(4), 800–804 (2011)
17. Özmen, B., Atıcı, B.: Learners views regarding the use of social networking sites in distance learning. Int. Rev. Res. Open Distrib. Learn. **15**(4), 161–177 (2014)
18. Roblyer, M.D., et al.: Findings on Facebook in higher education: A comparison of college faculty and student uses and perceptions of social networking sites. Internet High. Educ. **13**(3), 134–140 (2010)
19. Rodriguez, J.: Social media use in higher education: key areas to consider for educators. MERLOT J. Online Learn. Teach. **7**(4), 539–550 (2011)
20. Seaman, J., Tinti-Kane, H.: Social Media for Teaching and Learning. Pearson Learning Systems, UK (2013)
21. Taylor, K.: Can utilizing social media and visual programming increase retention of minorities in programming classes? In: Frontiers in Education Conference 2013, vol. 54 pp. 1046-1048. IEEE (2013)
22. Thoms, B., Eryilmaz, E., Gerbino, S.: Designing a peer support system for computer programming courses using online social networking software(HICSS), In: 47th Hawaii International Conference on System Sciences, IEEE (2014)
23. Veletsianos, G.: Higher education scholars participation and practices on Twitter. J. Comput. Assist. Learn. **28**(4), 336–349 (2012)
24. Veletsianos, G., Navarrete, C.: Online social networks as formal learning environments: Learner experiences and activities. Int. Rev. Res. Open Distrib. Learn. **13**(1), 144–166 (2012)
25. Washington Post. http://www.washingtonpost.com/news/the-intersect/wp/2014/06/02/myspace-still-exists-and-its-desperate-enough-to-blackmail-you-into-logging-in/

Social Network Analysis

An Analytic Study on Private SNS for Bonding Social Networking

Hyeonjung Ahn and Sangwon Lee[✉]

Department of Interaction Science, Sungkyunkwan University, Myeongnyun 3-ga,
Jongno-gu, Seoul, Republic of Korea
ahnhj77@gmail.com, upcircle@skku.edu

Abstract. In recent years, SNS(Social Network Service) has become one of the most effective communication tools for people. For instance, 'Facebook' contributes to the phenomenon, and various studies have already been made about the public SNS. However, public SNSs have some problems including privacy issues and information overload while being useful for connecting individuals. In short, the function of public SNSs may not be sufficient for bonding human relationships or protecting privacy. In contrast, private SNS has different functional features which compensate the defects of public SNS and promote bonding relationship with fewer people. Considering the increasing domestic popularity of private SNS domestically, this study conducted a comparative analysis of 12 typical private SNSs to find out common features of private SNSs by comparing them with the features of public SNSs. Specifically, we mainly referred to the honeycomb model of social media to serve the objective of our study. Finally, we analyze one private SNS called 'Band' based on the key traits of private SNS and make a suggestion to improve the current service. The present study may provide a theoretical standard about private SNSs for innovating SNSs that are under overcrowded condition and we can also judge whether the factors are in accordance with user's needs well in our future study.

Keywords: Private SNS · Public SNS · Social capital · Bonding relationship · Bridging relationship

1 Introduction

Nowadays, SNSs(Social Network Services) have been regarded as an essential tool in connecting networks online and sharing various information without any spatial-temporal constraints. SNSs have developed from the appearance of web service such as 'SixDegrees.com' which is considered as the first SNS that lasted from 1997 to 2001 [1]. Since then, more social network services, including 'Facebook' and 'Twitter', started its service and Facebook has attained over 1.3 billion users until now [2]. These public SNSs contributed the connection and the maintenance of networks. However, they have some problems such as privacy risks and information overload. Even though 'Facebook' incidentally provided privacy control functions which allow users to determine the size of

© Springer International Publishing Switzerland 2015
G. Meiselwitz (Ed.): SCSM 2015, LNCS 9182, pp. 107–117, 2015.
DOI: 10.1007/978-3-319-20367-6_12

privacy exposure (public, friends, only me), these functions are unfamiliar to the users in the sense of protecting privacy [3]. Most of those SNSs have no restrictions on the number of friends and the users can make friends online even though they have never met each other offline. Thus, the public SNS users tend to have lower sense of closeness among the members in the large networks [4]. Moreover, we can see many people who run the gauntlet of many unspecified people because of involuntarily written SNS posts, which is so-called 'SNS Phobia'. As a result, some of the public SNS users who are trying to make themselves look better than reality are censoring the contents before posting messages or visual materials to public SNS. For the side effects from using public SNSs, new types of SNS are becoming popular among SNS users. These new SNSs tend to have three attributes; 'reducing privacy risks', 'security of data', and 'guaranteed anonymity'. Some of them compensate the defects of public SNS by reducing privacy risks through restriction of the number of friends online. The present study focused on the aspect of 'reducing privacy risks' which is well known for private SNS such as Path and Band. Moreover, there are few studies about these private SNSs and finding a specific criteria to compare public SNS and private SNS is hard. This study mainly compares public SNS and private SNS by analyzing the key traits of 12 representative private SNSs.

The private SNSs are designed for communication with close acquaintances such as friends, family, or neighbors in small size communities. Since the initiation of private SNS called Band, the service has gained over ten million users in a year. According to one statistical data, the number of private SNS users has increased faster than public SNS users in Republic of Korea [5]. 'Path' and 'Band' are two major representative private SNSs which have the key features of private SNSs. The 'Path' (2010) is a complete closed-type social network service considered as the first private SNS in the United States of America. Specifically, Path limits the number of friends up to 150 for high-quality connections. This characteristic followed the theory of Dunbar's Number. According to Robin Dunbar (1993), the maximum of human relationships to maintain intimate social relationship is up to 150 people [6, 7]. Furthermore, the users can partly escape from useless information such as advertisement because 'Path' pursuits ad-free social network which is distinct from 'Facebook'.

Similarly, 'Band' (2012) is the most popular private SNS in the Republic of Korea and other countries in Asia and is also preparing to extend its service to the United States of America in 2014 [8]. Users can be involved in diverse groups online with various functions for get-together among acquaintances. In addition, users should get invitation from friends to join the groups. In addition to these two examples, we analyzed the functions of ten more private SNSs which have different characteristics to find out objective common features. Specifically, we referred to the honeycomb model of social media [9], which defines social media with seven core functional traits, to strengthen the objectivity of our analysis. In light of these backgrounds about private SNS, we conducted the study with the following research questions:

RQ1. What are the attributes of private SNS in the view of honeycomb model of social media?

RQ2. What are underlying factors of private SNS adoption compared to those of public SNSs?

The current study compared public SNS and private SNS specifically based on the analysis of 12 typical private SNSs which have different target users and functions. The result of this study will provide theoretical basis for better understanding of private SNS. Moreover, the author may help users to choose certain private SNS based on their own needs for enhanced satisfaction.

2 Background

In this section, we explain about basic knowledge of social network services, honeycomb model of social media, and factors of SNS usage for better understanding of our study about the private SNS.

2.1 Social Network Service

Nowadays, a variety of information including current issues spreads in a faster rate than the past through SNS globally. Specifically, 'Facebook' is one of the most popular SNS contributing to that phenomenon and there are a lot of studies relevant to this public SNS [10]. According to the previous studies, SNS(Social Network Sites) is defined as "web-based social network sites that allow SNS users to make a public or semi-public profile within a bounded system, articulate a list of other users with whom they share a connection, and view and traverse their list of connections and those made by others within the system" [1]. Above this, a lot of researchers have demonstrated diverse definitions of SNS. Moreover, six common functions of SNSs are identified by Richter and Koch (2008) through analysis of several SNSs and the results include identity management, context awareness, expert finding, network awareness, contact management, and exchange [11]. SNSs are considered as a social network service that individuals can interact, bridge, or bond with others online without any spatial or temporal restrictions. In these definitions of SNS, social capital is highly important concept as it is the main purpose of using SNS for building and maintaining personal relationship. Other findings also demonstrate that SNS users' main purpose is social relationship [12]. To be specific, the social capital means the resources formed by relationship among people in social networks [13]. The social capital serves two main purposes; bridging social relationship and bonding social relationship [15]. Bridging social capital means "weak ties" [16] which do not support close relationship between individuals and they can share new information one another through this connections [14]. In contrast, bonding social capital refers to "strong ties" [16] which demonstrates close and intimate relationship among families or close friends.

In the present study, we divided SNSs into two types; public SNS and private SNS. Public SNSs such as Facebook and Twitter are convenient tools bridging relationship with others including family, friends, and even complete strangers. In other words, it may not increase "strong ties" among users but may benefit in maintaining maintain "weak ties" [17]. In contrast, private SNSs are designed to interact with close acquaintances such as friends or family. Using private SNSs is a good way for increasing "strong ties". For example, some private SNSs (e.g., Path, Daybe) serve a function of limiting the number of friends in the services. Through this function, services do not allow users to have unrestricted number of friends and let users to manage their social capital more effectively.

2.2   Honeycomb Model of Social Media

Kietzmann et al. (2011) suggested honeycomb model which defines social media with seven core functional traits including identity, relationships, presence, sharing, reputation, conversations, and groups [9], [18]. Facebook, YouTube, and Foursquare are typical cases of social media having different functions. With the honeycomb model, they can be compared each other at a glance by increasing the understanding of social media. This study also presents guidelines about how firms should set up strategies for their social media platforms (Fig. 1).

Fig. 1.   Original honeycomb model of social media

In the current study, we narrowed the scope of this study about social media by focusing on private SNS. Specifically, we analyzed 12 representative private SNSs to find out key traits of private SNSs on the basis of honeycomb model of social media for the objectivity of our study. We sub-divided common traits of private SNS in Sect. 3 by comparing the ones with those of public SNSs.

2.3   Factors of SNS Usage

A lot of researchers have tried to find out SNS user's motivation, intention or usage patterns through online survey by targeting specific SNS users such as the users of Facebook, Twitter, and Myspace in different perspectives. According to Richter and Koch's findings (2008), SNS users have various purposes and expectations from using SNS including the following contents. "To keep in touch with others" accounts for the highest percentage of the purposes (87.1 %) and it is followed by "to share information" (80.2 %). Aside from these contents, "contact management", "to share visual materials", "expert search", "to get to know people", and "to present myself" are main purposes of using SNSs in order [11]. Similarly, Brandtzæg and Heim's findings (2009) presented that the highest percentage of SNS user's motivation is to expand social relationship because of its convenience and easy accessibility. In sequence, it is followed by "keeping in touch with friends", "Socializing", and "Access to information" [19]. Lin and Lu (2011) demonstrated the integrated theoretical framework which focuses on factors of SNS usage through combination of network externalities and motivation theory. The study suggests that network externalities including "perceived complementarity" and "number of peers" affect "perceived benefit" (usefulness and enjoyment) and enjoyment has a large impacts on "continued intention to use" by attracting users with inner pleasure [20]. Other researchers classified SNS usage motivation to "social motives" and "interest motives" which originates from "contact maintenance", "social searching" [21] and "contact interest", "topic interest" respectively [22]. Through these results, we can notice that SNS users' main purpose is social interaction with other people including peers, acquaintances, and new people. However, we predict that the main factors of using private SNS use are bonding relationship and privacy protection in the present study.

3   Key Features of Private SNS

In Sect. 3, we analyzed the key features of private SNSs and compared them with those of public SNSs based on the honeycomb model of social media. Prior to this, we chose 12 representative private SNSs which have the main purpose of bonding relationship according to their different main functions, features, and target users. We analyzed each of the characteristics that seemed to reflect the trends of private SNSs and the needs of users. Through the analysis, we suggest a specific criteria which compare public SNS and private SNS in Fig. 3 based on their main traits. Specifically, the features of SNS are characterized by the honeycomb framework. Through the following analysis of private SNSs, we aim to investigate key common characteristics of them.

Figure 2 represents many kinds of private SNSs which have different functions and community traits. The centerline in the Fig. 2 demonstrates the community size of each service. As the SNSs get closer to the right, they show smaller size of community in the service. Moreover, private SNSs in the proximity of the center line mean higher sense of belongings to the community in the service. For example, Next door is location based private SNS designed for communication among neighborhoods in the United States. Kakao Group and Kakao Story are connected to Kakao Talk which is the most popular messenger service having over 80 million users in the Republic of Korea. Kakao Group offers various functions under the management of group chairman. A User who gets invitation from the chairman can be a group member and this method clearly represents closed type of the service. Daybe is inactive social network service which set the limit of the number of friends to 50. Family Book is a family network service instantly inter-acting with family members by sharing information, photo, and schedules.

With the comparative analysis of these 12 private SNSs, we could find common features of private SNSs. Considering the 6 out of 7 traits of social media on the honey-comb model (i.e., relationships, groups, sharing, identity, reputation, and conversations), we suggest 17 key traits of private SNSs with a specific criteria between public SNS and private SNS. Imprecise items relevant to 'Presence' are not contained for the clear comparison between public SNS and private SNS.

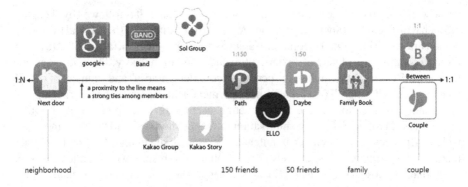

Fig. 2. A variety of private SNSs

- **Relationship:** (1) Main purpose of relationship; bridging or bonding relationship [23], (2) The degree of proximity among users; low or high [24], (3) Strength of relationship; weak ties or strong ties [16], (4) Multiplexity of relationship; high or low [9]
- **Groups:** (1) The number of friends; 1:1000 + or 1:N, 1:1, (2) The method of joining a group; open to anyone, approval required or get an invitation from others to join a group [9], (3) Social network size; large or small, (4) Friends on phonebook list; not contained or contained
- **Sharing:** (1) The range of information; wide or narrow, (2) Information load; high or low, (3) Type of resources; diverse or not diverse, (4) Information diffusion velocity; fast of slow
- **Identity:** (1) Disclosing personal profile: necessary or unnecessary, (2) Privacy exposure; good possibility or low possibility
- **Reputation:** (1) The number of followers; no restriction or restricted, (2) Social implications; significant or not significant
- **Conversations:** (1) Formal arrangement; required or not required

If the characteristics of specific SNS are positively associated with the latter, the SNS is close to the aspect of private SNS. Furthermore, we can evaluate the degree of enclosed type with the Fig. 3. As the more traits of private SNS are close to the right, the SNS shows the higher enclosed type.

4   Application Example

In this section, we aimed to analyze one private SNS specifically based on the attributes of private SNS in the Fig. 3 and presented recommendation to improve the functions. We chose Band as an example for the application because the Band provides more diverse functions than other private SNSs for bonding social networks. Moreover, the users of Band can create or manage various groups at a time. As we refer in Sect. 1, Band is the private SNS which has the largest number of users in the Republic of Korea. Band is designed by NAVER Corporation and originally targeted students for the purpose of facilitating all kinds of gathering. Contrary to expectations, Band attracted not only students but also the users in 30 s and 40 s after adding the function to search

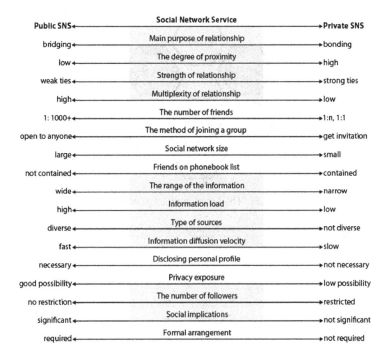

Fig. 3. Public SNS vs Private SNS

for alumnus. According to the main functions of Band, the users can be a member of diverse groups after they get invitation from members in each group. The invitations can be sent to specific person through various methods including sharing links, phone numbers, and particular messenger services. The users can maintain their social relationship online with various functions including group chatting, bulletin board system, photo, group calendar, and even voting for major decisions to make in the group. With these functions for get-together, the Band clarifies its concept of gathering online (Fig. 4).

Given honeycomb model of social media [9], the Band is the most specialized in relationships, sharing, groups, and conversations (Fig. 5).

| Joined groups | Noticeboard | Photo sharing | Group chatting | Group calendar | Voting for decisions |

Fig. 4. Main functions of Band

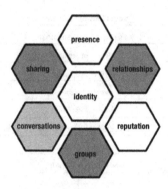

Fig. 5. The functionalities of band

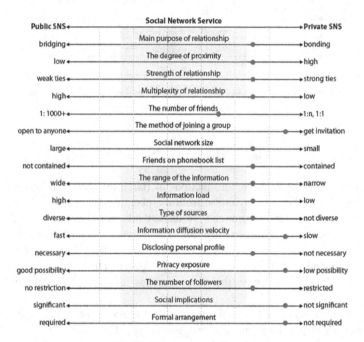

Public SNS	Social Network Service	Private SNS
bridging	Main purpose of relationship	bonding
low	The degree of proximity	high
weak ties	Strength of relationship	strong ties
high	Multiplexity of relationship	low
1: 1000+	The number of friends	1:n, 1:1
open to anyone	The method of joining a group	get invitation
large	Social network size	small
not contained	Friends on phonebook list	contained
wide	The range of the information	narrow
high	Information load	low
diverse	Type of sources	not diverse
fast	Information diffusion velocity	slow
necessary	Disclosing personal profile	not necessary
good possibility	Privacy exposure	low possibility
no restriction	The number of followers	restricted
significant	Social implications	not significant
required	Formal arrangement	not required

Fig. 6. The features of band

To be specific, Fig. 6 represents the relevant characteristics of Band by identifying the main attributes of Band and the degree of its enclosed-type. Similarly, we also analyzed Path in the same way because comparing Band and other private SNS may present other theoretical supports to upgrade each of the functions. We chose Path because of its considerably high satisfaction from the Path users. (Path has 7 times more users than Band and gets 4.4 out of 5 stars in the rating of satisfaction.) The Path demonstrates complete enclosed-type and functionalities of it are identical to Band (e.g., relationships, sharing, groups, and conversations). The Path mainly features limited size of community and respects privacy with a simple interface. A comparison between Band and Path clarifies important elements of private SNS.

Further analysis showed that one shortcoming of Band is maximum limits of groups because each group can invite up to 1,000 people. It is considered as the element which obscures the main concept of Band despite of its useful functions for get-together. In other words, it is hard to enhance connectedness in such a big community like public SNSs. However, if the users who want "strong ties" join small size of groups, they will get high satisfaction from using Band. Thus, we suggest that Band needs to reduce or limit the size of community like that of Path for the main concept of Band, high-quality connections.

As we have mentioned earlier, Band expects to expand its service to the United States. As Band has attracted different age groups by adding one function of searching alumnus, additional functions which reflect other cultural traits should be added for successful expansion of the service to other countries. This study will contribute users in other countries to notice the possibility of high-quality connections through private SNSs. To summarize, the present study suggests 17 key traits of private SNSs by comparing them with those of public SNSs. As these features reflected the common functions of classic 12 private SNSs, we were able to consider the results to upgrade or develop the other kinds of private SNSs having proper functions for the users.

5   Discussion

A lot of researchers in communication, psychology and computer science field have studied about SNS by focusing on its functions, social influence or human behavior while using it. However, a fair number of the studies focus on public SNSs such as Facebook and Twitter. In the current study, we studied on private SNSs which have different functions, features, and purposes of using it. First, we researched about the types of private SNSs and organized its functional traits by comparing them with those of public SNSs to better understand private SNS. We analyzed each of the features and interface elements in the most representative 12 private SNSs so far with 17 key features of SNS to find out popularity common factors. Specifically, we mainly referred to the honeycomb model of social media suggested by Kietzmann et al. to study more in depth and increase the objectivity of our study. The current study will provide theoretical basis about private SNS for innovation of SNS which is in overcrowded condition. This may give SNS developers some insights to improve their social network services by identifying how well the current private SNSs are reflecting the users' needs. Moreover, we may figure out how they can further satisfy private SNS users' needs through the analysis about ideal functions and traits of the SNS.

Aside from public SNS and private SNS, there are other kinds of SNS having different targets such as vertical SNS and anonymous SNS. As the sorts of SNS became far more diverse than ever, SNS usage patterns are also changed to use different SNSs together according to their functions and purposes. This means that we need to extend the scope of our study to those SNSs which may reflect other needs of the users. We also raised a question about how can we make the best use of SNS for our ideal social relationship. Moreover, it will be interesting to find out ideal social network size on private SNS for bonding relationship in the light of 'Path' and 'Daybe' which give the constraint to the size of community. For this study, we may refer to 'Dunbar's number' [7] and 'The new magic number' [25] which focused on community size with intimacy offline and online respectively.

6 Conclusion

Although private SNSs have rapidly gained popularity, public SNSs such as 'Facebook' is still in a superior condition than other SNSs. Specifically, the number of Facebook users is over 1.3 billion internationally and it is still increasing in number. Facebook also consistently updates its functions considering users' various needs. Furthermore, there are a fair number of users who are using those two types of SNS (public SNS and private SNS) together because of their different advantages. Through this point, we could notice that SNS users have multiple needs for social interaction with others by building and bonding own relationship at a time. In that various applications are already developed to satisfy user's diverse needs, there will be more attempts to enhance user's satisfaction in one social network service. Specifically, it is important to consider the advantages of each SNS with thorough analysis of user's requirements. According to Clay Shirky, the society with the most desirable network effects is taking advantages of high-density and low-density network evenly [26]. We recommend public SNS users to use private SNS together for effective social relationship by expanding and bonding social networks concurrently. Through this study, we predict a possibility of new trends of SNS to have each advantage of public SNS and private SNS before long for far more effective online social networking internationally.

Acknowledgment. This research was supported by the Ministry of Education, South Korea, under the Brain Korea 21 Plus Project (No.10Z20130000013) and Basic Science Research Program (No. NRF-2014R 1A 1A2054531).

References

1. Ellison, N.B.: Social network sites: Definition, history, and scholarship. J. Comput. Mediat. Commun. **13**, 210–230 (2007)
2. Facebook privacy policy. https://ko-kr.facebook.com/about/privacy/your-info-on-fb
3. Jones, H., Soltren, J.H.: Facebook: Threats to privacy. In: Project MAC: MIT Project on Mathematics and Computing **1** (2005)
4. Roberts, S.G., Dunbar, R.I., Pollet, T.V., Kuppens, T.: Exploring variation in active network size: constraints and ego characteristics. Social Networks. **31**, 138–146 (2009)
5. http://www.digieco.co.kr/KTFront/dataroom/dataroom_weekly_view.action?board_seq=9185&board_id=weekly
6. Dunbar, R.I.: Coevolution of neocortical size, group size and language in humans. Behav. Brain Sci. **16**, 681–694 (1993)
7. Hill, R.A., Dunbar, R.I.: Social network size in humans. Hum. Nat. **14**, 53–72 (2003)
8. How to use Band. http://www.band.us/home
9. Kietzmann, J.H., Hermkens, K., McCarthy, I.P., Silvestre, B.S.: Social media? get serious! understanding the functional building blocks of social media. Bus. Horiz. **54**, 241–251 (2011)

10. Wilson, R.E., Gosling, S.D., Graham, L.T.: A review of Facebook research in the social sciences. Perspect. Psychol. Sci. **7**, 203–220 (2012)
11. Richter, A., Koch, M.: Functions of social networking services. In: Proceedings of the International Conference on the Design of Cooperative Systems, pp. 87–98. Springer, May 2008
12. Steinfield, C., Ellison, N.B., Lampe, C.: Social capital, self-esteem, and use of online social network sites: a longitudinal analysis. J. Appl. Dev. Psychol. **29**, 434–445 (2008)
13. Portes, A.: Social capital: Its origins and applications in modern sociology. In: Lesser, E.L. (ed.) Knowledge and Social Capital, pp. 43–67. Butterworth-Heinemann, Boston (2000)
14. Pfeil, U., Arjan, R., Zaphiris, P.: Age differences in online social networking–a study of user profiles and the social capital divide among teenagers and older users in my space. Comput. Hum. Behav. **25**, 643–654 (2009)
15. Putnam, R.D.: Bowling Alone: The collapse and Revival of American Community. Simon and Schuster, New York (2000)
16. Granovetter, M.S.: The strength of weak ties. Am. j. Sociol. **78**(6), 1360–1380 (1973)
17. Donath, J., Boyd, D.: Public displays of connection. BT Technol. J. **22**, 71–82 (2004)
18. Kietzmann, J.H., Silvestre, B.S., McCarthy, I.P., Pitt, L.F.: Unpacking the social media phenomenon: towards a research agenda. J. Public Aff. **12**, 109–119 (2012)
19. Brandtzæg, P.B., Heim, J.: Why people use social networking sites. In: Proceedings of the Online communities and social computing, pp. 143–152. Springer, Heidelberg (2009)
20. Lin, K.Y., Lu, H.P.: Why people use social networking sites: an empirical study integrating network externalities and motivation theory. Comput. Hum. Behav. **27**, 1152–1161 (2011)
21. Lampe, C., Ellison, N., Steinfield, C.: A Face (book) in the crowd: social searching vs. social browsing. In: Proceedings of the 2006 20th anniversary conference on Computer supported cooperative work, pp. 167–170. ACM, November 2006
22. Brocke, J.V., Richter, D., Riemer, K.: Motives for using Social Network Sites (SNSs)–An analysis of SNS adoption among students (2009)
23. Norris, P.: The Bridging and Bonding Role of Online Communities. Sage Publications, Thousand Oaks (2004)
24. Kiesler, S., Cummings, J.N.: What do we know about proximity and distance in work groups? Legacy Res. Distrib. work. **1**, 57–80 (2002)
25. Zhao, J., Wu, J., Liu, G., Tao, D., Xu, K., Liu, C.: Being rational or aggressive? a revisit to Dunbar's number in online social networks. Neurocomputing **42**, 343–353 (2014)
26. Shirky, C.: Here comes everybody: The power of organizing without organizations. Penguin, USA (2008)

Simulation-Based Prediction and Analysis of Collective Emotional States

Charlotte Gerritsen[1(✉)] and Ward R.J. van Breda[2]

[1] Netherlands Institute for the Study of Crime and Law Enforcement, De Boelelaan 1077, 1081 HV Amsterdam, The Netherlands
CGerritsen@nscr.nl
[2] Sentimentics, NeedForward Research, Rotterdam, The Netherlands
ward@sentimentics.com

Abstract. The emergence of aggressive behaviour in crowds is not uncommon and is typically unpredictable and difficult to control. Since the availability of guardians for the prevention of aggression is typically limited, it would be useful if the emergence of unwanted behaviour could somehow be predicted. This paper presents a novel approach to predict the emergence of aggressive behaviour in crowds, based on a combination of sentiment analysis and agent-based simulation. The main idea is to use information from social media (in particular Twitter), analyse the sentiment of the messages and feed the resulting sentiments into a simulation model of social contagion. Based on these simulations, the system should be able to predict when and where unwanted behaviour will occur.

Keywords: Social media · Sentiment analysis · Crime prevention · Prediction · Agent-based modelling · Emotions · Social contagion

1 Introduction

It is April 30th, 2009. Today it is Queen's Day in the Netherlands, a day of national celebration of the Queen's birthday; a day and night in which Dutch people traditionally have fun and party. At one of these parties, in a bar in Amsterdam, a couple of friends are dancing. Suddenly, another visitor bumps into one of the girls and starts making accusations that the girl was in his way. In an attempt to protect the girl, her boyfriend responds that the man should go away. However, this makes the man even more aggressive, and a small riot emerges. The people surrounding the two men start to participate by pushing, name calling and eventually throwing their drinks at the man and his two friends, who have joined the riot. Because of the heated atmosphere and the limited space in the bar, other people start panicking and attempt to flee from the room. As a result, several people get injured by being pushed to the walls. The situation escalates and security has to enter the bar, stop the fight and escort several of the rioting people out of the bar.

Although this is just one example, it illustrates a problem that is often observed in events involving large crowds: the emergence of aggressive behaviour in crowds is often unpredictable and difficult to control. Whether it concerns sports festivities,

G. Meiselwitz (Ed.): SCSM 2015, LNCS 9182, pp. 118–126, 2015.
DOI: 10.1007/978-3-319-20367-6_13

demonstrations, or even dance events, in such contexts large-scale aggressive outbursts are not uncommon and are usually triggered by relatively small stimuli, such as a dispute between two people, or people trying to challenge the police [6, 14]. The amount of people involved in such incidents may grow quickly, and the larger the size of the group, the harder it is for the police to control the outburst.

Although significant progress has been made in understanding the mechanisms behind crowd behaviour [6], the (often) large number of people present makes it difficult for security personnel to oversee everything and to intervene in time to prevent unwanted behaviour.

In the Simulation-based Prediction and Analysis of Collective Emotional States (SPACES) project, that problem will be addressed by developing an intelligent system to help guardians predict and control the emergence of unwanted behaviour in crowds. This system makes use of a combination of two main techniques, namely sentiment analysis and agent-based simulation.

Regarding the former, sentiment analysis is a relatively recent method to extract meaning from text messages, and when applied to social media data this can provide an interesting new angle on monitoring the status of large crowds. Nowadays, many hi-tech solutions are already available to monitor crowds, e.g. using infrared cameras and sound detection. Unfortunately, these are both expensive, and (currently) have to be placed at a fixed location. In the current project, we propose the use of data available via social media, which constitutes a cost-effective and flexible solution. Social media are an interesting source of qualitative information and by analysing this information it should be possible to predict potential behaviour. Information posted on social media is available at low cost and analysing such data is a cost-effective means to get insight in what is exactly going on in a crowd, before, during and after large mass events.

Using this input based on sentiment analysis, SPACES will make a prediction of the development of a scenario in the near future. The main technique for making this prediction is agent-based simulation. Specifically, an agent-based simulation model will be developed that contains knowledge about the intra- and interpersonal dynamics of the (mental) states and actions of individuals in a crowd, such as emotion contagion, and (group) decision making. This model will be built upon an existing agent-based model for social contagion within crowds, called ASCRIBE [2, 5]. Based on this model, the system will be able to predict, for example, the emergence of aggressive outbursts, panicking behaviour, or congested areas in parts of a crowd.

Hence, the SPACES project envisions development and testing of a combination of innovative techniques, including dedicated methods to extract relevant information from the dataset in real-time; to match data patterns that are found to psychological states (e.g., fear, stress, anger); and to perform simulation and reasoning about these states to derive predictions about potential future developments. The intelligent system will use this output to provide support for police officers and (formal) guardians in both detecting, decreasing and avoiding (the number of) incidents in large-scale events. The current paper presents an overview of the project and explains our goals and methods to achieve these goals.

The remainder of this paper is structured as follows. Section 2 describes the sentiment analysis method used to extract emotional states from social media feed which provides the input of the social contagion model. Section 3 provides an overview of the ASCRIBE model for social contagion [2, 5]. Section 4 explains how both models are connected, and illustrates the functioning of the system by means of an example. Section 5 concludes the paper with a discussion.

2   Sentiment Analysis

2.1   Data Processing

As mentioned, the main source of information used within the project consists of messages posted on the Twitter platform [19]. This popular micro-blogging service provides a framework for people to publish and exchange short messages known as *tweets*. The tweets can be send using a wide array of mobile devices. The tweets have a maximum length of 140 characters, making them fast to publish and to the point, and given the functionalities of the Twitter platform, enable fast distribution of information. Furthermore, it provides services for capturing and analysing tweets in real-time using their API [17]. This makes Twitter an excellent source of input for the project. In a later stage we are interested in using other social media platforms as well (e.g., Facebook [20] or Instagram [18]).

The data processing framework used for the current study filters tweets from the Twitter environment using clusters of keywords related to topic domains that are identified as interesting for analysis. These topic clusters consists of one or more synonyms of the topic under analysis, such as names for an important sporting event, national holiday, or a city name. Also, it is possible to add feature clusters that represent different characteristics of the topic cluster, such as the name of a stadium related to a sporting event, or street names relate to a city name.

Given the set multidimensional clusters of topics and related characteristics, the framework stores and derives a number of variables related to the tweets and related to units of time. Some of the important variables that are stored, for each tweet, related to each cluster, are frequency of occurrence, geographical information, sentiment, and keyword related sentiment, and 32 distinct emotions, such as anger, disgust, aggressiveness and disapproval. For more information about the computation and accuracy of the sentiment and the distinct emotions, see [16]. Furthermore, other variables related to the tweets and its senders are stored.

Related to certain units of time, the framework further processes the tweet information. In the current project, the system needs to generate back information about dangerous situations on short notice; the data processing framework uses time units of one minute.

2.2   Data Gathering

Because the data collection process is in real-time, the framework needs to be configured for specific events on forehand. There are two possible approaches for collecting data, namely a top-down and a bottom-up approach.

In the top-down strategy, synonyms for certain high risk events are selected to be contained in topic clusters, such as (national holidays, sport events). Subsequently feature clusters can be selected containing keywords that represent the physical areas surrounding the events, such as city names, or street names, and related to these clusters, feature clusters representing negative situations, such as violence, intimidation, threat, and injury.

Using the bottom-up strategy, separate topic clusters to contain synonyms for negative situations are configured. Doing this, first negative situations in general are intentionally captured. Subsequently, high activity occurrences are detected, possibly containing identifiers for emergency situations. Although it is unknown if any irregularities will occur for our predefined set of events, using this approach we are still sure to end up with data containing negative situations.

After collecting sufficient amounts of temporal data containing high activity negative situations, we can explore which variables are possible predictors, and whether our agent model can accurately identify emergency situations using them. Here, the effect of the mathematical relations and corresponding weights on the performance of the predictions will be investigated. Also, the objectives of the model will be identified, i.e. the most important variables that it must predict. To further investigate the performance potential of the model, parameter tuning strategies will be used to optimize the agent model.

The output of the sentiment analysis model will be provided as input to the ASCRIBE model [2, 5]. This model will be explained in the next section.

3   The ASCRIBE Model for Social Contagion

The proposed model to predict the development of the crowd's mental states over time is an extension of the ASCRIBE model [2, 5]. The ASCRIBE model (which stands for Agent-based Social Contagion Regarding Intentions, Beliefs and Emotions) describes how mental states can spread over large crowds based on social contagion processes [2, 5]. The model is rooted in theories from the literature in neuroscience, including Damasio's Somatic Marker hypothesis [3] and the concept of mirror neurons [10].

The main ingredients of ASCRIBE are three types of mental states, namely *beliefs*, *intentions* and *emotions*. Beliefs refer to certain information about the world (e.g., an agent may have the belief that a fight is going on). Intentions may refer to planned actions (e.g., an agent may have the intention to join the fight or to escape). Emotions may refer to several types of emotional states (e.g., panic or aggression). All of these mental states are represented in terms of real-numbered variables in the domain $[0,1]$: for instance, an agent with an 'aggression state' of 0.1 is rather calm, whereas an agent with an 'aggression state' of 0.9 is highly aggressive. Next, all mental states of agents can be influenced by intra-agent processes (e.g., an agent's level of panic influences its beliefs) as well as inter-agent processes (e.g., agent A's panic level influences agent B's panic level). These influences are represented in terms of differential equations. Details are given in [2, 5], but the general idea is that the extent to which a mental state influences another mental state (of the same or another agent) depends on the current values of the mental states, as well as several additional parameters, such as the distance between the agent that transmits the mental state and the agent that receives it.

In [2], the ASCRIBE model was extended with mechanisms to determine individual agent movements, hence resulting in a crowd simulation model that goes beyond traditional approaches, in the sense that it contains sophisticated mechanisms to simulate the mental states of crowd members. Additionally, in [2] the model was applied to simulate a real world incident that took place in Amsterdam in 2010, and it was shown to outperform the influential model by Helbing and colleagues [4] due to its ability to address scenarios in which the mental processes of individual agents are a key determinant of the crowd's behaviour (for instance, a scenario where some people stop panicking as soon as they understand that the situation is not threatening anymore). Also in another study by different authors [11], ASCRIBE has been shown to perform equal and mostly superior to other models in the context of a protest scenario in Greece. Finally, ASCRIBE has been applied successfully to simulate various other cases in the emergency domain, including the London Bombings in 2005 [2].

The ASCRIBE model will form the basis of our simulation model. The input for the model will be provided by messages posted on Twitter [19], as mentioned in Sect. 2. In the next section the connection between both models will be explained.

4   Connection Between Models

In this section, the intended functionality of the combined model will be illustrated by means of a motivational example. Imagine a crowded pop concert, which takes place in a squared area[1] with a stage, a bar and some toilets (see Fig. 1a). For the purpose of the analysis, a grid structure is imposed onto the area, dividing it into a number of cells of equal size (e.g., 5×5 m); see Fig. 1b.

Once the pop concert starts, the sentiment analysis module described in Sect. 2 becomes active. By extracting sentiment out of the runtime Twitter data, and connecting this to the geographical information extracted from the same data, the module is able to create a two-dimensional map of particular states of the crowd. As an example, suppose we are interested in the distribution of the state of 'aggression' over the crowd during the pop concert. Then, the sentiment analysis module will focus on keywords related to aggressive behaviour (e.g., 'fight', 'beat', 'kick', etc.). Based on such information, the module assigns a 'level of aggressiveness' to each cell in the area. For instance, assume at a certain point in time a small riot emerges near the restrooms, and as a result bystanders start sending tweets about this, like "things are getting out of hand at the #toilets people getting mad! #pinkpop". By processing such tweets, the sentiment analysis module concludes that the cells in the vicinity of the restrooms have a relatively high level of aggressiveness (e.g., 0.8 on a scale from 0 to 1), whereas other cells relate to parts of the crowd with lower levels of aggressiveness.[2] As a result of this analysis, each cell can be assigned a

---

[1] For the sake of the example, it is assumed that the area consists of a single room with a squared shape. However, in principle the approach can be applied to any type of area (e.g., sports stadiums, streets, or even entire cities).

[2] In case no information about a particular cell is available, by default the average of the surrounding cells can be used.

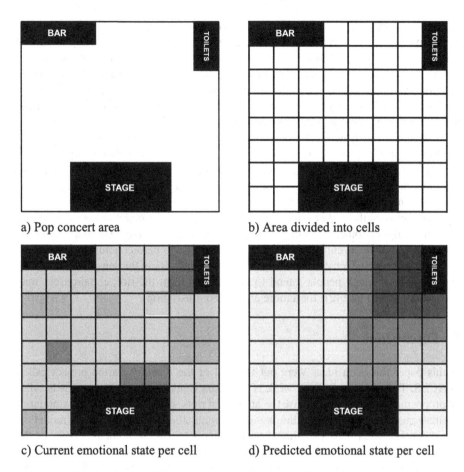

a) Pop concert area

b) Area divided into cells

c) Current emotional state per cell

d) Predicted emotional state per cell

Fig. 1. Illustration of the dynamics of the combined model for an area at a pop concert

numerical value that estimates its level of aggression (or any mental state, as will be explained below). This 'landscape of aggression' can be visualized as shown in Fig. 1c (where the darkness of the cells is proportional to the level of aggressiveness).

Next, the output of the sentiment analysis module is passed to the ASCRIBE model for social contagion, which makes a prediction of the dynamics of the mental state of the crowd in the near future. For instance, based on the situation depicted in Fig. 1c, ASCRIBE may predict that the initial riot that was detected next to the restrooms is likely to expand, thereby also increasing the state of aggressiveness of the adjacent cells (e.g., because the people in these cell are susceptible for aggression). On the other hand, the state of aggressiveness in other cells may decrease (e.g., because people are moving away from the riot). Hence, the social contagion model is able to calculate the dynamics of the mental states of the crowd over time, and as a result a similar picture can be created of the predicted situation in the near future (say, after 5 min), as shown in Fig. 1d. In this example, the riot has clearly expanded to a larger area in the neighbourhood of the restrooms and the stage.

To conclude, note that, although the current example focuses on the mental state of aggressiveness only, in reality a similar analysis can be made for a variety of mental states. In particular, ASCRIBE distinguishes between three categories of mental states, namely beliefs, intentions and emotions. Aggression can be considered one type of emotion, but when it comes to riots, other emotion types may play a role as well, in particular the emotion of fear (or panic). Additionally, several beliefs may influence the behaviour of the crowd as well. For instance, the belief 'that a riot is taking place near the restrooms' may trigger certain people to avoid that area, whereas it triggers others to approach it. Similarly, it may be valuable to have information about people's intentions (e.g., to party, to fight, to flee, etc.). Hence, with the help of ASCRIBE, ultimately a number of 'mental state maps' as shown in Fig. 1 can be produced. One step further, ASCRIBE not only predicts the dynamics of these states in isolation, but also takes the interplay between these states into account. For instance, the belief that a riot is taking place may trigger someone's emotion of fear, which in turn may lead to an increased intention to escape. Eventually, ASCRIBE is also able to predict actual actions of the people in question, which can be used to predict the dynamics of the density of the crowd. For example, if many people intend to move away from the riot, certain areas may become congested (see [2]) for a more elaborated illustration).

5   Discussion

In this paper the main ideas were put forward of the recently started project called SPACES. The main goal of our work is to make events involving large crowds safer, by proposing a method to decrease the number of riots while using a limited amount of (formal) guardians. To achieve this, we will integrate the existing ASCRIBE model for social contagion [2] with a sentiment analysis module. Based on the outcomes of the sentiment analysis we are able to perform agent based simulations regarding the spread of mental states, like beliefs, intentions and emotions. This gives us predictions of the development of the mental state of a crowd over time and space, and serves as an input to guide the behaviour of guardians. For instance, guardians can use this information to determine where they should go to de-escalate situations, or to decide which areas are in need for other types of support (e.g., providing directions on where to go in case of congestion [1] or alterations in light or music to calm people down [15]).

This is not the first project regarding this societal problem [8, 9, 12]. Li et al. [7] monitored emotions in a crowded area by using an app. The visitors had to rate their emotion at fixed time periods by using the EmoApp [7]. Their findings revealed that both movement and emotions were consistent with the activities at the festival indicating that the users answered truthfully. The main difference between this work and our project is the way of collecting information about the mental state of the crowd. While Li et al. [7] asked specifically for the level of emotion we are able to unobtrusively extract emotions (as well as other mental states) from social media. In Ahuja et al. [1] the authors present a different way of monitoring the crowd. They propose the use of drones when certain areas are overcrowded or congested. These drones are able to give suggestions to the visitors, to escape the crowd. The main goal of Ahuja et al. [1] is somewhat different from the goal in the SPACES project but it is an interesting approach of controlling the crowd. Both Li et al. [7] and Ahuja et al. [1] visualize the data at run time but they do not combine the data on emotions with a predictive model as we do with the ASCRIBE model [2]. The work by Van Dyke Parunak et al. [13] comes closest to the SPACES project. They make predictions of crowd behaviour using Twitter data as well, and also combine this information with a predictive model. The main difference is that we provide a more detailed analysis of the different mental states of the crowd, and their interactions.

The proposed project is still in an early stage. Although the conceptual framework has been developed, much of the actual implementation work remains to be done. As a first step we will refine the sentiment analysis and the ASCRIBE model, by extending them and tuning them to the needs of our project. Once that has been established the connection between both models will be implemented and the system will be tested using simple case studies. The last phase of the project consists of an evaluation of the system based on a real life event, and the development of support methods.

Acknowledgments. The authors are grateful to Tibor Bosse for fruitful discussions about the project.

References

1. Ahuja, G., Karlapalem, K.: Managing multi robotic agents to avoid congestion and stampedes. In: Elkind, B., Yolum, W., (eds.), Proceedings of the 14th International Conference on Autonomous Agents and Multiagent Systems (AAMAS 2015), ACM Press (2015)
2. Bosse, T., Hoogendoorn, M., Klein, M.C.A., Treur, J., van der Wal, C.N., van Wissen, A.: Modelling collective decision making in groups and crowds: integrating social contagion and interacting emotions, beliefs and intentions. Auton. Agent. Multi-Agent Syst. J. **27**, 52–84 (2012)
3. Damasio, A.R., Everitt, B.J., Bishop, D.: The somatic marker hypothesis and the possible functions of the prefrontal cortex. Philos. Trans. R. Soc. Lond. B: Biol. Sci. **351**(1346), 1413–1420 (1996)
4. Helbing, D., Farkas, I., Vicsek, T.: Simulating dynamical features of escape panic. Nature **407**(6803), 487–490 (2000)
5. Hoogendoorn, M., Treur, J., van der Wal, C.N., van Wissen, A.: Modelling the interplay of emotions, beliefs and intentions within collective decision making based on insights from social neuroscience. In: Wong, K.K.W, Mendis, B.S.U., Bouzerdoum, A. (eds.) ICONIP 2010, Part I. LNCS, vol. 6443, pp. 196–206. Springer, Heidelberg (2010)
6. Knutsson, J., Madensen, T.D.: Preventing Crowd Violence. Lynne Rienner Pub., Boulder (2011)
7. Li, J., Erkin, Z., de.Ridder, H., Vermeeren, A.: A field study on real-time self-reported emotions in crowds. In: proceedings of ICT OPEN, eindhoven, The Netherlands, pp. 80–84 (2013)
8. Mitleton-Kelly, E., Deschenaux, I., Maag, C., Fullerton, M., Celikkaya, N.: Enhancing crowd evacuation and traffic management through ami technologies: a review of the literature. In: Mitleton-Kelly, E. (ed.) Co-evolution of Intelligent Socio-Technical Systems, pp. 19–41. Springer, Heidelberg (2013)

9. Nagy, A. Stamberger, J.: Crowd sentiment detection during disasters and crises. In: Rothkrantz, L., Ristvej, J., Franco, Z., (eds.), Proceedings of the 9th International ISCRAM Conference – Vancouver, Canada, April 2012
10. Rizzolatti, G., Sinigaglia, C., Anderson, F.T.: Mirrors in the Brain How our Minds Share Actions and Emotions. Oxford University Press, Oxford (2008)
11. Tsai, J., Bowring, E., Marsella, S., Tambe, M.: Empirical evaluation of computational emotional contagion models. In: Vilhjálmsson, H.H., Kopp, S., Marsella, S., Thórisson, K.R. (eds.) IVA 2011. LNCS, vol. 6895, pp. 384–397. Springer, Heidelberg (2011)
12. Tsai, J., Fridman, N., Bowring, E., Brown, M., Epstein, S., Kaminka, G., Marsella, S., Ogden, A., Rika, I., Sheel, A., Taylor, M.E., Wang, X., Zilka, A., Tambe, M.: ESCAPES—evacuation simulation with children, authorities, parents, emotions, and social comparison. In: Tumer, K., Yolum, P., Sonenberg, L., Stone, P., (eds.), Proceedings of the 10th International Conference on Autonomous Agents and Multiagent Systems (AAMAS 2011). Valencia: Innovative Applications Track. (2011)
13. Parunak, H.V.D., Brooks, S.H., Brueckner, S., Gupta, R.: Dynamically tracking the real world in an agent-based model. In: Alam, S.J., Parunak, H.V.D. (eds.) MABS 2013. LNAI, vol. 8235, pp. 3–16. Springer Verlag, Heidelberg (2014)
14. http://nl.wikipedia.org/wiki/Strandrellen_in_Hoek_van_Holland
15. http://www.de-escalate.nl
16. http://www.sentimentics.com
17. https://dev.twitter.com
18. https://instagram.com
19. https://twitter.com
20. https://www.facebook.com

Analysing Yammer Usage Pattern in the Context of Social Collaborative Activity Performance by Knowledge Workers

Jordan Hall[(⊠)] and Bee Bee Chua

University of Technology, Sydney, Australia
Jordan.Hall@live.com.au, choiceno1@mailcity.com

Abstract. This study investigates the impact and trend of the Yammer utilisation pattern by multi-generational knowledge workers employed in the risk service department of a multi-national enterprise. In contrast to the existing literature, our results highlight the experiences between the different levels of management in their adoption of a new technology. In our study, senior management used Yammer for post creation more frequently than did the junior management. Furthermore, the more senior the employee was, the higher the chance he or she would access Yammer. Senior management was less concerned about Yammer's usability and functionality compared to junior management. The Yammer usage rate may increase if the tool is well integrated with other in-house compatible tools. Finally, workers may benefit from high-quality coaching about Yammer's benefits and values.

1 Literature Review on Enterprise Social Networks

An Enterprise Social Network (ESN) called the Hub has reported benefits of reduced time taken to collaborate and communicate and improved access to expertise when Yammer was used [1–6]. In a study evaluating an ESN tool, the researchers concluded that Yammer generated an extremely high risk-adjusted return on investment of 365 % [7, 8]; however, as the study was commissioned by Yammer, it may have been biased. No data were collected showing Yammer use and suitability by knowledge workers.

Our paper is structured as follows: Sect. 1 provides an overview of the case study and background, while Sect. 2 describes the research methodologies that were employed. Section 3 presents the results of the data collection, which was accomplished by means of survey and interviews. Last but not least, Sect. 4 discusses the results and draws a conclusion.

2 The Case Study Background and Objectives

The study investigates the Yammer utilisation pattern is of a leading Australian based consulting firm. The company reported a profit of more than a billion dollars in 2013. The business activities include providing audit, tax, consulting, and financial advisory services to clients across numerous industry sectors. The firm prides itself as a leader in

© Springer International Publishing Switzerland 2015
G. Meiselwitz (Ed.): SCSM 2015, LNCS 9182, pp. 127–137, 2015.
DOI: 10.1007/978-3-319-20367-6_14

the use of social media. In 2011 the firm won a Forrester Groundswell industry award for its business transformation with Yammer [8], which is an enterprise social network (ESN) that allows people to share knowledge, information and ideas with their co-workers. It was one of the first large companies to use Yammer; first as a trial by the innovation team, latter in specific projects, and is now available across the whole organisation [9, 10].

There is evidence to support the use of ESNs in business [1–5]. However, in order to maximise the efficiencies and benefits of Yammer, there needs to be maximum utilisation by employees. The study aims to identify trends in the employee utilisation of Yammer that are currently unknown. Our investigation includes three objectives:

1. To identify the utilisation rate of Yammer within the Risk Services department of the auditing firm.
2. To categorise employees by their utilisation of Yammer and determine any trends in the usage rates of Yammer.
3. To determine ways in which the usage rates of Yammer could be increased within the organisation.

3   Research Methodologies

In order to meet these objectives the study used a mixed research methodology [10–12]. Firstly, a survey (see Sect. 3.1) was conducted that included the collection of both qualitative and quantitative data. This data was then analysed and used to give the thematic direction to several follow-up semi-structured interviews (see Sect. 3.2) that collected qualitative data to enable a more thorough investigation of Yammer utilisation (see Table 1).

Table 1. Outlines how the objectives of the study were achieved using the data collected by the survey and interviews

Objective	Question type
To identify the utilisation rate of Yammer	Closed quantitative usage questions in survey
To determine any trends in the utilisation rates of Yammer	Analysis of closed demographic questions, closed quantitative usage questions and open qualitative usage questions in survey
	Analysis of qualitative interview responses
To determine ways in which utilisation rates of Yammer could be increased	Analysis of open qualitative questions in survey
	Analysis of qualitative interview responses

The analysis of the data generated by both the survey and interviews enabled the objectives to be met and conclusions formed in regard to the utilisation rates of Yammer. Relevant future research and recommendations for the firm in regard to Yammer use is also discussed. This knowledge will be beneficial to the consulting firm as it may then be possible to recommend ways in which Yammer's utilisation could be increased in order to realise its full business potential. The knowledge gained from this study could also be applied in a global context as the consulting firm operated more than 150 countries and has implemented Yammer across its entire organisation. In addition, ESNs are becoming increasingly common right across the global business environment.

3.1 Survey Structure

The survey was formulated with questions that accurately met each objective of the study. Three employees piloted the survey. The pilot survey found that a few of the questions were ambiguous and thus needed to be re-worded to clear any confusion. The department partner approved the final version of the survey and it was distributed via email with an introductory explanation to the entire Risk Services Department (approx. 200 employees).

Questions 1 to 3 in the survey were demographic questions to categorise employees. They determined the gender of the respondent, the seniority level of the respondent and the duration in which the respondent had been at the organisation. Demographics are extremely useful in identifying trends; for instance, the determination of a correlation between seniority level and Yammer usage. Question 4 asked whether the respondent was an employee at Deloitte when Yammer was first introduced. This aimed at identifying if this was a significant determination factor for Yammer usage.

In question 5 respondents evaluated a series of statements and placed them on a scale of usage. The statements included; 'I use Yammer', 'I go to the Yammer site', 'I make posts on Yammer' and 'I comment on Yammer posts'. The scale was expressed as; 'Never', 'Rarely', 'Sometimes', 'Often' or 'Very Frequently'. In analysis 'Never' was coded quantitatively as this section formed the foundation for the respondents Yammer usage. Question 6 was concerned with the functionality of Yammer and thus asked respondents their reasons for using Yammer. Options included a list of pre-set answers which were formulated from the functions identified in the studies by Riemer et al. [13] and Reimer and Tavakoli [14]. In addition the respondents had the opportunity to add additional uses in the 'other' section.

Question 7 was a follow-up to question 5 for respondents who had indicated that they do not use Yammer. This question aimed to identify the reason why some employees do not use Yammer and hence determine ways to improve usage. Respondents were given answer options based on the pilot questions feedback and similar to question 6, had the opportunity to personalise their response.

The survey was constructed to measure the usage component qualitatively, however, in analysis this measure is coded into a quantified scale where 0 represents 'never' used and 4 represents 'Very Frequently' used. This quantified measure is allows trends and correlations to be observed.

In order to encourage a greater number of participants the length of the survey was deliberately constructed in a way so that it would not take long to be completed but at the same time collect the required data. A limitation of this approach, however, is the lack of detail in the open question responses. In order to compensate for this limitation and enhance the information that was generated from the surveys, interviews were conducted with some of the respondents as a follow-up to the survey. Five employees were interviewed that represented each of the employee levels. Section 4 provides an overview of respondents' feedback results of each question.

3.2 Interviews

The interviews were conducted in an informal setting with only the participant's position recorded to facilitate anonymity. The sessions were conducted in a short time frame so as to not be a hindrance for work productivity. In each interview the interviewee was asked:

- "What could be done to increase the usage of Yammer in this organisation?"
- "Is Yammer beneficial to the organisation?"
- "Are you encouraged by management to use Yammer?"

The interviews were semi-structured and were organized around the three pre-determined open questions, with other questions emerging from the dialogue. The face-to-face interview facilitated the opportunity to collect accurate, relevant and in-depth data. A total of five employees were interviewed that represented each of the employee levels within the Risk Services department of the firm.

The resulting data was organised into a readable format for analysis. Data analysis was conducted using simple descriptive statistics and by correlations to identify trends. Simple descriptive statistics include converting the data received into percentages. Percentages are useful to be able to categorise data [15]. From percentages graphical analysis was also created. Measures of central tendency assisted in identifying trends [15]. Details of interview is discussed in Sect. 4.

4 Survey and Interview Results

4.1 Part 1 – Survey Results

The survey was completed by 68 employees from the Risk Services Department in the firm. This represents a sample size of approximately 25 % of the unit. Of the 68 persons who responded, 28 respondents were female (41 %) and 40 were male (59 %). The survey had respondents from each employee level, with the graduate/analyst level having the highest number of participants (23 persons 34 %). Figure 1 below shows survey responses for employee type and demographic.

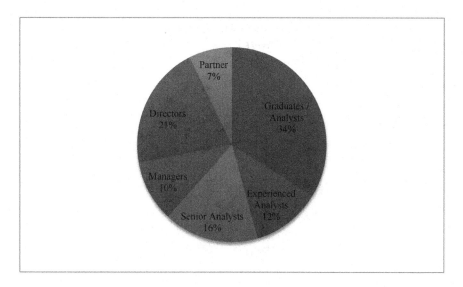

Fig. 1. Employee type and demographic

53 % of respondents indicated that they either rarely or never used Yammer. This equated to a codified average usage rate of 1.5 out of 4, with rarely being the most popular option selected. Usage decreased when respondents were asked if they make posts on Yammer. The average rating for making posts was 0.91 out of 4, with 75 % of respondents answering never or rarely. 53 respondents answered that they never or rarely comment on yammer posts (78 %), this is the lowest utilisation with a codified average rating of 0.90 out of 4 (see Figs. 2 and 3).

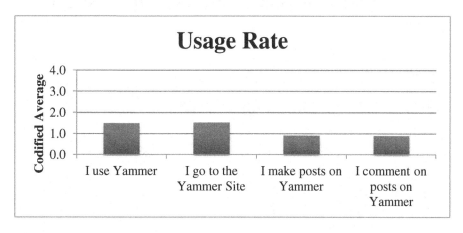

Fig. 2. Usage rate on each Yammer type used

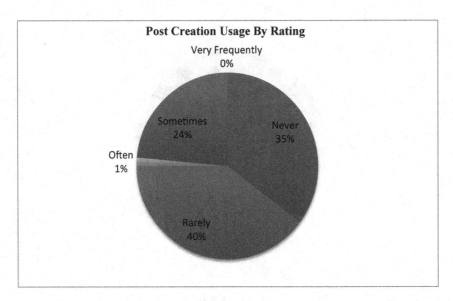

Fig. 3. Post creation usage by rating

The Yammer usage rate for post creation was recorded for each employee type. The majority of Graduates/Analysts of them indicated that they rarely or never make posts (85 %). In comparison, 40 % of Partners answered rarely or never. In general, the more senior the employee was, the higher the chance he or she would access Yammer (see Fig. 4).

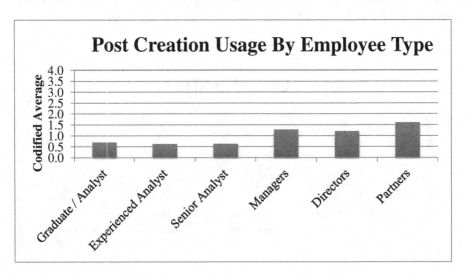

Fig. 4. Post creation usage by employee type

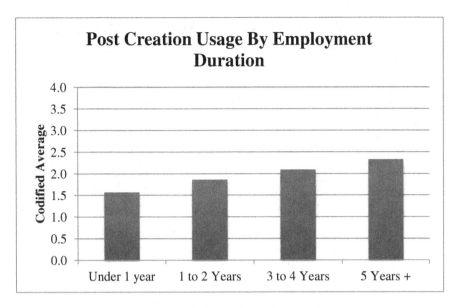

Fig. 5. Post creation usage by employment duration

Yammer utilisation rate for post creation was also compared with duration of employment (see Fig. 5). Employees who had been working for under a year at the firm had an average usage of 1.57/4.00 for post creation. Employees working for 1 to 2 years had an average rating of 1.86/4.00 for post creation with 38 % answering never (see Fig. 3). Employees working for 3 to 4 years at the organisation had an average usage rating of 2.09/4.00 for post creation, with 18 % answering never. Employees who had been working for 5 years or above had the highest rating with an average utilisation rate of 2.33/4.00 for post creation, with 13 % of those respondents answering never.

A comparison between the creation of posts for graduates/analysts, experienced analysts and senior analysts have a combined utilisation rate of 0.67 out of 4. Managers, directors and partners, have a combined average utilisation of 1.31 out of 4. This is shown in Fig. 6 below. This 95 % increase in usage could be due to a number of factors, such as the different responsibilities of the positions or their familiarity of Yammer.

60 of the 68 respondents answered question 6, which asked what Yammer was used for. 60 % of those indicated that Yammer was used for information sharing, 48 % selected the problem solving/seeking advice option. 40 % selected the community Building/social Engagement option. 27 % selected idea generation/crowd sourcing, while 10 % selected task co-ordination and another 18 % selected the 'Other' option (see Fig. 7).

Other uses that were specified included, 'to tick the box', 'the partners tell us to', 'when we are told by the partners to use it', 'to nominate people for awards'. Two answers also suggested that they do not use Yammer in this other category.

44 respondents answered question 7 which asked why individuals don't use Yammer. 30 respondents answered "Not enough time" this represented 68.18 % of respondents or 44.12 % of the entire sample. A further 15 people answered that they "Don't see the benefit" which is 34.09 % of the people that answered the question or

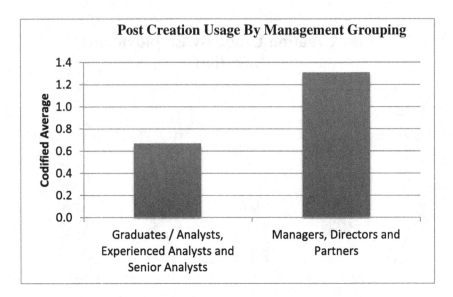

Fig. 6. Post creation usage by management grouping

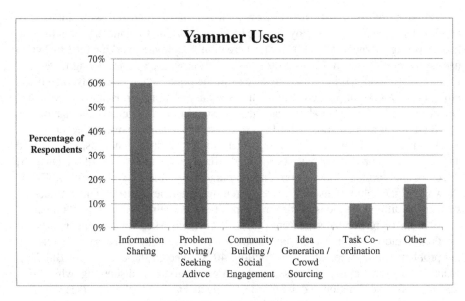

Fig. 7. How Yammer is used

22.06 % of the whole sample. No respondents answered that they did not know how to use Yammer. For the 14 people that selected 'Other', common themes were grouped. 4 respondents indicated that it was not easy to find information. 6 surveys also suggested that Yammer is not well integrated into the organisation or there are easier ways to connect. The 6 answers indicating integration as an issue is 14 % of the people that answered the question or 9 % of the full 68 sample size. Refer to the results in Table 2.

Table 2. Reasons for not using Yammer.

Reasons for not using Yammer	Number of people	Percentage
Not enough time	30	68 %
Don't see the benefit	15	34 %
Other (please specify)	14	32 %
I don't know how	0	0 %

4.2   Part 2 – Interview Results

Increasing Yammer Usage. 3 of the 5 people interviewed suggested that usage could be increased by integrating it more with other in-house communication tools. Some suggestions included a single sign on, integration with Lync and other communication tools. 3 out of the 5 interviewees also suggested that a way to improve usage would be more experience and training, such as a short course. One respondent suggested that enticements to get people actively engaged such as competitions. Refer to the Fig. 8.

The Benefits of Using Yammer. 3 out of 5 respondents indicated that there are benefits in using Yammer, while the remaining 2 indicated to the contrary. Of the two users who did not see the benefit, one stated that they preferred other communication tools, the other stated they did not use it use because they did not have enough time.

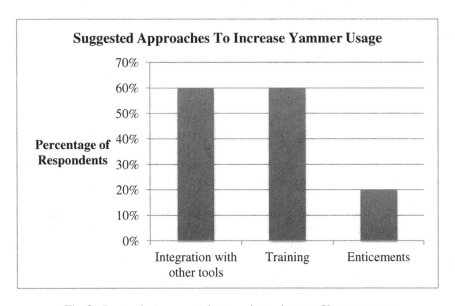

Fig. 8. Respondents suggested approaches to increase Yammer usage

Encouragement by Management to Use Yammer. All interviewees indicated that they had been encouraged by more senior employee to use Yammer. Of those, 4 of the respondents suggested that this was due to the importance of the firm being perceived as an innovative company that has a competitive edge in technology use.

5   Conclusions and Future Work

Our findings are limited by factors such as sample size and survey techniques utilised. While a significant number of people participated, all participants were from one division within the company. Analysis however, shows that approximately 25 % of the department and a wide range of respondents, including, employees from all different role levels, different genders and different times employed at the organisation completed the survey. The relatively large percentage of respondents with a variety of demographics assists to counter the limitation. An assumption of this study is that ESNs, such as Yammer, are beneficial to the workforce. The articles and documentation that are analysed as part of this study do substantiate this assumption, however more investigation should be conducted. It is also assumed that the responses provided by participants were accurate representations of usage.

Based on the above-mentioned results, we propose several recommendations. The first recommendation is that Yammer must be able to be incorporated into existing tools. This could be achieved, for instance, by implementing a single sign-on feature so that users don't have to log on individually. The second recommendation aimed at improving the usage rate of Yammer is to integrate Yammer's functionality with Lync, which is an instant messaging service. Yammer and Lync are both owned by Microsoft (Yammer 2014), so it is possible that the functions of the two ESNs will be integrated and/or combined to make them more user friendly and thus encourage increased usage of both applications. The third recommendation concerns any organisation that is planning or has already implemented an ESN: Providing an orientation course to junior and senior management not only instructs them on how to use the application but also communicates information about its many benefits. This will assist in ensuring a more productive business environment.

Our findings may also be useful for many other service-driven industries that rely on a client base to generate revenue. These industries include but are not limited to consulting, finance, hospitality, health care and entertainment. Many of these industries strive to be leaders of technological innovation, which may give them a competitive edge and therefore increase the probability of maximum utilisation by employees. Moreover, these industries may have multi-generational tiers that could face similar challenges in using Yammer.

Finally, this study is valuable for all businesses because it is a good example of how business professionals need to continually assess the functioning of their technology applications. Technology is constantly evolving, and improvements are very often possible. The integration of Yammer with other applications such as Lync, as indicated by this investigation, would be one such improvement.

References

1. Hughes, C., Chapel, A.: Connect, communicate, collaborate and create: implementing an enterprise-wide social collaboration platform at KPMG - part two: realizing value. Bus. Inf. Rev. **30**(4), 191–195 (2013)
2. Leftheriotis, I., Giannakos, M.N.: Using social media for work: losing your time or improving your work. Comput. Hum. Behav. **31**(1), 134–142 (2014)
3. Razmerita, L., Kirchner, K., Nabeth, T.: Social media in organizations: leveraging personal and collective knowledge processes. J. Organ. Comput. Electron. Commer. **24**(1), 74–93 (2014)
4. Qian, L., Nagel, N., Sun, L.: Migrating to agility 2.0: how social computing creates strategic value. Organ. Dyn. **40**(2), 119–126 (2011)
5. Chui, M., Manyika, J., Bughin, J., Dobbs, R., Roxburgh, C., Sarrazin, H., Sands, G., Westergren, M.: The Social Economy: Unlocking Value and Productivity Through Social Technologies. McKinsey Global Institute, Washington (2012)
6. Howarth, B.: social tools tearing down the silos, The Australian, 20 November, viewed 12 April 2014. http://www.theaustralian.com.au/technology/special-reports/social-tools-tearing-down-the-silos/story-fn8lu7wm-1226519807619#
7. Forrester Consulting: The Total Economic Impact of Yammer, Forrester Research, Cambridge (2011)
8. Forrester Research, Deloitte Australia Yammer Network, viewed 3 April 2014. http://groundswelldiscussion.com/groundswell/awards/detail.php?id=636
9. Yammer 2014, What is Yammer, viewed 25 May 2014. https://about.yammer.com
10. Cameron, R., Molina-Azorin, J.: The acceptance of mixed methods in business and management research. Int. J. Organ. Anal. **19**(3), 256–271 (2011)
11. Creswell, J.: Educational Research: Planning, Conducting and Evaluating Quantitative and Qualitative Research, 3rd edn. Pearson Education, Boston (2008)
12. Creswell, J., Plano Clark, V.: Designing and Conducting Mixed Methods Research, 2nd edn. Thousand Oaks, California (2011)
13. Riemer, K., Tavakoli, A.: The role of groups as local context in large Enterprise Social Networks: A Case Study of Yammer at Deloitte Australia. Business Information Systems Working Paper Series, University of Sydney (2013)
14. Riemer, K., Scifleet, P., Reddig, R.: Powercrowd: Enterprise Social Networking in Professional Service Work: A Case Study of Yammer at Deloitte Australia. Business Information Systems Working Paper Series, University of Sydney (2012)
15. Polgar, S., Thomas, S.: Introduction to Research in the Health Sciences, 5th edn. Churchchill Livingstone Elsevier, London (2008)

Ensemble Selection for Community Detection in Complex Networks

Rushed Kanawati[(✉)]

LIPN, CNRS UMR 7030, University Paris 13, Sorbonne Paris Cité,
Villetaneuse, France
rushed.kanawati@lipn.univ-paris13.fr
http://www-lipn.univ-paris13.fr/kanawati

Abstract. Ensemble clustering approaches have been recently applied, in a variety of ways, in order to enhance the quality and/or the execution time of community detection tasks. The quality gain that can be obtained from applying ensemble approaches is known to be tightly linked to both quality and diversity of the applied clusterings. However, most of existing work simply ignore this important issue of ensemble selection. In this paper we intend to fill this gap. We propose a graph-based ensemble selection approach that allow to take into account both criteria of quality and diversity. Different quality measures are also considered: cluster-oriented quality and network-oriented quality functions. Experiments on real network datasets show the validity of our approach.

Keywords: Community detection · Complex networks · Ensemble clustering · Ensemble selection

1 Introduction

Complex networks are frequently used for modeling interactions in real-world systems in diverse areas, such as sociology, biology, information spreading and exchanging and many other different areas. One key topological feature of real-world complex networks is that nodes are arranged in tightly knit groups that are loosely connected one to each other. Such groups are called *communities*. Nodes composing a community are generally admitted to share common proprieties and/or be involved in a same function and/or having a same role. Hence, unfolding the community structure of a network could give us much insights about the overall structure a complex network. Comprehensive review of the state of the art can be found in [6,24]. Different algorithms have different execution times and yield results of various quality.

The large-size of today available networks makes most of existing algorithms hard to apply. In addition, most of existing low time complexity algorithms show generally low robustness. Different executions of the same algorithm on the same network may leads to detecting highly different partitions of the network. This is for instance the case of the *Louvain* approach [2] which is sensitive to the order

© Springer International Publishing Switzerland 2015
G. Meiselwitz (Ed.): SCSM 2015, LNCS 9182, pp. 138–147, 2015.
DOI: 10.1007/978-3-319-20367-6_15

in which nodes of the network are parsed. Another very known exemple is the high speed label propagation algorithm the exhibits, in its original version [18], a very high instability.

Ensemble clustering approaches have been proposed as a mean for both graph coarsening and graph clustering enhancing. Graph coarsening refers to the process of reducing the scale of a graph by replacing a group of cohesive nodes in the graph by a single node [22]. High quality community detection algorithms, with higher computational complexity, can then be applied on the reduced graph. Results are then expanded to the initial graph. Ensemble clustering can directly be applied in order to merge different clustering obtained by applying different algorithms or by applying an unstable algorithm several times [21]. However, the quality gain that can be obtained from applying ensemble approaches is known to be tightly linked to both quality and diversity of the applied clusterings [1,4]. Most of existing work simply ignore this important issue of ensemble selection. In this paper we intend to fill this gap.

The remainder of this paper is organized as follows. Next in Sect. 2, we first define the problem of ensemble clustering, discuss main approaches for consensus clustering computation and show applications in the field of community detection in complex networks. In Sect. 3 we define the problem of ensemble selection and quickly review main ensemble selection approaches. The proposed graph-based ensemble selection algorithm is presented in Sect. 3.2. Experiments and results are reported and commented in Sect. 4. Finally we conclude in Sect. 5.

2   Applying Ensemble Clustering to Community Detection

2.1   Ensemble Clustering Approaches

Let $G = <V,E>$ be a undirected simple graph where V is the set of nodes and E is the set of edges. Let π_i be a partition of the set V. We have by definition $\pi_i = \{\pi_i^1, \ldots, \pi_i^l\}$ where $\pi_i^j \subseteq V$, and $\bigcup_j \pi_i^j = V$ and $\forall j, k \in [1, l] \pi_i^j \cap \pi_i^k = \emptyset$.

We consider a set of a different partitions $\mathcal{P} = \{\pi_1, \ldots, \pi_n\}$ defined over the same set V. The goal of an ensemble clustering function is to compute a consensus clustering π_* that minimize the number of disagreements with each base partition π_i. In a formal way we have:

$$\pi_* = \underset{\pi_i \in \mathcal{P}}{\arg\min} \, dist(\pi_*, \pi_i) \tag{1}$$

Where $dist()$ is a distance function measuring disagreement between two partitions. Some exemples of such distance functions are given in Sect. 3.

Different consensus clustering functions have been proposed in the literature. Existing functions can be roughly classified into two classes: *evidence accumulation based functions* [7] and *graph-based functions* [23]. The first family of approaches is based on computing a clustering-based similarity between nodes of the graph. One widely applied method is based on constructing a **consensus graph** out of the set of partitions to be combined [5,23]. The consensus graph G_{cons} is defined over the same set of nodes of the initial graph G. Two nodes $v_i, v_j \in V$ are linked in G_{cons} if there is at least one partition $P^y_{Q_x}$ where both nodes are in a same cluster. Each link (v_i, v_j) is weighted by the frequency of instances that nodes v_i, v_j are placed in the same cluster. Notice that the obtained graph is not necessarily a connected one. Different approaches can be applied in order to compute the aggregated clustering out from the consensus graph:

- In [23], authors transform the graph into a complete one by adding missing links with a null weight, then nodes are finally partitioned into clusters using agglomerative hierarchical clustering with some linkage rule, or by using a classical graph partitioning method such as the Kernighan-Lin algorithm [16].
- In [3] a similar approach is applied but with enforcing that nodes in the same result clusters should be connected in the initial graph by a sufficiently short path.
- In [20] authors propose a simple but effective method that consists on pruning links in the obtained consensus graph whose weights (frequency) is under a given threshold $\alpha \in [0, 1]$. The set of obtained connected components is taken to be the aggregated partition. The main problem of this approach is the problem of defining the value of the threshold α to use.

2.2   Ensemble Clustering-Based Community Detection

Ensemble clustering approaches have been used for various goals in the field of community detection in complex networks. One first direct application is to allow merging different partitions of the same graph obtained by applying a fast but low quality community detection algorithm, such as the label propagation algorithm [20]. Another application, to reduce the size of large-scale graphs. Let $G = < V, E >$ be a large)scale graphe. The idea is compute a set of n different low quality partitions of a graphe : $\Pi = \{\pi_1, \ldots, \pi_n\}$. A strict consigns graph is defined over the set of nodes V such that, $v \in V$ are linked if and only if they are grouped together in a same cluster in all partitions $\pi_i \in \Pi$. The obtained graph is usually composed of a large number of small connected components. Nodes composing each connected component are reduced to form only one node reducing hence the scale of the whole graph. The reduction phase can allow applying high quality community detection algorithms to the reduced graphe [22]. In [12] ensemble selection approaches are proposed in order to relaxe the constraint on connecting nodes if the frequency of being clustered together in all n partitions is higher than a given threshold $0 < \delta < 1$.

In [11], ensemble clustering approaches have been applied in order to implement multi-objective local community identification. In [10] an ensemble clustering approach is applied in order to compute a graph partition out of a set of bi-partitions of the graph computed after identifying local-communities of a set of seed nodes carefully selected to represent different points of view on the target graph.

Few work has addressed the problem of ensemble selection before applying the ensemble clustering process. In next section we introduce the problem of ensemble selection and we show how this can enhance the output of the ensemble clustering process.

3   Ensemble Selection

3.1   Problem Definition

Different works have showed that the quality of the output of an ensemble clustering is tightly related to both the *quality* of each partition in the base partitions set and *diversity* of these partitions.

Let Π be a set of n base clusterings. An ensemble selection function $\mathcal{ES}$ aims at selecting a subset of $\tilde{\Pi} \subseteq \Pi$ such that all partitions $\pi_i \in \tilde{\Pi}$ are of high quality and diverse. The diversity of partitions can be measured applying clustering comparison metrics such as the Adjusted Rand Index (ARI) [9], or information-based metrics such as the NMI [15].

The ARI index is based on counting the number of pairs of elements that are clustered in the same clusters in both compared partitions. Let $P_i = \{P_i^1, \dots, P_i^l\}$, $P_j = \{P_j^1, \dots, P_j^k\}$ be two partitions of a set of nodes V. The set of all (unordered) pairs of nodes of V can be partitioned into the following four disjoint sets:

- $S_{11} = \{$pairs that are in the same cluster under P_i and $P_j\}$
- $S_{00} = \{$pairs that are in different clusters under P_i and $P_j\}$
- $S_{10} = \{$pairs that are in the same cluster under P_i but in different ones under $P_j\}$
- $S_{01} = \{$pairs that are in different clusters under P_i but in the same under $P_j\}$

Let $n_{ab} = |S_{ab}|, a, b \in \{0, 1\}$, be the respective sizes of the above defined sets. The rand index, initially defined in [19] is simply given by :

$$\mathcal{R}(P_i, P_j) = \frac{2 \times (n_{11} + n_{00})}{n \times (n - 1)}$$

In [9], authors show that the expected value of the Rand Index of two random partitions does not take a constant value (e.g. zero). They proposed an adjusted version which assumes a generalized hypergeometric distribution as null hypothesis: the two clusterings are drawn randomly with a fixed number of clusters and a fixed number of eleme nts in each cluster (the number of clusters in the two clusterings need not be the same). Then the adjusted Rand Index is the normalized difference of the Rand Index and its expected value under the null hypothesis. It is defined as follows:

$$ARI(P_i, P_j) = \frac{\sum_{x=1}^{l} \sum_{y=1}^{k} \binom{P_i^x \cap P_j^y}{2} - t_3}{\frac{1}{2}(t_1 + t_2) - t_3} \qquad (2)$$

where:

$$t_1 = \sum_{x=1}^{l} \binom{P_i^x}{2} , t_2 = \sum_{y=1}^{k} \binom{P_j^y}{2} , t_3 = \frac{2t_1 t_2}{n(n-1)}$$

This index has expected value zero for independent clusterings and maximum value 1 for identical clusterings.

Another family of partitions comparisons functions is the one based on the notion of mutual information. A partition P is assimilated to a random variable. We seek to quantify how much we reduce the uncertainty of the clustering of randomly picked element from V in a partition P_j if we know P_i. The Shanon's entropy of a partition P_i is given by:

$$H(P_i) = -\sum_{x=1}^{l} \frac{|P_i^x|}{n} log_2(\frac{|P_i^x|}{n})$$

Notice that $\frac{|P_i^x|}{n}$ is the probability that a randomly picked element from V be clustered in P_i^x. The mutual information between two random variables X,Y is given by the general formula:

$$MI(X,Y) = H(X) + H(Y) - H(X,Y) \tag{3}$$

This can then be applied to measure the mutual information between two partitions P_i, P_j. The mutual information defines a metric on the space of all clusterings and is bounded by the entropies of involved partitions. In [23], authors propose a normalized version given by:

$$NMI(X,Y) = \frac{MI(X,Y)}{\sqrt{H(X)H(Y)}} \tag{4}$$

The evaluation of the quality of a clustering is much harder, than the diversity, in unsupervised settings. In [1] authors propose to evaluate the quality of a partition $\pi_i \in \Pi$ by computing its distance (using ARI or NMI) from the consensus partition computed over the whole set Π. In [5], the quality of a partition $\pi_i \in \Pi$ us computed as follows: $Q(\pi) = \sum_{\pi \in \Pi} NMI(\pi, \pi_i)$.

In graph settings, external partition quality functions can be used to measure the equity of a partition. The well known *modularity* function is one option [8].

3.2   Proposed Approach

We propose here an original graph-based approach to cope with the problem of cluster ensemble selection. Algorithm 1 sketchs the general outlines of the proposed approach.

The algorithm is structured into four main steps. Having as an input a set of r base clusterings, we first compute an $r \times r$ pair-wise clustering similarity matrix M. An entry $M[i,j] = sim(r_i, r_j)$ gives the similarity between two base clusterings r_i and r_j. Different similarity functions can be used such as the

Algorithm 1. Graph-based cluster ensemble selection algorithm

---

Require: $G < V, E >$ a connected graph
Require: $\Pi = \{\pi_1, \ldots, \pi_r\}$ a base clusterings
Require: Q A partition quality function
 1: $\Pi^* \leftarrow \emptyset$
 2: $M \leftarrow$ **compute_pairwise_similarity_Matrix**(Π)
 3: $\mathrm{GV} \leftarrow$ **construct_graph(M)**
 4: $\mathcal{C} = \{c_1, \ldots, c_k\} \leftarrow$ **community_detection(GV)**
 5: **for all** $c \in \mathcal{C}$ **do**
 6:    $\hat{\pi} \leftarrow \arg\max_{\pi \in c} Q(\pi)$
 7:    $\Pi^* \leftarrow \Pi^* \cup \{\hat{\pi}\}$
 8: **end for**
 9: **return** Π^*

---

normalized mutual information (NMI), Adaptive Rand index (ARI) index or information variation (IV) [15,17]. The obtained matrix is then used to define a similarity graph GV over the set of base clusterings. Different kinds of similarity graphs can be defined. These include:

- ϵ-**Neighborhood Graph:** Here we connect all points whose pairwise distances are smaller than ϵ. As the distances between all connected points are roughly of the same scale ("at most"), weighting the edges would not incorporate more information about the data to the graph. Hence, the ϵ-neighborhood graph is usually considered as an unweighted graph.
- k-**Nearest Neighbor Graph:** Here the goal is to connect vertex v_i with vertex v_j if v_j is among the k-nearest neighbors of v_i. However, this definition leads to a directed graph, as the neighborhood relationship is not symmetric. There are two ways of making this graph undirected. The first way is to simply ignore the directions of the edges, that is we connect v_i and v_j with an undirected edge if v_i is among the k-nearest neighbors of v_j or if v_j is among the k-nearest neighbors of vi. The resulting graph is what is usually called the k-nearest neighbor graph. The second choice is to connect vertices v_i and v_j if both v_i is among the k-nearest neighbors of v_j and v_j is among the k-nearest neighbors of v_i. The resulting graph is called the mutual k-nearest neighbor graph. In both cases, after connecting the appropriate vertices we weight the edges by the similarity of their endpoints.
- **Relative Neighborhood Graph:** Relative neighborhood graph (RNG) has been initially proposed in [25]. The choice of RNG graph is motivated by the topological characteristics of these graphs that are connexe and sparse. To build an RNG graph, we first compute a similarity matrix between couple of items in the dataset. This results in a symmetric square matrix of size $n \times n$ where n is the number of items in the dataset. A RNG graph is defined by the following simple construction rule: two points x_i and x_j are connected by an edge if they satisfy the following property:

$$d(x_i, x_j) \leq \max_l \{d(x_i, x_l), d(x_j, x_l)\}, \forall l \neq i, j \tag{5}$$

where $d(x_i, x_j)$ is the distance function. A community detection algorithm is applied on the obtained graph in order to cluster the given examples. Clustering evaluation criteria can then be used to compare different algorithms.

In this work, we have selected to build a relative neighborhood graph since it is the only approach that guarantee having a connected and sparse graph.

4   Experiments

In this section we evaluate the utility of the proposed ensemble selection approach for enhancing community detection in real world complex networks. The evaluation process is the following: given a network for which we know a ground truth partition into communities we apply first the label propagation approach 100 times. We then compute a consensus partition applying a CSPA ensemble clustering approach on the whole set of obtained partitions and on the set of partitions selected by applying our approach. The quality of obtained communities is evaluated using the ARI and NMI metrics with respect to the ground truth partition.

A set of three widely used benchmark networks for which a ground-truth decomposition into communities are known are used. These are the following:

- **Zachary's Karate Club:** This network is a social network of friendships between 34 members of a karate club at a US university in 1970 [26]. Following a dispute the network was divided into 2 groups between the club's administrator and the club's instructor. The dispute ended in the instructor creating his own club and taking about half of the initial club with him. The network can hence be divided into two main communities.
- **Dolphins Social Network:** This network is an undirected social network resulting from observations of a community of 62 dolphins over a period of 7 years [14]. Nodes represent dolphins and edges represent frequent associations between dolphin pairs occurring more often than expected by chance. Analysis of the data revealed two main groups.
- **American Political Books:** This is a political books co-purchasing network. Nodes represent books about US politics sold by the online bookseller *Amazon.com*. Edges represent frequent co-purchasing of books by the same buyers, as indicated by the "customers who bought this book also bought these other books" feature on Amazon. Books are classified into three disjoint classes: liberal, neutral or conservative. The classification was made separately by Mark Newman based on a reading of the descriptions and reviews of the books posted on Amazon.

Next figure shows the structure of the selected networks with real communities indicated by the color code. In Table 1 we summarize basic characteristics of selected benchmark real networks (Fig. 1).

For all three datasets, the ensemble selection process enhance the quality of the obtained final partition (Table 2).

Zachary Karate Club Network [26]   US Politics books network [13]

Dolphins social network [14]

Fig. 1. Real community structure of the selected benchmark networks

Table 1. Characteristics of some well-known benchmark networks

Network	# nodes	# edges	# com	reference
Zachary club	34	78	2	[26]
Political books	100	441	3	[13]
Dolphins	62	159	2	[14]

Table 2. Evaluation if he proposed graph-based ensemble selection

Dataset	Approach	NMI	ARI	Q	# Communities
Zachary	Ensemble clustering without selection	0.57	0.46	0.40	5
	Ensemble clustering with selection	**0.77**	0.69	0.34	2
US Politics	Ensemble clustering without selection	0.55	0.68	0.51	5
	Ensemble clustering with selection	**0.68**	0.67	0.42	6
Dolphins	Ensemble clustering without selection	0.55	0.39	0.51	5
	Ensemble clustering with selection	**0.58**	0.59	0.53	3

5   Conclusion

Ensemble clustering approaches are proposed as mean to cope with the robustness issue. of high speed community detection algorithms. In this work, we have proposed a new approach for enhancing the output of ensemble clustering by applying an ensemble selection process. An original graph-based ensemble selection approach is studied. Results show that the overall quality of detected communities is enhanced when applying ensemble selection process. Experiments on large-scale datasets are planned in order to confirm these first but promising results. Comparisons with other ensemble selection approaches based on implicit quality estimation are also scheduled.

References

1. Azimi, J., Fern, X.: Adaptive cluster ensemble selection. In: Boutilier, C. (ed.) IJCAI, pp. 992–997 (2009)
2. Blondel, V.D., Guillaume, J.I., Lefebvre, E.: Fast unfolding of communities in large networks. J. Stat. Mech. Theory Exp. **2008**, P10008 (2008)
3. Dahlin, J., Svenson, P.: Ensemble approaches for improving community detection methods. CoRR abs/1309.0242 (2013)
4. Fern, X.Z., Lin, W.: Cluster ensemble selection. Stat. Anal. Data Min. **1**(3), 128–141 (2008)
5. Fern, X.Z., Brodley, C.E.: Solving cluster ensemble problems by bipartite graph partitioning. In: Brodley, C.E. (ed.) ICML. ACM International Conference Proceeding Series, vol. 69. ACM (2004)
6. Fortunato, S.: Community detection in graphs. Phys. Rep. **486**(3–5), 75–174 (2010)
7. Fred, A.L.N., Jain, A.K.: Combining multiple clusterings using evidence accumulation. IEEE Trans. Pattern Anal. Mach. Intell. **27**(6), 835–850 (2005)
8. Girvan, M., Newman, M.E.J.: Community structure in social and biological networks. PNAS **99**(12), 7821–7826 (2002)
9. Hubert, L., Arabie, P.: Comparing partitions. J. Classif. **2**(1), 192–218 (1985)
10. Kanawati, R.: YASCA: an ensemble-based approach for community detection in complex networks. In: Cai, Z., Zelikovsky, A., Bourgeois, A. (eds.) COCOON 2014. LNCS, vol. 8591, pp. 657–666. Springer, Heidelberg (2014)
11. Kanawati, R.: Empirical evaluation of applying ensemble methods to ego-centered community identification in complex networks. Neurocomputing **150**, **B**, 417–427 (2015)
12. Kanawati, R.: Ensemble selection for enhancing graph coarsening quality. In: Proceedings of 5th International Workshop on Social Network Analysis. Capri, April 2015
13. Krebs, V.: Political books network. http://www.orgnet.com
14. Lusseau, D., Schneider, K., Boisseau, O.J., Haase, P., Slooten, E., Dawson, S.M.: The bottlenose dolphin community of doubtful sound features a large proportion of long-lasting associations. Behav. Ecol. Sociobiol. **54**, 396–405 (2003)
15. Meila, M.: Comparing clusterings by the variation of information. In: Schölkopf, B., Warmuth, M.K. (eds.) COLT/Kernel 2003. LNCS (LNAI), vol. 2777, pp. 173–187. Springer, Heidelberg (2003)
16. Newman, M.: Networks: An Introduction. Oxford University Press, Oxford (2010)
17. Nguyen, X.V., Epps, J., Bailey, J.: Information theoretic measures for clusterings comparison: variants, properties, normalization and correction for chance. J. Mach. Learn. Res. **11**, 2837–2854 (2010)
18. Raghavan, U.N., Albert, R., Kumara, S.: Near linear time algorithm to detect community structures in large-scale networks. Phys. Rev. E **76**, 1–12 (2007)

19. Rand, W.M.: Objective criteria for the evaluation of clustering methods. J. Am. Stat. Assoc. **66**, 846–850 (1971)
20. Seifi, M.: Cœurs stables de communautés dans les graphes de terrain. Ph.D. thesis, Université Pierre et marie Curie (paris 6) (2012)
21. Seifi, M., Guillaume, J.L.: Community cores in evolving networks. In: Mille, A., Gandon, F.L., Misselis, J., Rabinovich, M., Staab, S. (eds.) WWW (Companion Volume), pp. 1173–1180. ACM, New York (2012)
22. Staudt, C., Meyerhenke, H.: Engineering high-performance community detection heuristics for massive graphs. In: ICPP, pp. 180–189. IEEE (2013)
23. Strehl, A., Ghosh, J.: Cluster ensembles: a knowledge reuse framework for combining multiple partitions. J. Mach. Learn. Res. **3**, 583–617 (2003)
24. Tang, L., Liu, H.: Community Detection and Mining in Social Media. Synthesis Lectures on Data Mining and Knowledge Discovery. Morgan & Claypool Publishers, San Rafael (2010)
25. Toussaint, G., Bhattacharya, B.K.: Optimal algorithms for computing the minimum distance between two finite planar sets. Pattern Recogn. Lett. **2**(2), 79–82 (1981)
26. Zachary, W.W.: An information flow model for conflict and fission in small groups. J. Anthropol. Res. **33**, 452–473 (1977)

Analysis of Online Social Networks Posts to Investigate Suspects Using SEMCON

Zenun Kastrati$^{(\boxtimes)}$, Ali Shariq Imran, Sule Yildirim-Yayilgan,
and Fisnik Dalipi

Faculty of Computer Science and Media Technology,
GjøVik University College, GjøVik, Norway
{zenun.kastrati,ali.imran,sule.yayilgan,fisnik.dalipi}@hig.no

Abstract. Analysing users' behaviour and social activity for investigating suspects is an area of great interest nowadays, particularly investigating the activities of users on Online Social Networks (OSNs) for crimes. The criminal activity analysis provides a useful source of information for law enforcement and intelligence agencies across the globe. Current approaches dealing with the social criminal activity analysis mainly rely on the contextual analysis of data using only co-occurrence of terms appearing in a document to find the relationship between criminal activities in a network. In this paper, we propose a model for automated social network analysis in order to assist law enforcement and intelligence agencies to predict whether a user is a possible suspect or not. The model uses web crawlers suited to retrieve users' data such as *posts*, *feeds*, *comments*, etc., and exploits them semantically and contextually using an ontology enhancement objective metric SEMCON. The output of the model is a probability value of a user being a suspect which is computed by finding the similarity between the terms obtained from the SEMCON and the concepts of criminal ontology. An experiment on analysing the public information of 20 Facebook users is conducted to evaluate the proposed model.

Keywords: Ontology · Online social networks · Facebook · SEMCON

1 Introduction

In recent years, the usage of Online Social Networks (OSNs) has increased rapidly throughout all layers of society. Law enforcement and intelligence agencies analyse traces of digital evidence in order to solve crimes and capture criminals whom are also OSNs users during their investigation activities. Particularly analysing contents shared by users on social networks such as Facebook, Twitter and LinkedIn are of interest. Several approaches of analysis aiming at extracting useful information, modelling users profile, and understanding users behaviour and social activity have been proposed [1].

Analysing users behaviour and social activity for investigating suspects is also an interesting area of research, particularly investigating the activities of users on OSN for crimes. The criminal activity analysis provides a useful source of information for law enforcement and intelligence agencies across the globe.

© Springer International Publishing Switzerland 2015
G. Meiselwitz (Ed.): SCSM 2015, LNCS 9182, pp. 148–157, 2015.
DOI: 10.1007/978-3-319-20367-6_16

Some agencies are now using social media as a crime-solving tool [2]. Digital traces from social media such as Facebook is gaining fast acceptance for use as evidence in courts [3]. According to a survey by LexisNexis in 2012 [4], there are more than 950 law enforcement professionals with federal, state, and local agencies in United States whom use social media, particularly Facebook and YouTube, to obtain evidence to deepen their criminal investigation. Other similar criminal cases have been reported recently where digital evidence from OSNs is used as support for digital investigation [5,6].

Criminal activity analysis consists of different stages such as data processing, transformation, analysis, and visualization. Many of these stages are done manually. Thus, it takes much time and human effort to extract the required evidence from the massive amount of information.

Recently some research has been done to automate the social criminal activity analysis to help law enforcement and intelligence agencies discover the criminal networks. In this light, a framework for the forensic analysis of user interaction in OSNs is proposed in [7]. The framework enables searching for actor activities and filtering them further for temporal and geographical analysis. The authors in [8] proposed a framework that consists of major components of a network analysis process: network creation, network partition, structural analysis, and network visualization. Based on this framework, the authors developed a system called *CrimeNet Explorer*. The system has structural analysis functionality to detect subgroups from a network, identifying central members of subgroups, and extracting interaction patterns between subgroups. The authors in [9,10] used data mining approach for analyzing criminal groups. They used data mining in multiple social networks data to discover criminal networks.

However current approaches to automating the social criminal activity analysis have some limitations. They mainly rely on the contextual analysis using only co-occurrence of terms appearing in a document to find the relationship between criminal activities in a network [8]. Moreover, some of the approaches perform experiment using no real-world datasets [9].

In this paper, we try to fill this gap by proposing a framework for automated social network analysis. This framework will assists law enforcement and intelligence agencies to predict efficiently and effectively whether a user is a possible suspect or not. This is achieved by exploiting users' *posts*, *feeds* and *comments*, semantically and contextually using SEMCON [11]. SEMCON is a context and semantic based ontology enhancement model developed at our lab originally for the purpose of enriching an ontology from posts of multimedia documents.

The rest of the paper is organized as follows. In Sect. 2 we illustrate in detail our proposed model. Section 3 describes the setting for experimental procedure whereas Sect. 4 illustrates the experimental results and their analysis. Lastly, in Sect. 5 we sketch conclusions and future work.

2   Proposed Model and Methodology

The proposed model, illustrated in Fig. 1, aims at performing the analysis of social networks profiles. Information such as *posts*, *feeds* and *comments* are extracted

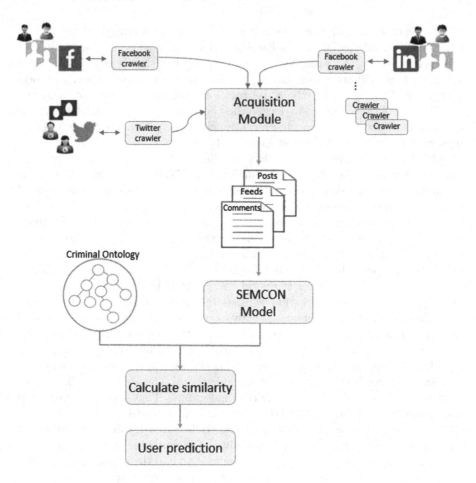

Fig. 1. Flow chart of the proposed model

and analysed, considering in particular both the context and the semantics of terms used by users. The model is explained in the following sections.

2.1 Acquisition Module

The module use web crawlers suited to retrieve and manage data coming from particular social networks such as Facebook, Twitter, LinkedIn, etc. In our case we have used Facebook crawler for managing Facebook posts. Facebook crawler is based on the Facebook Graph APIs and Facebook Query Language (FQL). To fetch Facebook messages and making queries, this paper uses RestFB [12] which is a simple and flexible Facebook Graph API client written in Java. The crawler uses an opaque string called Facebook access token that identifies a user, application, or page and can be used by the application to make graph API calls. In this work, the Facebook crawler is dedicated to fetch only *posts*, *feeds* and *comments* of a user. Facebook imposes some limitations on the number of *posts*, *feeds* and *comments* retrievable through its APIs according to the data access policy of Facebook. It does not allow to retrieve the information of more than 25 *posts*, *feeds* and *comments* per user. The restrictions on the maximum number of retrievable information are overcome by using specific parameters which enables to filter and page through the connection data.

2.2   SEMCON Module

The information fetched by Acquisition Module is used as input to the SEMCON Module. The SEMCON module treats each *post, feed* and *comment* basically as an independent document-passage and it performs the following steps.

   Initially a morpho-syntatic analysis using TreeTagger [13] is performed where the partitioned passages are tokenized and lemmatized. The potential terms that are obtained as a result can either be a noun, verb, adverb or adjectives. These are different parts-of-speech (POS) of a language. It is a well-known fact that nouns represent the most meaningful terms in a document [14], thus, our focus is on extracting only common noun terms t for further consideration.

   The next step is the calculation of the observation matrix. The observation matrix is formed by calculating the frequency of occurrences of each term t, its font type (*bold, underline, italic*) and its font size (*title, level* 1, *level* 2) as given in Eq. 1.

$$O_{i,j} = \sum_{i \in t} \sum_{j \in p} (Freq_{i,j} + Type_{i,j} + Size_{i,j}) \tag{1}$$

where, t and p indicate the set of terms and passages, respectively. $Freq_{i,j}$ denotes the frequency of occurrences of term t_i in passage, p_j, $Type_{i,j}$ denotes font type of term t_i in passage p_j, and $Size_{i,j}$ indicates font size of term t_i in passage p_j.

   The observation matrix is used as input to compute the contextual and semantic similarity between two terms.

   Term to term contextual score (S_{con}) is calculated using the cosine similarity metric with respect to the passages, and it is given in Eq. 2.

$$S_{con}(t_i, t_j) = \frac{t_i \cdot t_j}{\| t_i \| \| t_j \|} \tag{2}$$

A term square matrix is used to store the contextual(S_{con}) values among all extracted terms t.

   The next step is the computation of the semantic score (S_{sem}). The semantic score is calculated using the Wu&Palmer algorithm [15] and the score is computed using the Eq. 3.

$$S_{sem}(t_i, t_j) = \frac{2 * depth(lcs)}{depth(t_i) + depth(t_j)} \tag{3}$$

where t_i and t_j indicate terms extracted from the passage, *depth(lcs)* indicates least common subsumer of t_i and t_j, *depth*(t_i) and *depth*(t_j) indicate the path's depth of t_i and t_j, respectively. Go through the all terms, we take all possible pairs and compute the semantic score $S_{sem}(t_i, t_j)$, for each pair t_i and t_j, where $t_i, t_j \in C$ and C is the set of terms extracted from the corpus.

The overall correlation between two terms t_i and t_j extracted from the the passage is computed using the contextual and semantic score. Mathematically, the overall score is given in Eq. 4.

$$S_{overall}(t_i, t_j) = w * S_{con}(t_i, t_j) + (1 - w) * S_{sem}(t_i, t_j) \tag{4}$$

where S_{con} is the contextual score, S_{sem} is the semantic score and w is a parameter with value set as 0.5 in our case, based on the empirical analysis from the data set. The overall score is in the range (0,1]. The overall score is 1 if two extracted terms are the same.

2.3   User Prediction Module

The prediction of a user as a suspect or not depends on the similarity score between the terms extracted from the user' *posts*, *feeds* and *comments* via SEM-CON module and concepts extracted by the criminal ontology. The higher the score, the closer the user is considered as a suspect user.

The similar calculation is performed using the cosine similarity measurement. More formally, it is given in Eq. 5.

$$Similarity(O_c, u_i) = \frac{\vec{O}_c \times \vec{u}_i}{\| \vec{O}_c \| \cdot \| \vec{u}_i \|} \tag{5}$$

where, O_c indicates concepts extracted from the criminal ontology and u_i indicates terms extracted by the user postings.

The output of the system is a probability value P, of a user being a suspect s. If the P_s is greater than a specified threshold t then the user is labelled as a suspect.

3   Experimental Setting

We have performed the investigation of suspects using the public users' *posts*, *feeds* and *comments*. The facebook crawler is established to collect the data for the period starting from 1 January till 31 December 2014. The posts are extracted from news and media.

The posts from social networks contain usually noisy text, e.g. null values, therefore we filtered out only the posts which comply with the standard rules of orthography, syntax and semantics. After this process, we created a corpus which consists of 198 posts published by 20 users. The average number of posts per user is 10. The total number of terms used is 8493 with an average of 43 terms for each post. Finally, from these terms we identified and extracted 1042 nouns (singular and plural). The detailed information for each user is shown in Table 1.

Table 1. The corpus data

User	# of Posts	# of Terms	# of Nouns
1	11	929	55
2	3	121	11
3	12	301	58
4	5	130	25
5	8	376	56
6	4	1550	140
7	11	366	48
8	9	383	51
9	16	600	58
10	11	270	40
11	12	313	46
12	6	117	21
13	21	567	102
14	9	344	46
15	12	336	43
16	8	317	42
17	12	494	58
18	9	307	44
19	10	298	42
20	8	374	56
Total	198	8493	1042

We have also created a criminal ontology shown in Fig. 3. Basically it is used to predict if a user is a suspect by comparing its concepts with the terms outputted by the SEMCON as described in Sect. 2.3. However, the criminal ontology may also be used for visualization of criminal information by displaying concise overviews of its concepts and their hierarchical relations using treemaps.

4 Results and Analysis

In order to evaluate a user being as a suspect or not, we have performed an experiment on 20 Facebook users by analysing their public postings. For each user, we initially computed an overall score by aggregating the semantic and contextual score for each term (noun) extracted. The overall scores of terms are used to find the similarities of the terms with the criminal ontology concepts. Figure 2 illustrates the terms score obtained by SEMCON for the *User* #13 as depicted in Table 1. As can be seen from the graph, the contextual score indicated by the blue curve is much lower then the semantic score denoted by

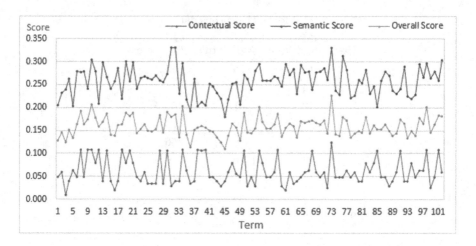

Fig. 2. Scores obtained by SEMCON for a user in investigation

Table 2. The probability of users being suspects

User	Probability	User	Probability
1	0.990	11	0.992
2	0.727	12	0.000
3	1.000	13	1.000
4	0.892	14	0.772
5	0.578	15	0.784
6	0.820	16	0.800
7	1.000	17	0.799
8	0.000	18	0.000
9	0.933	19	1.000
10	1.000	20	0.800

the orange curve. This may have happened due to the fact that the user has posted or commented in different topics. However, terms used in these posts have high semantic correlation with each other.

In the next step we found out how likely that a user is a suspect. This is achieved by comparing the user overall score obtained by SEMCON module and the scores of concepts of criminal ontology. User suspicion is represented by a probability value. The obtained probabilities for users being a suspect are shown in Table 2. The probability value 0.000 represents the users whose posts does not contain any of the criminal ontology concepts. Thus, these users are considered as unsuspected users. The probability value 1.000 indicates the users whose posts contain some of the concepts of the criminal ontology, i.e. *gun*, *rifle*, *shooting*, *threat* and *death*. These users are considered to be highly suspected users.

Table 3. Categorization of user prediction

	Unsuspected	Moderate suspected	Highly suspected
User	8, 12, 18	2, 4, 5, 6, 14	1, 3, 7, 10
		15, 16, 17, 20	11, 13, 19

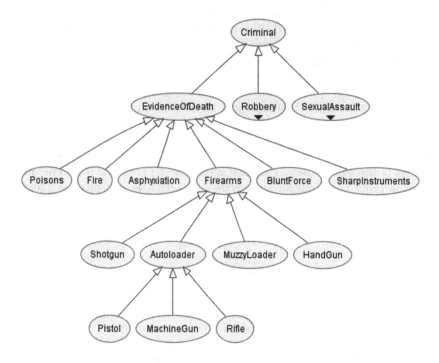

Fig. 3. A part of criminal ontology

Based on the obtained probability results, we can identify three major categories of users; users classified as unsuspected users, moderate suspected users and the highly suspected users. More precisely, if the probability score of user exceeds a given positive threshold value (in our case 0.90) we classify his/her as being a highly suspected user; if his/her probability score is 0.00 we label him/her as unsuspected user, otherwise he/she is considered as being a moderate suspected user. The labelling of users in particular categories is shown in Table 3.

5   Conclusion and Future Work

In this paper, we have proposed a new approach to investigating if a user is a suspect by analysing the OSNs data. We used Facebook as a case study of OSNs and Facebook user' *posts, feeds* and *comments* have been the object of the study. The approach employs the SEMCON to provide a semantic and contextual data-mining analysis for automatically monitoring users' activity through textual analysis. We initially built a domain ontology called criminal ontology. The prediction of a user as a suspect or not is computed by finding the similarity score between terms extracted from user' *posts*, *feeds* and *comments* via SEMCON module and the concepts extracted by the criminal ontology.

From the experiment conducted by analysing the postings published within a year by 20 users, we identified three categories of users: unsuspected, moderate suspected and highly suspected users. The categorization of users can assist law enforcement and intelligence agencies to narrow the investigation, identify and focus only on suspected users in order to prevent or solve crimes.

In the future we plan to further extend our proposed approach. Terms obtained from the SEMCON model will be used to build a user ontology. The user ontology can be used to create a history based user activity profile which may actually put light on otherwise invisible relations between a particular social network user and his/her network, and the dependence among a user's various activities. It also can be used by the law enforcement personnels for deeper investigation in order to search for suspicious user activities and filtering them for temporal and geographical analysis.

References

1. Adamic, L., Adar, E.: Friends and neighbors on the web. Soc. Netw. **25**, 211–230 (2001)
2. Knibbs, K.: In the online hunt for criminals, social media is the ultimate snitch. http://www.digitaltrends.com/social-media/the-new-inside-source-for-police-forces-social-networks/. Accessed on 11th February 2015
3. The New York Criminal Law Blog: Assault Fugitive Who Was Found Via Facebook Is Back In NY. http://newyorkcriminallawyersblog.com/2010/03/assault-criminal-who-was-found-via-facebook-is-back-in-ny.html. Accessed on 16th October 2014
4. LexisNexis: Social media use in law enforcement agencies. http://www.lexisnexis.com/government/investigations/. Accessed on 16th October 2014
5. McGuire, M.: Technology, Crime and Justice: The Question Concerning Technomia. Routledge, New York (2012)
6. Binham, C., and Croft, J.: Twitter fuels debate over super-injunctions. Financial Times (2011)
7. Abdalla, A., Yayilgan, S.Y.: A review of using online social networks for investigative activities. In: Meiselwitz, G. (ed.) SCSM 2014. LNCS, vol. 8531, pp. 3–12. Springer, Heidelberg (2014)
8. Xu, J., Chen, H.: CrimeNet explorer: a framework for criminal network knowledge discovery. ACM Trans. Inf. Syst. (TOIS) **23**, 201–226 (2005)
9. Fard, A.M., Ester, M.: Collaborative mining in multiple social networks data for criminal group discovery. In: Proceedings of International Conference on Computational Science and Engineering, Vancouver, Canada (2009)
10. Shang, X., Yuan, Y.: Social network analysis in multiple social networks data for criminal group discovery. In: Proceedings of International Conference on Cyber-Enabled Distributed Computing and Knowledge Discover, Sanya, China (2012)

11. Kastrati, Z., Imran, A.S., Yayilgan, S.Y.: SEMCON: semantic and contextual objective metric. In: Proceedings of the 9th IEEE International Conference on Semantic Computing, Anaheim, California, USA (2015)

12. RestFB: RestFB facebook graph API. www.restfb.com. Accessed on 10th February 2015

13. Schmid, H.: Probabilistic part-of-speech tagging using decision trees. In: Proceedings of International Conference on New Methods in Language Processing (1994)

14. Li, H., Tian, Y., Ye, B., Cai, Q.: Comparison of current semantic similarity methods in wordnet. In: International Conference on Computer Application and System Modeling, vol. 4, pp. 4008-4011 (2010)

15. Wu, Z., Palmer, M.: Verb semantics and lexical selection. In: Proceedings of the 32nd Annual Meeting of the Associations for Computational Linguistics, pp. 133–138 (1994)

Language-Independent Sentiment Analysis
with Surrounding Context Extension

Tomáš Kincl[1(✉)], Michal Novák[1], Jiří Přibil[1], and Pavel Štrach[2]

[1] University of Economics, Prague, Czech Republic
{tomas.kincl,michal.novak,jiri.pribil}@vse.cz
[2] Upper Austria University of Applied Sciences, Steyr, Austria
pavel.strach@fh-steyr.at

Abstract. Expressing attitudes and opinions towards various entities (i.e. products, companies, people and events) has become pervasive with the recent proliferation of social media. Monitoring of what customers think is a key task for marketing research and opinion surveys, while measuring customers' preferences or media monitoring have become a fundamental part of corporate activities. Most experiments on automated sentiment analysis focus on major languages (English, but also Chinese); minor or morphologically rich languages are addressed rather sparsely. Moreover, to improve the performance of machine-learning based classifiers, the models are often complemented with language-dependent components (i.e. sentiment lexicons). Such combined approaches provide a high level of accuracy but are limited to a single language or a single thematic domain.

This paper aims to contribute to this field and introduces an experiment utilizing a language– and domain– independent model for sentiment analysis. The model has been previously tested on multiple corpora, providing a trade-off between generality and the classification performance of the model. In this paper, we suggest a further extension of the model utilizing the surrounding context of the classified documents.

Keywords: Sentiment analysis · Cross-domain · Cross-language · Document surrounding context

1 Introduction

Expressing attitudes and opinions towards various entities such as products, companies, people and events has become an instant phenomenon with the proliferation of social media. Nowadays, the monitoring of what customers think is a key task of marketing research. Opinion surveys, measuring customers' preferences or media monitoring have become a fundamental part of corporate activities [1]. Recognizing opinion polarity and finding out about people's attitudes has become a challenge, which is addressed by (automated) sentiment analysis [2]. The literature highlights two main approaches to this issue [3]. The first approach is based on utilizing a dictionary of words (opinion lexicon) to recognize the sentiment polarity (lexicon-based approaches [4]). The second group of approaches to sentiment analysis is based on (supervised) machine learning [5]. Such methods usually require labeled training set to build the classifier [6].

© Springer International Publishing Switzerland 2015
G. Meiselwitz (Ed.): SCSM 2015, LNCS 9182, pp. 158–168, 2015.
DOI: 10.1007/978-3-319-20367-6_17

Most experiments on automated sentiment analysis focus on major languages (English, but also Chinese); minor or morphologically rich languages are rarely addressed [7]. Moreover, to improve the performance of machine-learning based classifiers, the models are often complemented with language-dependent components (i.e. sentiment lexicons). Such combined approaches provide a high level of accuracy but are also limited to a single language or a single thematic domain.

This paper aims to contribute in this field and introduces an experiment utilizing a language– and domain– independent model for sentiment analysis. The model has been previously tested on multiple corpora [8], providing a trade-off between generality and the classification performance of the model. In this paper, we suggest a further extension of the model utilizing the surrounding context of the classified documents.

2 The Surrounding Context Correction

From the marketing communications perspective, negative comments are more important than positive ones. This is not to say that the positive remarks from customers are not important—i.e. when spread by word-of-mouth to encourage potential customers—although these do not usually require any immediate (re-)action from the company, as is in the case of negative comments. Moreover, customers tend to share a negative experience which often initiates further activity of other disappointed or frustrated users, thereby creating a snowball effect. Negative emotions not only strengthen and prolong discussions but can also influence or even disrupt communication between community members and/or a company [9]. Therefore discovering a negative comment or an expression of negative emotions could enable a faster and more appropriate reaction by the company to a potentially emerging problem.

Common approaches to the sentiment analysis problem usually classify the comments (or documents in general) separately [2]. However, incorporating the sentiment of surrounding comments could provide additional information to further improve classification accuracy. When the classifier cannot detect the sentiment of the analyzed comment with high confidence, it could look around for the prevailing sentiment of surrounding comments. If there are more surrounding negative comments, this could indicate that the sentiment of the analyzed comment is also rather negative [10]. The surrounding context could be either local (i.e. the comments are in the same discussion or thread) or chronological (i.e. the comments addressing a similar issue appear in the same time frame but on different locations).

Therefore the model includes a correction to further improve the accuracy of the analyzed comments. For each classified comment, the classifier computes two values c_{neg}, $c_{pos} \in [0, 1]$; $c_{neg} = 1 - c_{pos}$ which express the confidence that the classified comment belongs to the given class of sentiment [11]. If the confidence of the classifier is high (c_{neg}, c_{pos} values are far from 0.5), the correction plays only a marginal to no role in the classification. However, when the classifier has low confidence in the sentiment of the analyzed comment (c_{neg}, c_{pos} values are very close to 0.5), the correction is applied. The extent of the correction applied according to the c_{neg} value is displayed in Fig. 1.

If the c_{neg} value is close to the value 0.5 (the level of the classifier's confidence in assigning a comment to a positive/negative class is low), then the correction (*corr*) is applied to the full extent. However with an increasing distance from $c_{neg} = 0.5$, the amount of correction applied declines rapidly. The z parameter influences the extent of which is the correction applied with the increasing distance from the point where $c_{neg} = 0.5$. In the current setting described in Fig. 1, the correction doesn't play any important role for $c_{neg} \notin (0.4, 0.6)$. The z parameter has been experimentally set to $z = 500$. However, such an approach is only heuristic and the value can be set up differently according to the classification task.

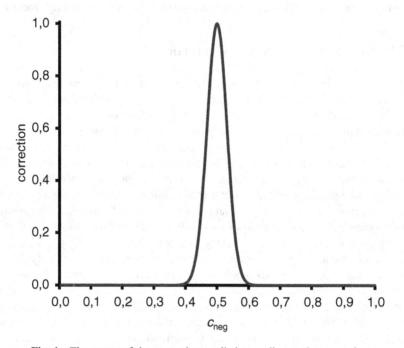

Fig. 1. The extent of the correction applied according to the c_{neg} value

The correction (*corr*) can be expressed as in the Eq. (1):

$$corr = e^{-z \cdot (c_{neg} - 0.5)^2} \tag{1}$$

The correction mechanism has been designed to take into account two various effects. The first effect (E_1) represents the predominant sentiment of related comments published from the when the topic first appeared. The related comments can be represented by a discussion in one thread in a discussion group or on a social network, or by comments published on various sites but still discussing the same topic (identified i.e. by topic keywords).

The second effect (E_2) includes the current trend of sentiment polarity. This exclusively takes into account the sentiment of recently published comments. The number of comments representing the trend is $n - k$ and can be set up differently according to the classification task. Again, the comments can be represented either by a discussion in one thread or by comments addressing the same topic. Both effects are demonstrated in Fig. 2.

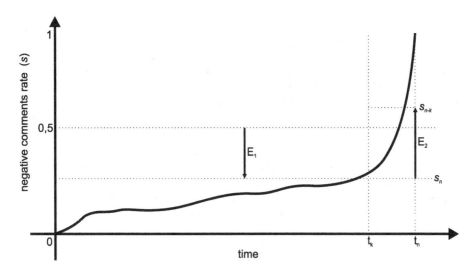

Fig. 2. An example of both sentiment correction components E_1 and E_2

The horizontal axis represents the time sequence of the comments published. The vertical axis represents the relative share of comments (s) that were assigned to the negative class by the classifier. Figure 2 illustrates an example where the positive comments are prevailing at the beginning of the discussion (the share of negative comments is less than 0.5). Subsequently, the overall mood in the discussion shifts and many negative comments are made (comments k to n). The task is to classify the $n + 1$ comment.

First, the classifier evaluates the $n + 1$ comment regardless of the surrounding context. If the c_{neg} is far from the 0.5 value (the classifier has high confidence in the polarity of the analyzed comment), the correction doesn't apply. However, if the c_{neg} is close to 0.5, the correction (including effects E_1 and E_2) is applied to the extent according to Eq. (1).

The first E_1 (prevailing surrounding sentiment) effect is included in the model as expressed in the Eq. (2):

$$E_1 = s_n - 0,5 \tag{2}$$

The first E_1 effect is the relative share of negative comments (s_n) from the beginning of the discussion until now, minus 0.5. For $E_1 < 0$, the predominant sentiment of analyzed comments is positive (the relative share of negative comments in the discussion is less than 0.5) and the $E1$ effect will be reflected in lowering the c_{neg}. For $E_1 > 0$, the corrected c_{neg} will be higher, since the negative sentiment is prevailing (the relative share of negative comments s_n is more than 0.5).

The second effect compares the relative share of negative comments s_{n-k} in last $n - k$ cases according to the cumulative share of negative comments for all analyzed cases s_n. The E_2 effect is included in the model as expressed in the Eq. (3):

$$E_2 = \frac{\frac{n \cdot s_n - k \cdot s_k}{n-k}}{s_n} - 1 \tag{3}$$

For $E_2 > 0$ is the relative share of negative comments s_{n-k} for last $n - k$ cases is higher than for all analyzed comments s_n. Therefore it could be expected that the share of negative comments will continue to increase in the near future. The effect will contribute to the increase of c_{neg} for the classified comment. For $E_2 < 0$, the corrected c_{neg} will be lower since the relative share of negative comments is lower for the last $n - k$ cases. The E_2 effect could even rise beyond value 1 (in case that a recent rise in negative comments is highly significant). If so, the effect value counts as 1.

The correction mechanism also includes weights for both effects. By default, the weights were chosen identically for both effects as $w_1 = w_2 = 0.5$. The corrected c_{neg} – $ccor_{\text{neg}}$ – can therefore be expressed as in the Eq. (4).

$$ccor_{\text{neg}} = c_{\text{neg}} + corr \cdot (w_1 \cdot E_1 + w_2 \cdot E_2) \tag{4}$$

3 Results

Several datasets were used to validate the model. The first corpus data were obtained from the Czech-Slovak Film Database available at http://www.csfd.cz. CSFD is the largest community-driven online database of reviews and information in the Czech (Slovak) language related to films, television programs, including cast, production crew and biographies. CSFD is often considered as a local alternative to the Internet Movie Database (IMDb). This dataset has been chosen to compare the results on local language with studies conducted on similar (i.e. IMDb) corpora. The second dataset was obtained from mall.cz, the second largest [12] Czech e-shop. Mall.cz offers various products ranging from electronics and home appliances to sports gear and supplies for hobbies and pets. This dataset has been chosen to validate how the model deals with cross-domain sentiment classification [2]. The third dataset was the Large Movie Review Dataset [13] based on the IMDb data (movie reviews). This dataset has been chosen not only to compare the results on CSFD corpus, but also to compare the model performance with other studies (since the corpus is publicly available and often utilized as a sentiment analysis dataset).

The last dataset contained reader reviews retrieved from Amazon websites in multiple languages. All reviews related to the 2012 bestselling book, Fifty Shades of Grey by E.L. James (all versions – hardcover, paperback, kindle or audio version) were obtained.

The languages included English (amazon.co.uk; 7,255 reviews), German (amazon.de; 4,154 reviews) and French (amazon.fr; 1,258 reviews). The dataset has been chosen to test how the model deals with cross-language sentiment classification [2].

3.1 Czech-Slovak Film Database Results

The training set contained 3,000 positive (4 - and 5-star reviews) and 3,000 negative comments (0-, 1- and 2-star reviews). Then the trained model was validated on a randomly selected set of 120,000 comments (20,000 from each star-rating). The results of the classification (without the correction applied) are summarized in Table 1.

Table 1. Classification results on CSFD validation set

Star rating	Predicted negative	Predicted positive
0	89.57 %	10.44 %
1	86.17 %	13.83 %
2	74.60 %	25.40 %
3	46.44 %	53.56 %
4	21.98 %	78.03 %
5	15.73 %	84.28 %

The classification accuracy without the correction mechanism applied (computed on 0-, 1-, 2-, 4-, and 5-star comments since 3-star comments were considered as neutral and therefore without any sentiment) reached 82.53 %. Subsequently, the correction including the surrounding context has been applied. The context to the CSDF data was considered as the previously published comments to the same movie. There was more than one comment about 12,000 movies in the test dataset. The highest number of comments about one single movie was 175. The dataset contained various movies, from The Shawshank Redemption (2nd most popular movie on CSFD) to Playgirls (considered as the 14th worst movie of all time). The classification results with the suggested correction applied are summarized in Table 2.

Table 2. Classification results on CSFD validation set (correction applied)

Star rating	Predicted negative	Predicted positive
0	91.58 %	8.42 %
1	87.87 %	12.14 %
2	76.22 %	23.78 %
3	47.31 %	52.69 %
4	21.87 %	78.14 %
5	15.11 %	84.89 %

The classification accuracy with the correction mechanism applied (computed on 0-, 1-, 2-, 4-, and 5-star comments since 3-star comments were considered as neutral and therefore without any sentiment) reached 83.74 %. Therefore the correction applied improves the classification accuracy by 1.21 %.

3.2   Large Movie Review Dataset (IMDb) Results

The IMDb allows users to review the movies on a scale ranging from 1- to 10-stars. The training set from [13] contained 12,500 positive (7- to 10-star reviews) and 12,500 negative comments (1- to 4-star reviews). The validation set contained the same amount of comments – 12,500 positive and 12,500 negative reviews. The results of the classification (without the correction applied) are summarized in Table 3.

Table 3. Classification results on IMDb validation set

Star rating	Predicted negative	Predicted positive
1	92.49 %	7.51 %
2	88.79 %	11.21 %
3	82.88 %	17.12 %
4	74.80 %	25.20 %
5	23.54 %	76.46 %
6	13.96 %	86.04 %
7	11.31 %	88.69 %
8	8.98 %	91.02 %
9	92.49 %	7.51 %
10	88.79 %	11.21 %

The classification accuracy without the correction mechanism applied (computed on 1-to 4- and 7- to 10-star comments) reached 86.44 %. Subsequently, the correction including the surrounding context has been applied. Similarly to the CSFD data, the comments to the same movie were considered as a context to apply the correction. The classification results with the suggested correction applied are summarized in Table 4.

Table 4. Classification results on IMDb validation set (correction applied)

Star rating	Predicted negative	Predicted positive
1	93.65 %	6.35 %
2	90.83 %	9.17 %
3	84.65 %	15.35 %
4	77.00 %	23.00 %
5	21.20 %	78.80 %
6	12.32 %	87.68 %
7	9.26 %	90.74 %
8	8.04 %	91.96 %
9	93.65 %	6.35 %
10	90.83 %	9.17 %

The classification accuracy with the correction mechanism applied reached 87.88 %. Therefore, the correction applied improves the classification accuracy by 1.44 %. Studies conducted on the same dataset reached similar performance (i.e. 88.33 % in [13]). However the model suggested in our experiment does not utilize any language- or domain-dependent components (i.e. sentiment vocabularies or ontologies) and therefore could be used to address cross-language or cross-domain sentiment classification.

3.3   Mall.Cz Results

The mall.cz dataset has been analyzed to validate the model on data from multiple domains (product reviews from various product categories). The training set contained 3,000 positive (4- and 5-star reviews) and 3,000 negative comments (1- and 2-star reviews). Then the trained model was validated on a randomly selected set of 100,000 comments (20,000 from each star-rating). The results of the classification (without the correction applied) are summarized in Table 5.

Table 5. Classification results on mall.cz validation set

Star rating	Predicted negative	Predicted positive
1	81.38 %	18.62 %
2	73.67 %	26.33 %
3	57.09 %	42.91 %
4	32.58 %	67.42 %
5	20.50 %	79.50 %

The classification accuracy without the correction mechanism applied (computed on 1, 2-, 4- and 5-star comments) reached 76.71 %. Subsequently, the correction including the surrounding context has been applied. As a context, reviews previously commenting on the same product were considered. The classification results with the suggested correction applied are summarized in Table 6.

Table 6. Classification results on mall.cz validation set (correction applied)

Star rating	Predicted negative	Predicted positive
1	82.89 %	17.11 %
2	75.51 %	24.49 %
3	50.81 %	49.19 %
4	27.42 %	72.58 %
5	17.04 %	82.96 %

The classification accuracy with the correction mechanism applied reached 78.95 %. Therefore, the correction applied improves the classification accuracy by 2.24 %. The performance of the model on mall.cz dataset did not reach such values as in the previous cases. However, the model still performed on a satisfactory level considering that the data came from multiple domains, Czech is a morphologically rich language and the model does not utilize any language-dependent component to improve the classification.

3.4   Amazon Results

For the experiment on Amazon data, 100 positive (4- and 5-star reviews) and 100 negative (1- and 2-star reviews) comments from each language were used to train the model. Even though the amount of data obtained from the Amazon websites was much higher, there were only a limited number of French negative comments collected. This was also the reason why a separate training and validation set could not be used. In this case, the model utilized the 10-cross fold validation. All three languages were merged together into one and treated as one single dataset. The aim of this experiment was to discover how the model deals with cross-language sentiment classification. The results of the classification (without the correction applied) are summarized in Table 7.

Table 7. Classification results on Amazon multilingual set

Star rating	Predicted negative	Predicted positive
1	89.00 %	11.00 %
2	88.00 %	12.00 %
3	57.33 %	42.67 %
4	19.00 %	81.00 %
5	7.67 %	92.33 %

The classification accuracy without the correction mechanism applied (computed on 1, 2-, 4- and 5-star comments) reached 87.58 %. Subsequently, the correction including the surrounding context has been applied. The classification results with the suggested correction applied are summarized in Table 8.

Table 8. Classification results on Amazon multilingual set (correction applied)

Star rating	Predicted negative	Predicted positive
1	90.33 %	9.67 %
2	89.67 %	10.33 %
3	59.00 %	41.00 %
4	19.67 %	80.33 %
5	8.00 %	92.00 %

The classification accuracy with the correction mechanism applied reached 88.08 %. Therefore the correction applied improves the classification accuracy by 0.50 %. Even though the model does not utilize any language-dependent components, it performs very well on multilingual data. Moreover, the correction we suggest was able to further improve the classification accuracy of the model.

4   Discussion and Conclusion

The results indicate that the performance of the sentiment classification model could be improved even without utilizing language-dependent components. The paper suggests a correction based on incorporating the surrounding context of the analyzed document. This context is either local (i.e. the comments are in the same discussion or thread) or chronological (i.e. the comments addressing a similar issue appear in the same time frame but on different locations). The extended model has been tested on several corpora to reveal how the suggested approach deals with the usual sentiment analysis problems (i.e. cross-domain, cross-language sentiment analysis or sentiment analysis on morphologically rich or minor languages). The results of the experiments are encouraging and summarized in Table 9.

Table 9. Results summary

Corpus	Corpus characteristics	Model performance
Mall.cz	Czech (morphologically rich) language, multiple thematic domains (product reviews in various categories).	76.71 % correctly classified cases without the correction applied. With the knowledge of the surrounding context, the model reached 78.95 %. 2.24 % overall improvement
CSFD	Czech (morphologically rich) language. One thematic domain (movie reviews)	82.53 % correctly classified cases without the correction applied. With the knowledge of the surrounding context, the model reached 83.74 %. 1.21 % overall improvement.
IMDb	English language. One thematic domain (movie reviews).	86.44 % correctly classified cases without the correction applied. With the knowledge of the surrounding context, the model reached 88.33 %. 1.44 % overall improvement.
Amazon	Multiple (English, German, French) languages. One thematic domain (book reviews).	87.58 % correctly classified cases without the correction applied. With the knowledge of the surrounding context, the model reached 88.08 %. 0.55 % overall improvement.

The results suggest that the model performs well on multiple languages even though it does not utilize any language-dependent component (for a further description of the model please see [8]). It performs well on major languages (English, German or French) as well as on a morphologically rich language (Czech). The performance of the model could be easily improved by including the surrounding context of the analyzed document. The model also achieves comparable results with studies conducted on similar datasets [13].

It may represent an opportunity for a subsequent research inquiry to address the limitation of the effect of the previously reached performance and on the nature of the analyzed data on the magnitude of correction outcomes. The higher the previously reached performance, the lesser the correction contributes to further classification improvement.

References

1. CyberAlert. http://www.cyberalert.com/downloads/media_monitoring_whitepaper.pdf
2. Liu, B.: Sentiment analysis and opinion mining. Synth. Lect. Hum. Lang. Technol. **5**, 1–167 (2012)
3. Balahur, A.: Sentiment analysis in social media texts. In: WASSA 2013, p. 120 (2013)
4. Feldman, R.: Techniques and applications for sentiment analysis. Commun. ACM **56**, 82–89 (2013)
5. Pang, B., Lee, L., Vaithyanathan, S.: Thumbs up?: sentiment classification using machine learning techniques. In: Proceedings of the ACL-02 Conference on Empirical Methods in Natural Language Processing, vol. 10, pp. 79–86 (2002)
6. Pak, A., Paroubek, P.: Twitter as a corpus for sentiment analysis and opinion mining. In: Proceedings of the International Conference on Language Resources and Evaluation, LREC, pp. 1320-1326 (2010)
7. Tsarfaty, R., Seddah, D., Goldberg, Y., Kuebler, S., Candito, M., Foster, J., Versley, Y., Rehbein, I., Tounsi, L.: Statistical parsing of morphologically rich languages (SPMRL): what, how and whither. In: Proceedings of the First Workshop on Statistical Parsing of Morphologically-Rich Languages, NAACL HLT 2010, pp. 1–12. Association for Computational Linguistics (2010)
8. Kincl, T., Novák, M., Přibil, J.: Getting inside the minds of the customers: automated sentiment analysis. In: European Conference on Management Leadership and Governance ECMLG 2013, pp. 122–129. Alpen-Adria Universität Klagenfurt, Austria (2013)
9. Chmiel, A., Sienkiewicz, J., Thelwall, M., Paltoglou, G., Buckley, K., Kappas, A., Hołyst, J.A.: Collective emotions online and their influence on community life. PLoS ONE **6**, e22207 (2011)
10. Brychcín, T., Habernal, I.: Unsupervised improving of sentiment analysis using global target context. In: International Conference Recent Advances in Natural Language Processing (RANLP 2013) (2013)
11. Chang, C.C., Lin, C.J.: LIBSVM: a library for support vector machines. ACM Trans. Intel. Syst. Technol. (TIST) **2**, 1–39 (2011)
12. http://byznys.ihned.cz/c1-54991650-cesko-je-e-shopovou-velmoci-internetove-obchody-vygeneruji-37-miliard-obratu
13. Maas, A.L., Daly, R.E., Pham, P.T., Huang, D., Ng, A.Y., Potts, C.: Learning word vectors for sentiment analysis. In: Proceedings of the 49th Annual Meeting of the Association for Computational Linguistics: Human Language Technologies, vol. 1, pp. 142–150. Association for Computational Linguistics (2011)

Hashtag Popularity on Twitter: Analyzing Co-occurrence of Multiple Hashtags

Nargis Pervin[1]([⊠]), Tuan Quang Phan[1], Anindya Datta[1], Hideaki Takeda[2], and Fujio Toriumi[3]

[1] National University of Singapore, Singapore, Singapore
{nargisp,phantq,datta}@comp.nus.edu.sg
[2] National Institute of Informatics, Tokyo, Japan
takeda@nii.ac.jp
[3] The Tokyo University, Tokyo, Japan
tori@sys.t.u-tokyo.ac.jp

Abstract. Hashtags increase the reachability of a tweet to manifolds and consequently, has the potential to create a wider market for brands. The frequent use of a hashtag features it in the Twitter trending list. In this study we want to understand what contributes to the popularity of a hashtag. Further, hashtags generally come in groups in a tweet. In fact, an investigation on a real world dataset of Great Eastern Japan Earthquake reveals that 50 % of hashtags appear in a tweet with at least another hashtag. How this co-occurrence of hashtags affects its popularity is also not addressed heretofore, which is the focus herein. Results indicate that if a hashtag appears with one or more other similar hashtags, popularity of the hashtag increases. In contrast, if a hashtag appears with dissimilar hashtags, popularity of the focal hashtag decreases. The results reverse when dissimilar hashtags come along with a URL.

Keywords: Twitter · Hashtag · Hashtag co-occurrence · Metacognitive experience

1 Introduction

In August 2007, Chris Messina tweeted on his Twitter account "how do you feel about using # (pound) for groups? As in #barcamp [msg]?" It was claimed as the first ever hashtag [19] on Twitter and since then this became a unique strategy for categorizing messages which can properly lead individuals to conversations and discussions pertaining to a specific topic [7,15]. Social media is fast paced and no one has the time all day long to sift through his timeline to read everything being posted. That is where hashtags are significant. It can generate immediate, live, and interactive reactions and responses to specific topics. People use hashtags while watching their favorite TV program, listening to a debate on the radio, promoting a product, or running a campaign. It has been shown that when individuals used a hashtag within their tweet, engagement can increase as much as 100 % and for brands it could get an increase of 50 % [6]. This is because

© Springer International Publishing Switzerland 2015
G. Meiselwitz (Ed.): SCSM 2015, LNCS 9182, pp. 169–182, 2015.
DOI: 10.1007/978-3-319-20367-6_18

a hashtag immediately expands the reach of the tweet beyond followers of the tweet author and hence is reachable to anyone interested in that hashtag phrase or keyword.

During the 2012 presidential election, both Obama and Romney used hashtags to campaign through social media. The craze for hashtags is so high that people are willing to pay even $3,000 to rent a "social media wedding concierge" [8].

From the preceding discussion, it is transparent that the importance of hashtags is enormous, which motivates us to investigate the characteristics of these hashtags. The abundance of information to which we are exposed through online social networks exceeds the amount of information we can consume. Hence, the hashtags compete with each other to attain our limited attention. Users can remember a bounded number of different hashtags at a time, which suggests that one hashtag is remembered by the users at the expense of others [23]. How many users will adopt a hashtag determines its popularity. This adoption solely depends on how people find it meaningful and attractive which is concluded from their metacognitive experience. Metacognitive experiences are those experiences that are related to the current, on-going cognitive endeavor while metacognition refers to a level of thinking that involves active control over the process of thinking that is used in learning situations [12,13]. The detailed discussion of metacognition can be found in the literature review section.

On inspecting tweets containing hashtags, one can notice that hashtags usually come in groups, i.e., a single tweet contains more than one hashtag. A preliminary analysis on our data set reveals that tweets containing multiple hashtags get diffused more compared to tweets having a single hashtag. Here the decisive question arises whether the characteristics of the hashtags appeared together are random or it carries certain pattern, which is the focus of this study. The popularity of one hashtag might boost the popularity of others when they appear together. For instance, say hashtag h becomes trendy on Twitter. Now, users start using h with h_1 which increases the discoverability of h_1 also. In such circumstances, we believe that there can be three main possibilities: a) popularity of h takes off further, b) hashtag h_1 becomes more popular, and c) hashtag h_1 replaces hashtag h. To understand this phenomenon, it is necessary to investigate the change of popularity of a hashtag h when co-appeared with other hashtags h_1, h_2, etc. We investigate the popularity of a hashtag measured by the number of distinct users who have adopted / used it and model the popularity using regression technique considering both network variables and content variables of hashtag.

We postulate that when a hashtag appears with multiple hashtags, it increases the popularity of the focal hashtag. Next, we investigate the nature of these co-appearing hashtags in terms of similarity. Dissimilar hashtags increase the metacognitive difficulty of the users [11], but when used with URLs it adds more information and brings surprisingness to the tweet, which in turn increases the popularity of hashtags. Earlier studies [9] have shown that when hashtags appeared with a URL in a tweet, retweetability of that tweet escalates which is in line with our hypothesis. We examine this phenomenon using the Great

Eastern Japan earthquake data set and also check whether the external event (e.g., earthquake) has any impact on this process.

Our investigation on hashtag popularity supports both the hypotheses. Further, it has been shown that only hashtag content can predict the popularity of hashtags and network variables turned out insignificant in popularity prediction, which is in agreement with [21]. Running the model in three different windows we found that direction of the impact of the independent variables on popularity are same, though the strength of impacts (coefficients) was larger at the time of the event which reduced again back to normal after the event.

Moreover, we have investigated these properties at a granular level. We model hashtag retweetability at the dyad (user-retweeter pair) level. This model will allow us to understand the user level attributes that play role in popularity.

2   Literature Review

What does motivate people to share information? Sharing information with friends is considered to be a communal act in online social network sites. People share YouTube videos, Facebook posts, or tweets on Twitter. While a massive amount of information gets generated online, only a handful of them get noticed and shared. This leads to the straightforward question what makes a piece of content more share-worthy than others. Researches have been carried in the viral-marketing area to unfold the characteristics of the content that goes viral [1–3]. However, the main query lies in why people share information in the first place and what type of content gets shared. Consumers might share some content online for several reasons, e.g., altruistic reasons (e.g., to help others) or for self-enhancement purposes (e.g., to appear knowledgeable, see [25]).

Human reasoning is accompanied by metacognitive experiences. The assumptions about what makes it easy or difficult to think of certain things or to process new information contribute to what exactly people conclude from their metacognitive experiences. Researches showed evidence that people are more likely to advocate a statement as true when the color in which it is printed makes it easy to read (e.g., [12,13]). [14] describes that accessibility and processing fluency both pertain to the ease of recalling and processing new information. Moreover, repeated exposures lead to the subjective feeling of perceptual fluency, which in turn influences liking [13]. On the other hand, [11] experimentally showed that metacognitive difficulty increases the attractiveness of a product by making it appear unique or uncommon.

In this work we want to investigate why some hashtags go more viral than others? A hashtag is a word or phrase preceded by a hash sign (#), used on Twitter to identify messages on a specific topic. This works as a user-defined index term to link several topics or events together. [26] examined the dual effect of hashtags on Twitter: a) a symbol of a community membership and b) a bookmark. In this paper they investigated which of the two reasons strive people to adopt a hashtag. The prediction using SVM technique incorporates social network variables like indegree, outdegree of nodes (number of people retweeted the hashtag), relevance, popularity of the hashtags, length (number of characters), age of the hashtag. The dataset used in this study was Twitter data on politics.

Popularity of the hashtag determines how many users will adopt a particular hashtag. Using a 25 week Twitter data, [21] reported hashtag frequency prediction on a weekly basis using regression technique. Features used in the regression model were extracted from the hashtag itself (e.g., number of characters in the hashtag) and their experiment shows that hashtag popularity can be predicted using only the content features of the hashtags instead of using the costly graphical features extracted from tweets. However, [10] claimed that contextual features are more effective than content features which can be explained by the fact that community graph plays an important role in information diffusion. Clarity of hashtag, number of words in a hashtag, user count, tweet count, etc. were used to predict the popularity. However, on Twitter a large number of hashtags are generated every day and people cannot remember all of them. Using an agent-based simulation model, [23] claimed that the users can remember a bounded number of different memes at a time, which suggests that one meme is remembered by the users at the expense of others. The proposed retweet model assumes the finite memory of the users where memes are registered and by the friend and follower links, some other users can read the meme posted. However, a careful investigation of the usage of hashtags needs to be done. On inspecting tweets containing hashtags, one can notice that hashtags usually come in groups, i.e., a single tweet contains more than one hashtag. A preliminary analysis reveals that tweets containing multiple hashtags get diffused more than tweets having a single hashtag. It will be interesting to investigate "Are these characteristics of the hashtags appeared together random or does it carry certain patterns?" Moreover, in the time of emergency, the adoption of hashtags might change. Using a 2011 Japan earthquake data, this chapter investigates how a hashtag becomes popular.

3   Dataset Description

In this study, we have used data set from the 2011 Japan earthquake. We used a Twitter dataset collected during the earthquake in 2011 described thoroughly in [20]. Dataset collection procedure has been discussed briefly here:

- First, a set of tweets has been collected from Twitter streaming API for tweets during the event.
- Next, for all these tweets the user details has been crawled using the same API along with the follower IDS.
- For all these users the tweets are collected for 20 days of time period.

The dataset covers a period of 20 days (from 5th March, 2011 to 24th March, 2011), and consists of 362,435,649 tweets posted by 2,711,473 users in Japan. This dataset is remarkable by its completeness: 80 % to 90 % of all published tweets by these users were present in this dataset. It should be noted that the dataset consists of tweets of Japanese Twitter users. Hence, major proportion of tweets (98 %)in the data set is written in Japanese.

4   Solution Details

4.1   Building Research Hypotheses

Synonymous hashtags when appeared together, it will increase the visibility of the tweet contrary to dissimilar hashtags. Dissimilar hashtags will increase the metacognitive difficulty of the users [11], but when used with URLs it would add more information, bring surprisingness to the tweet, and could increase the popularity of hashtags. Thus, we postulate two hypotheses:

Hypothesis 1. *Hashtag popularity increases when it appears with other hashtags.*

Hypothesis 2. *When co-appearing hashtags are dissimilar, presence of URLs increases hashtag popularity.*

We have investigated what happens when the hashtags co-appear. First, we examine whether the co-occurrence of hashtags plays any role in hashtag popularity and then we calculate the distance among the co-appearing hashtags to test whether the distance among the tags has any impact on its popularity. Additionally, we have also considered the interaction effect of the URL and the distance among the co-appearing hashtags. We have modeled hashtag popularity using the content variables of hashtags and the user specific variables. We have presented two models, one with only the hashtag specific variables, and another model with the hashtag specific and dyad specific variables.

4.2   Factors Considered for Hashtag Popularity

To investigate the factors impacting popularity hashtag specific, dyad specific, and control variables are considered as follows:

Hashtag Specific Variables

Length of Hashtag: The hashtag has been extracted from the tweet content by searching words that start with "#". For all hashtags we counted the number of characters in that hashtag. Very long hashtags are not economical in the Twitter perspective as tweets are limited to only 140 characters. On the other hand, very small hashtags (e.g., abbreviated hashtags containing only 2 or three letters) do not contain sufficient information to understand.

Number of Words: Clarity of the hashtag is important for its adoption. Hashtags, which contain multiple words are easy in order to follow the context from the hashtag itself. However, finding the word segments from a hashtag in the Twitter context is not straightforward as Twitter users use Twitter specific lingual. For the same reason, we counted the number of words in the hashtag by separating the capital letters or other special separator characters (e.g., underscore (_), plus (+) etc.).

Contains Capital Letters: This is a boolean variable computing the presence of capital letters in the hashtag. The value of the variable = 1 if the hashtag contains capital letters and 0 otherwise.

Contains Digits: This is a boolean variable denoting the presence of digits in the hashtag. The value of the variable = 1 if the hashtag contains digits and 0 otherwise.

Contains Other Separators: This is a boolean variable computing the presence of other separators in the hashtag, e.g., underscore (_), plus (+). The value of the variable = 1 if the hashtag contains other separators and 0 otherwise.

Appeared with Other Hashtag: This determines whether a hashtag appeared with other hashtags or not. If the hashtag appears with other hashtags then the value of the variable is the number of hashtags it appeared with and 0 otherwise. This is a time series variable indicating that the value of the variable determines in a particular time unit, whether the hashtag appeared with others or not.

Distance: For the co-appearing hashtags we compute the distance between the hashtag pairs. If more than two hashtags appear with the focal hashtag then the average distance of the hashtag pairs are considered. For each pair of hashtags we have calculated the Levenshtein distance [24] among them.

Inclusion of URLs: Earlier studies [18] have shown that inclusion of URLs in the tweet increases a tweet's retweetability. Our previous study also supports this finding (as described in the previous chapter, Chap. 3). Moreover, we also observed that the presence of both hashtags and URLs in the tweet increases its popularity. Therefore, we compute this variable as a boolean variable denoting the presence of URLs in the tweet. URL = 1 if the tweet contains a URL, 0 otherwise. If a hashtag appears in more than one tweet, we compute the average number of times the focal hashtag appeared with URLs. We place URL = 1 if the average number of tweets > 0, 0 otherwise.

DistanceXURL: To examine the moderating effect of the URL on distance of co-appearing hashtags we compute the interaction variable of distance and boolean URL.

$DistanceXURL = distance \times URL$

Frequency of Hashtag: For each hashtag h we calculate the frequency of hashtag as the number of times h has been retweeted per minute.

Age of Hashtag: For each hashtag h we compute the age of the hashtag since it has been used by some user. Unit of time used here is an hour.

Dyad Specific Variables

Frequency of Dyad: For each hashtag h we calculate the frequency of hashtag at the dyad level. Hence, dyad frequency (per minute) is computed as the number of times user $u_{retweeter}$ retweets a tweet by u_{author}, that contains hashtag h.

PageRank of Author and Retweeter: Each user on Twitter has a number of followers and followees which can be thought of as incoming and outgoing links from a web page. Similar to web pages, we can also compute the PageRank of a user to enumerate his popularity. However, in our case we formulated the retweet network of the users where direction indicates the reverse direction of information flow from (retweeter → author). Instead of using the PageRank computed on the follower-followee network, we computed the PageRank based on the retweet network. In this case, unlike otherwise, computed PageRank determines the activeness and actual influence of the users.

For both author and retweeter of the tweet, we compute the PageRank ($PageRank_{author}$ and $PageRank_{retweeter}$).

Betweenness Centrality of Author and Retweeter: Betweenness centrality is a measure of a node's centrality in a network. It is equal to the number of shortest paths from all vertices to all others that pass through that node. We have measured the betweenness centrality of the users on the retweet network.

For both author and retweeter of the tweet, we compute the betweenness centrality ($betweenness_{author}$ and $betweenness_{retweeter}$).

Relationship between Dyad (Author and Retweeter): On Twitter, a tweet can be retweeted by author's followers or friends. However, if a tweet becomes popular, this can be retweeted by retweeters even if they do not have any relationship with the author of the tweet.

Control Variables

Below are two control variables used in the model:

Day of Week: Day of the week [22] might have an impact on the popularity of the hashtag. [22] finds that day of the week controls traffic on Twitter, while Monday to Thursday the tweet volume increases, Friday it slows down. On Mondays users usually use Monday specific hashtags more frequently (#Monday, #mondayfever). On the other hand, on Saturdays and Sundays people write more fun-filled hashtags like #supersunday, #saturdaysale.

Time of the Day: Twitter gets the most traffic during 9am-3pm from Monday to Thursday [22]. We also include this as a control variable in the popularity model (Table 1).

Model Specifications. In this model the dependent variable is the retweet count of tweets containing a specific hashtag for a specific dyad (retweeter → author pair).

$RetweetCount_{i,j,t} = \alpha + \sum_i H(i,t) + \sum_j D(j,t) + \sum_k C(k,t) + \varepsilon$

$H(i,t), D(j,t), C(k,t)$ refer to the vector of hashtag specific variables, dyad specific variables, control variables respectively.

Table 1. Variables affecting hashtag popularity

	Variable	Meaning
Dependent variable	numDistinctUsers	number of distinct users who adopted/used the hashtag
Network variables	PageRank	average PageRank of the users using the hashtag in retweet network
	betweenness	average betweenness centrality of the users using the hashtag in retweet network
Content variables	hasCaps	value = 1 if the hashtag contains capital letters, = 0, otherwise
	hasDigits	value = 1 if the hashtag contains digits, = 0, otherwise
	hasOther	value = 1 if the hashtag contains other separators, = 0, otherwise
	numWords	number of words in the hashtag
	length	length of the hashtag
	appearedWithOthers	number of hashtags #h appeared with
	distance(h,H)	average distance of #h with all hashtags in H
	isURL	boolean variable indicating if the tweet contains URLs
Control variables	timeOfDay	24 hours have been divided into 5 time-windows, morning(7am-10am), noon (11am-3pm), afternoon (4pm-7pm), evening (8pm-11pm), night (12am -6am)
	dayOfWeek	day of the week is coded as dummy variable
	tagAge	time since the tweet is composed (in hour)
	tagFreq	frequency of the hashtag per unit time (minute)
Dyad specific variables	dyadFreq	dyad (retweeter → author) frequency per unit time (measured in minute)
	relationship	boolean variable denoting follower-followee relationship, value = 1 if relationship exists and 0 otherwise

$$H(i,t) = [hasDigits, hasCaps, numWords]'_i$$
$$+ [distance, appearedWithOthers, isURL, distanceXisURL]'_{i,t}$$
$$D(j,t) = [Pagerank_{author}, betweenness_{author}, Pagerank_{retweeter},$$
$$betweenness_{retweeter}]'_{j,t} + [relationship]_j$$
$$C(k,t) = [dayOfWeek, timeOfDay, age]'_{k,t}$$

Table 2. Hashtag popularity model at the dyad level

Variable	Pre-event	During-event	Post-event
$dyadFreq$	0.001***	0.002***	0.005***
$length$	-0.004***	-0.004***	-0.004***
$numWords$	-0.006***	0.002	0.017***
$length^2$	0.001***	0.001***	0.001***
$numWords^2$	0.001**	0.000	-0.005***
$tweetCount$	0.009***	0.046***	0.016***
$hasCaps$	0.013***	0.010***	0.029***
$hasDigits$	-0.028***	-0.027***	-0.039***
$hasOther$	0.005***	0.024***	0.029***
$appearedWithOthers$	0.008***	0.003***	0.001***
$tagAge$	-7.7E-05***	-7E-05***	-5.3E-05***
$tagFreq$	3.63E-05***	1.07E-05***	9.83E-06***
$distance$	-0.001***	-0.004***	-0.002***
$isURL$	0.085***	0.093***	0.104***
$distancesXisURL$	0.004***	0.012***	0.006***
$PageRank_{author}$	0.037	0.214	-0.672
$betweenness_{author}$	0.001E-10***	0.001E-10***	-3.01E-10***
$PageRank_{retweeter}$	0.317	-2.173***	-1736.72***
$betweenness_{retweeter}$	0.001E-09***	0.001E-09***	-1.21E-09***
$relationship$	0.772***	0.868***	0.911***

***$p < 0.01$, **$p < 0.05$, *$p < 0.1$

5   Data Analysis and Findings

The Great Eastern Japan earthquake dataset has been used to examine this phenomena. The dataset consists of 1.3 million observations with 521028 hashtags from 0.1 million users. The model investigates the effect of URLs in hashtag popularity at two levels - first at the hashtag level and second at the dyad (user-retweeter pair) level.

5.1   Data Preparation

Using the Twitter dataset, we found the hashtags from each tweet by simply searching words that start with "#". From the primary tweet dataset we prepared a dataset where each row contains the timestamp of the tweet, the list of hashtags in the tweet, author of the tweet, boolean variable indicating whether the tweet contains URLs. Our tweet dataset (5th-24th March) has been divided into three time windows, pre-earthquake ($5^{th} - 10^{th} March$), during-earthquake ($11^{th} - 16^{th} March$), and post-earthquake ($17^{th} - 24^{th} March$).

5.2   Data Analysis

We formed the retweet network from the tweets in our database, where the nodes represent the users and directed links represent the reverse of direction (retweeter $\rightarrow$ user) of information flow. Network variables such as PageRank, betweenness centrality are measured using the retweet network.

Besides network variables, hashtag contents have been analyzed. Since tweets are limited to 140 characters, each character in the tweet is very costly. Therefore, very long hashtags are not preferable. Moreover, long and complex hashtag increases the cognitive load and are not easy to understand [16,17]. For the same reason, the hashtag is analyzed and the number of words in the hashtag is counted. The intuition behind this is that number of words in a hashtag increases its clarity and the hashtag itself carries more contextual information about the tweet itself. If the words are separated by special characters or by capital letters it is easy to determine the words in the hashtag.

There tends to be more than one hashtag in a tweet. A preliminary analysis has shown that if a hashtag appears with others, popularity of the focal hashtag increases. Moreover, we included the distance among the co-appearing hashtags to examine the effect of distance on its popularity. Previous studies have experimented that inclusion of URLs and hashtags increase the chance of retweetability [4]. In this study, we have included the boolean variable for URL to examine its effect on similarity/dissimilarity of hashtags.

Next, we examine whether there is an effect of an event on popularity and Japan earthquake data is used for that reason. The effects of the variables are investigated in all the three time periods (pre-, during- and post-event time-windows) independently.

5.3   Findings and Discussion

To understand the effect of hashtag popularity at user level, we modeled retweet-ability of a hashtag for dyads, where each dyad consists of the user who tweeted and the one who is retweeted. The model is run with the hashtag and dyad specific variables along with the control variables as listed earlier. Retweet count (per hashtag per dyad) is considered as the dependent variable. We have divided the dataset into three different time-windows and regression technique has been used in all cases. Results for the three time-windows have been shown in Table 2. The findings show that dyad specific and hashtag specific variables considered in the model have significant impacts on retweet count. The dyad frequency have significant positive impact on retweet count per unit time, which suggests that the users retweet hashtags from Twitter users they usually retweet from. Moreover, in the Twitter world if the user and retweeter has follower-followee relationship, then retweet count of a hashtag increases opposed to retweet practices from non-follower/friend relationship.

It is also clear from our dataset that length does not have a significant impact on popularity, however, the number of words in a hashtag has inverse u-shaped impact. While the number of words has a positive impact on popularity, too many

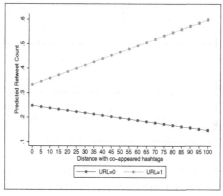

(a) Pre-event Time Window

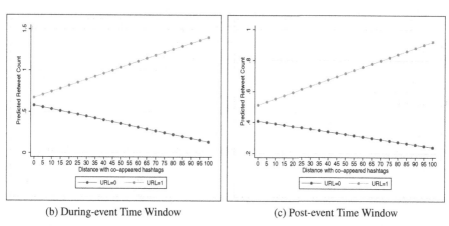

(b) During-event Time Window   (c) Post-event Time Window

Fig. 1. Interaction plot on distance and URLs in pre-, during-, and post-event window (dyad Level)

words in a hashtag have a negative impact. Intuitively, this is comprehensible as the number of words increases the clarity of hashtag at first, but as the number of words grows in abundant the hashtag becomes complex. Further, the presence of digits or capital letters in the hashtag has negative impact on popularity, but popular hashtags mostly contain other separators to segregate the words in hashtag phrases.

On the other hand, while hashtag frequency (for a specific dyad) has a positive impact, which suggests that user retweets tweet containing specific hashtags many times. Above all, we have examined the interaction effect of hashtag dissimilarity with presence of URLs and we receive similar impact as seen in model 1 at hashtag level.

Figure 1a plots the interaction effect of URLs on distance in the pre-event time-window at the dyad level.

It shows that when there is a URL in a tweet (along with a hashtag), the retweet count of that hashtag by a specific dyad is more compared to when there is no URLs in the tweet. In this case, when the distance among the co-appearing hashtags is higher, introduction of a URL results in higher retweet count, compared to when a URL appears with similar hashtags.

To determine if the patterns characterizing the significant interactions conform to the directions as proposed in the research hypotheses, we have plotted the interaction effects (Fig. 1a, b, and c) for all three time-windows. This procedure was introduced by [5] for all interaction cases. Figure 1a, b, and c show the disordinal (or crossover) interaction of URLs on the relationships of hashtag similarity with hashtag popularity. Figure 1b and Fig. 1c plot the interaction effect of URLs on similarity with retweetability of a hashtag at dyad level in the during-event and post-event windows respectively. Similar to hashtag level analysis, one can note that the retweet count at dyad level has similar result as in Fig. 1a. The appearance of URLs when the hashtags are similar has significantly less impact compared to when the hashtags are dissimilar.

Overall, we can see that the presence of URLs with similarity (or dissimilarity) of hashtags has significant impact at dyad level, which suggests that choice of hashtag is driven by individual metacognitive experiences.

6   Conclusion

Hashtag in a tweet starts with a # symbol and is used before a relevant keyword or phrase in a tweet, which facilitates to categorize the tweets into different topics. Consequently, it becomes convenient to search them in a Twitter search. However, in practice hashtags mostly come in groups, i.e., one can find more than one hashtag in a tweet. Are these co-appearing hashtags random or do they carry certain patterns? In this study, we have investigated the characteristics of the co-appearing hashtags. Findings show that the popularity of a hashtag increases when a hashtag appears with other hashtags. Moreover, the similarity / dissimilarity of the hashtags plays crucial role in hashtag popularity. Results indicate that when similar hashtags appear together the hashtag popularity increases as opposed to dissimilar hashtags. To our surprise when the dissimilar hashtags appear with a URL, then the effect is reversed. This phenomenon can be explained by the fact that when dissimilar items co-appear it increases the meta-cognitive load and introduces confusion, but with the provision of extra information (e.g., URL), this becomes surprising and interesting to users resulting adoption of those hashtags together. These findings can help to diffuse new hashtags by coupling with similar popular hashtags or adding the pinch of surprise with dissimilar hashtags and a URL. It also can help the practitioners implement efficient policy making for product advertisement with brand hashtags.

In this study we have analyzed how these effects change due to an event and observed that due to event the trend of the effect was the same. However, to generalize the effect of the event on this phenomenon, it will be interesting to investigate on a separate data set. We plan to investigate this in our future research.

References

1. Aral, S., Muchnik, L., Sundararajan, A.: Distinguishing influence-based contagion from homophily-driven diffusion in dynamic networks. Proc. Nat. Acad. Sci. **106**(51), 21544–21549 (2009)
2. Berger, J., Milkman, K.L.: What makes online content viral? J. Mark. Res. **49**(2), 192–205 (2012)
3. Berger, J., Milkman, K.: Social transmission, emotion, and the virality of online content. Wharton research paper (2010)
4. Boyd, D., Golder, S., Lotan, G.: Tweet, tweet, retweet: conversational aspects of retweeting on twitter. In: Proceedings of the 2010 43rd Hawaii International Conference on System Sciences, HICSS 2010, pp. 1–10. IEEE Computer Society, Washington, DC, USA (2010)
5. Cohen, J., Cohen, P., West, S., Aiken, L.: Applied Multiple Regression/Correlation Analysis for the Social Sciences. L. Erlbaum Associates, Hillsdale (1983)
6. Cooper, S.: Big mistake: making fun of hashtags instead of using them. October 2013. http://www.forbes.com/sites/stevecooper/2013/10/17/big-mistake-making-fun-of-hashtags-instead-of-using-them/. Accessed 2nd August 2014
7. Doctor, V.: What's the point of all these hashtags? December 2012. http://www.hashtags.org/platforms/twitter/whats-the-point-of-all-these-hashtags/. Accessed 2nd August 2014
8. Hathaway, J.: Now you can get a $3,000 "social media concierge" for your wedding, March 2014
9. Hughes, A., Palen, L.: Twitter adoption and use in mass convergence and emergency events. Int. J. Emerg. Manage. **6**(3), 248–260 (2009)
10. Ma, Z., Sun, A., Cong, G.: On predicting the popularity of newly emerging hashtags in twitter. J. Am. Soc. Inf. Sci. Technol. **64**(7), 1399–1410 (2013)
11. Pocheptsova, A., Labroo, A.A., Dhar, R.: Making products feel special: when metacognitive difficulty enhances evaluation. J. Mark. Res. **47**(6), 1059–1069 (2010)
12. Reber, R., Schwarz, N.: Effects of perceptual fluency on judgments of truth. Conscious. Cogn. **8**(3), 338–342 (1999)
13. Reber, R., Winkielman, P., Schwarz, N.: Effects of perceptual fluency on affective judgments. Psychol. Sci. **9**(1), 45–48 (1998)
14. Schwarz, N.: Metacognitive experiences in consumer judgment and decision making. J. Consum. Psychol. **14**(4), 332–348 (2004)
15. Shirley, T.: Why hashtags are so important. August 2014. http://www.thelasthurdle.co.uk/hashtags-important/. Accessed 2nd August 2014
16. Song, H., Schwarz, N.: If it's hard to read, it's hard to do processing fluency affects effort prediction and motivation. Psychol. Sci. **19**(10), 986–988 (2008)
17. Song, H., Schwarz, N.: If it's difficult to pronounce, it must be risky fluency, familiarity, and risk perception. Psychol. Sci. **20**(2), 135–138 (2009)
18. Suh, B., Hong, L., Pirolli, P., Chi, E.H.: Want to be retweeted? large scale analytics on factors impacting retweet in twitter network. In: Proceedings of the 2010 IEEE Second International Conference on Social Computing, SOCIALCOM 2010, pp. 177–184. IEEE Computer Society, Washington, DC, USA (2010)
19. Sweeney, D.: Can you legally own a twitter hashtag? March 2012. http://www.socialmediatoday.com/content/can-you-legally-own-twitter-hashtag. Accessed 2nd August 2014

20. Toriumi, F., Sakaki, T., Shinoda, K., Kazama, K., Kurihara, S., Noda, I.: Information sharing on twitter during the 2011 catastrophic earthquake. In: Proceedings of the 22nd International Conference on World Wide Web companion, WWW 2013 Companion, pp. 1025–1028. International World Wide Web Conferences Steering Committee, Republic and Canton of Geneva, Switzerland (2013)
21. Tsur, O., Rappoport, A.: What's in a hashtag?: content based prediction of the spread of ideas in microblogging communities. In: Proceedings of the Fifth ACM International Conference on Web Search and Data Mining, WSDM 2012, pp. 643–652. ACM, New York, NY, USA (2012). http://doi.acm.org/10.1145/2124295.2124320
22. TweetSmarter: The ultimate guide to finding the best time to tweet (2011). http://blog.tweetsmarter.com/retweeting/when-is-the-best-time-to-tweet/
23. Weng, L., Flammini, A., Vespignani, A., Menczer, F.: Competition among memes in a world with limited attention. Scientific reports 2 (2012)
24. Wikipedia: Levenshtein distance, July 2014
25. Wojnicki, A.C., Godes, D.: Word-of-mouth as self-enhancement. HBS marketing research paper (2008)
26. Yang, L., Sun, T., Zhang, M., Mei, Q.: We know what@ you# tag: does the dual role affect hashtag adoption? In: Proceedings of the 21st International Conference on World Wide Web. pp. 261–270. ACM (2012)

Individual and Group Behaviour in Social Media

It's Not About the Risks, I'm just Used to Doing It: Disclosure of Personal Information on Facebook Among Adolescent Dutch Users

Ardion D. Beldad[✉] and Ruud Koehorst

Department of Corporate and Marketing Communication,
University of Twente, Enschede, The Netherlands
a.d.beldad@utwente.nl

Abstract. A paper-based survey was conducted with 560 students of a high school in the eastern part of the Netherlands to determine the factors influencing their personal information disclosure behavior on Facebook. Results of the path analysis reveal that habits and perceived control strongly predict information disclosure of research respondents. Furthermore, information-related benefits also contribute to disclosure among adolescent Dutch Facebook users. Moreover, perceived control positively influences respondents' trust (in Facebook and in their network members).

Keywords: Personal information disclosure · Habit · Perceived control · Trust

1 Introduction

Reports from the Office for National Statistics (ONS) in the UK and from the Eurostat indicated that the Netherlands, alongside the United Kingdom and Sweden, topped the list of countries with the highest proportion of social network users in Europe [46]. It has also reported that 65 % of the Dutch population are using either Facebook or Twitter, or even both. The Dutch Centraal Bureau voor de Statistiek [7] reported that in 2012, over 80 % of people between the ages of 12 and 18 were active users of either Facebook or Twitter or both. Since adolescents are significantly present in online social networking (OSN) sites, the quantity of personal information they share on those sites can also be enormous, as they, according to Christofides, Muise, and Desmarais [10], tend to share more information than adult OSN site users.

Active participation in OSN sites, through identity creation and management and social conversation engagement, according to a number of researchers [9, 31], requires users to constantly share various types of information such as photos, updates of their activities, and their thoughts on issues and things. In Beldad, De Jong, and Steehouder's [3] framework for personal information-related behaviors on the Internet, it is proposed that people's willingness to share personal information is predicated on several factors such as trust, benefits, habits, and context relevance.

Previous studies into information disclosure on Facebook have indicated that the benefits that can be derived from information sharing (e.g. self-presentation,

© Springer International Publishing Switzerland 2015
G. Meiselwitz (Ed.): SCSM 2015, LNCS 9182, pp. 185–195, 2015.
DOI: 10.1007/978-3-319-20367-6_19

maintenance of social ties) [23] can increase disclosure, while perceived risks can result in people's disinclination to share information [12]. What remains unknown, however, is the exact nature of the relationship between factors such as habits and perceived control and the disclosure of various types of personal information on OSN sites. Furthermore, while researchers [9, 23] have investigated the determinants of information disclosure among young adults, there is still less attention to the mechanisms behind information sharing among adolescent users of an OSN site. These are the two gaps that the study aimed at addressing.

2   Determinants of Information Disclosure on Facebook

2.1   Benefits

People's decision to join online social networking (OSN) sites, such as Facebook and Flickr, is often predicated on several considerations such as communication and relationship maintenance [17, 23, 25, 34], relationship building [23], and personal information publication [25, 42]. Additionally, OSN sites also enable users to actively participate in civil and political activities [41]. In this study, the benefits of disclosing personal information on OSN sites are categorized into two, namely, information-related (e.g. transmission of information about one's daily activities and thoughts on things) and impression management-related (e.g. posting information to shape other people's view of the person posting).

Previous studies have shown that these benefits lower OSN site users' resistance to the idea of sharing complete and correct personal information [6, 23], since information withholding and fabrication reduce users' ability to engage in online self-presentation and communication with multiple individuals [10]. This prompts the first set of research hypotheses.

H1 : The perceived (a) information-related and (b) impression management-related benefits of disclosing personal information on Facebook positively influence personal information disclosure among adolescent Dutch users.

2.2   Trust

Personal information disclosed online is susceptible to abuse. In the context of OSN site use, disclosed personal information could be exploited not only by the OSN site but also by members of the network of the one disclosing and third parties such as commercial organizations [1, 22]. These risks necessitate the cultivation of trust, as trust is relevant only when actions could be pursued without any certainty [24]. Mayer, Davis, and Schoorman [27] define trust as 'the willingness of a party to be vulnerable to the actions of another party based on the expectation that the other will perform a particular action important to the trustor, irrespective of the ability to monitor or control that other party' (p. 712).

The impact of trust in the party receiving personal information has been reported to significantly influence information disclosure in various online transactions, such as e-government [5] and e-commerce [14, 28]. It is also likely that the level of trust OSN site users have in Facebook and in their network members, two primary recipients of shared information, could also influence users' personal information sharing behavior. This supposition results in the second hypothesis.

H2 : The levels of trust adolescent Dutch Facebook users have in (a) Facebook and in their (b) social network members positively influence their personal information disclosure behavior.

The negative relationship between trust and risk perception is well-established in the literature. Previous studies have shown that people's level of trust lowers their sensitivity to risk considerations [18] and reduces their perceptions of the risks of engaging in an exchange with the trusted party [2, 4, 20]. This leads to the third research hypothesis.

H3 : Adolescent Dutch Facebook users' levels of trust in Facebook and in their social network members negatively influence their perception of the risks of disclosing personal information to (a) Facebook and to their (b) social network members, respectively.

2.3 Perceived Control

Central to the definition of privacy is the concept of control [29, 39] – that is, control over who should have access to one's personal information though the creation of a 'privacy zone' [40]. The notion of control in relation to Facebook use is realized through the platform's effort to extend the needed technical possibility for users to define who would have access to their disclosed information, in the form of privacy settings. As people believe that they own their personal information [33], they are less likely to hesitate sharing their information if they know that they can decide how much information to make accessible to whom. The next research hypothesis is predicated on this assertion.

H4 : Perception of control among adolescent Dutch Facebook users positively influences their personal information disclosure behavior.

Managing one's information privacy in OSN use context is possible when OSN sites provide their users with the possibility to define who should have access to their information through technical means such as privacy settings [45]. This perception of control has been noted to influence OSN users' perceptions of control [38], just as this perception, through available privacy management tools, could trigger users' trust in their network members [23]. On the contrary, when users do not feel that they have control over their personal information, they will most likely assume that disclosing personal information is a risky enterprise [11]. Based on these results, hypotheses 5 and 6 are advanced.

H5 : Perception of control among adolescent Dutch Facebook users positively influences their trust in (a) Facebook and in their (b) social network members.

H6 : Perception of control among adolescent Dutch Facebook users negatively influences their perception of the risks of disclosing personal information to (a) Facebook and to their (b) social network members.

2.4 Habit

Thus far, the first three described predictors of information disclosure on Facebook are primarily tied to the rational mechanism behind the decision to share information. What remains unclear and unknown, however, is the extent to which a non-rational predictor, such as habit, contributes to information disclosure. The shortage in studies that consider habit as a determinant of any OSN use-related behavior prompted Cheung and Lee [8] to suggest the inclusion of habit in models intending to capture the performance of an OSN site-related behavior.

The assumption that information disclosure is not always anchored on a rational ground is based on the finding that despite people's preference to keep their information private they still opt to share those information not only for the benefits derived from sharing but also for the 'taste' of disclosure [36]. Additionally, Strater and Richter [37] reported that people tend not to be very sure about the reasons why they share information online, with some indicating that they have been so used to completing online forms that they do not think twice anymore when supplying the information requested by an online organization. These findings somehow trigger the premise that people's decision to share personal information might also be hinged on habits. Thus, the seventh hypothesis is advanced.

H7 : The habit of sharing information positively influences adolescent Dutch Facebook users' personal information disclosure behavior.

3   Deterrent of Information Disclosure on Facebook

3.1   Risk Perception

As previously mentioned, the risks associated with the decision to share personal information to an OSN site are copious. In her book 'I Know Who You Are and I Saw What You Did: Social Networking and the Death of Privacy', Andrews [1] argues that users of online social network sites have confronted different problems of varying levels of severity as a consequence of information disclosure on such sites.

Considering the complexity in studying risk as an objective reality, researchers advanced that 'perceived risk' should be the appropriate object of investigation [32, 44]. Pavlou [32, p. 109], citing Bauer, defines risk perception as the 'subjective belief of suffering a loss in pursuit of a desired outcome'. Risk perception certainly matters since the degree of such a perception (whether high or low) predicts the extent to which an individual will perform a certain behavior [13]. In online exchanges, the perceived risks of disclosing personal information have been found to lower people's decision to share personal information to an online entity [14, 26, 30]. One can also expect that beliefs in the riskiness of sharing information to an OSN site might lower Facebook users' levels of personal information disclosure. The last research hypotheses are hinged on these findings.

H8 : The perceived risks of sharing information online attributed to the actions of (a) Facebook and (b) users' network members negatively influence adolescent Dutch Facebook users' personal information disclosure behavior.

4   Method

4.1   Sampling and Respondents

To test the research hypotheses, a paper-based survey was implemented with students of a high school in the eastern part of the Netherlands. The school offers several levels of education either to prepare students for practical training or for university education. During the implementation of the survey, approximately 1,300 students, between the age of 12 and 18, were enrolled in the school. Official approval from the school administration was acquired which made the wide scale distribution of questionnaires to target respondents possible.

With the help of some teachers, 921 students were approached to complete the questionnaire for a two-week period. Questionnaires from 66 students were eventually excluded from the dataset as they were not completed. As the study was primarily focused on students who were using Facebook at the time of the survey, questionnaires from 225 respondents who did not have Facebook accounts and from 70 students who stopped using Facebook were also removed. The two-phase exclusion of some respondent data resulted in 560 completed questionnaires that were used for statistical analysis.

Of the 560 respondents whose questionnaires were subjected to analysis, 305 (54.5 %) were females. Respondents' age ranged from 12 to 17, with a mean age of 14.43 (SD = 1.34). This age range signifies that all respondents were all adolescents – the target group for this research.

4.2   Measurements

The dependent variable 'personal information disclosure' was operationalized as the frequency of posting various types of personal information such as updates of activities, opinions, likes, and photos. Five newly formulated items were used to measure the construct. Examples of items to measure the dependent variable included 'I often share my opinion on Facebook' and 'I often share photos I am in on Facebook'.

The 'benefits' construct was split into two sub-constructs: information-related benefits (e.g. using Facebook to communicate with friends) and impression management-related benefits (e.g. using Facebook to increase one's popularity). Items used to measure the two sub-constructs were derived from the scales of Ellison et al. [16] and Krasnova et al. [23]. The second predictor 'trust' was also split into two: trust in Facebook (e.g. 'I trust that Facebook has the expertise in protecting my information'.) and trust in network members (e.g. 'I trust that my Facebook friends will not jeopardize my personal information'). Items from the trust scale of Krasnova et al. [23] inspired the formulation of items used to measure both trust constructs.

'Perceived control' was measured with four items partly based on the scale of Krasnova et al. [23]. Examples of items used to measure the construct included 'With the privacy settings, I can determine who can see my personal information' and 'I keep control over information I share on Facebook'. 'Habit' was measured with four items based on the scale by Verplanken and Orbell [43]. A typical example of an item to measure the construct is 'I share information without thinking about it'. All items were measured on a five-point Likert scale with 5 representing 'strongly agree' and 1 'strongly disagree'.

To see whether the statements selected for the constructs really measured those constructs, confirmatory factor analysis using SPSS was executed. Results of the principal component analysis (PCA) using the 29 items selected for the constructs revealed that the correlations among those items were sufficiently high for PCA, as indicated by

Table 1. Reliability scores and mean and standard deviation values of the different research constructs after PCA

Constructs	No. of items	α	Mean	SD
Personal information disclosure	5	.82	2.73	.93
Information-related benefits	3	.68	3.22	.85
Impression management-related benefits	2	.77	2.04	.98
Trust in Facebook and in network members	7	.84	3.66	.73
Perceived control	4	.75	4.02	.84
Habits	4	.74	2.18	.82
Perception of risks attributed to the actions of Facebook and those of network members	6	.83	2.22	.77

a Kaiser-Meyer Olkin Measure Sampling of Adequacy value of. 82 (higher than the recommended value of .60) and the Bartlett's Test of Sphericity value of X^2 $(435) = 6,275.44$, $p < .001$.

Furthermore, results of PCA indicated that the items measuring 'information disclosure behavior', 'information-related benefits', 'impression management-related benefits', 'perceived control', and 'habits' really loaded into the respective constructs they were supposed to measure. The items measuring 'trust in Facebook' and 'trust in network members' loaded into one factor resulting in the merging of these items into a single construct (trust). A similar thing happened to the items measuring 'perceived risks attributed to the actions of Facebook' and 'perceived risks attributed to actions of network members'. These items were also merged into one construct (perception of risks). These decisions led to the reformulation of hypotheses 2, 3, 5, 6, and 8 (from two sub-hypotheses to just one). Table 1 presents the Cronbach's alpha scores, mean and standard deviation values for the new constructs after PCA.

5 Results

Path analysis using AMOS 19.0 was performed to determine the significant predictors of personal information disclosure on Facebook and to test the hypothesized relationship among perceived control, trust, and risk perception. To assess the fit of the model, the following indices proposed by Kline [21] were used: model chi-square, comparative fit index (CFI), standardized root mean square (SRMR), and root mean square error of approximation (RMSEA). A model with a good fit has a CFI value > .95 and SRMR < . 08 [19] and RMSEA < .07 [35]. Test of the original model indicated that it has a poor fit: $X^2(12) = 195.39$, $X^2/df = 16.28$, CFI = .60, SRMR = .09, RMSEA = .17.

Inspection of the modification indices revealed that fit could be improved by correlating the construct 'habit' with 'information-related benefits' and 'impression management-related benefits' and by correlating the two benefit constructs. The modification resulted in an improved fit, though still unacceptable: $X^2(9) = 77.69$, $X^2/df = 8.63$, CFI = .85, SRMR = .06, RMSEA = .12. Analysis shows that personal information disclosure on Facebook among adolescent Dutch users is positively influenced by 'habit' ($\beta = .33$, p < .001), 'perceived control' ($\beta = .32$, p < .001), and 'information-related benefits' ($\beta = .18$, p < .001), Hypotheses 7, 4, and 1a are therefore, supported; while hypotheses 1b, 2, and 8 are not.

Additionally, 'trust' negatively influences 'risk perception' ($\beta = -.30$, p < .001), while 'perceived control' positively influences 'trust' ($\beta = .30$, p < .001). 'Perceived control', however, does not negatively influence 'risk perception'. Hence, hypotheses 3 and 5 are also supported, while hypothesis 6 not. Moreover, 'habit' positively correlates with 'information-related benefits' ($\beta = .17$) and 'impression management-related benefits' ($\beta = .25$), while the two benefit constructs also positively correlate with each other ($\beta = .24$).

As the results indicate that only the positive determinants (habit, perceived control, and information-related benefits) and not the negative determinant (risk perception) have statistically significant effect on the dependent variable of interest, the model was further modified by removing the 'risk perception' construct to see whether or not its fit would improve. The removal of that construct in the model resulted in a substantially good fit: $X^2(6) = 22.37$, $X^2/df = 3.73$, CFI = .96, SRMR = .03, RMSEA = .07.

This final model shows that information disclosure is still positively influenced by 'habit' ($\beta = .33$, p < .001), 'perceived control' ($\beta = .32$, p < .001), and 'information-related benefits' ($\beta = .18$, p < .001). 'Perceived control' still positively influences 'trust' ($\beta = .30$, p < .001). Moreover, the correlations between 'habit' and the two benefit construct ($\beta = .17$ for information and $\beta = .25$ for impression management) and between information- and impression management-related benefits ($\beta = .24$) are still significant. Finally, even with the removal of 'risk perception' in the model, the effect of 'trust' on personal information disclosure remains statistically insignificant.

6   Discussion and Future Research Directions

As underscored in the introduction, approximately 80 % of the total number of individuals aged 12 to 18 in Netherlands are active users of Facebook, with 93 % of people in that age category active in other social media platforms [7]. With this massive number of active OSN site users, one can only wonder at the amount of personal information that is somehow made public through Facebook. Despite what has been known about the negative consequences of information disclosure on OSN sites such as Facebook, however, sharing and posting various types of personal information on such sites are unlikely to go downhill in the next few years. This study investigated the determinants and the deterrent of personal information disclosure on Facebook among adolescent Dutch users.

Attention to 'habits' as a predictor of personal information disclosure has not been very high in previous studies, which tended to take a more rational view on the mechanism behind people's information disclosure behavior. From a highly rational standpoint, personal disclosure on OSN sites is believed to be influenced by factors such as trust [10] and the benefits offered by disclosure [23]. It has been known, however, that some people are so used to completing online forms that they do not think twice anymore whenever they are asked to supply personal information in a totally different situation [37].

Results of this study reveal that 'habit' strongly predicts the personal information disclosure behavior of adolescent Dutch FB users. Nonetheless, the finding that respondents' perception of control over their personal information also determines information disclosure seems to suggest that respondents do not just habitually and blindly share information without taking into account the possible negative consequences of disclosure. The fact that both 'habit' and 'perceived control' contribute to disclosure on Facebook implies that although respondents may have been accustomed to sharing personal online, this decision to share is also governed by a consideration of the degree of control they have over their information.

Information-related benefits, such as transmitting information to network members, are also statistically significant predictors of information disclosure. What is surprising, however, is the statistically insignificant effect of impression management-related benefits on disclosure, considering that adolescents are claimed to have a strong propensity to present themselves to their social networks as a way to affirm their emerging identities [15]. These results somehow echo the findings of Krasnova et al.'s [23] study – that while relationship building through information exchange prompts the decision to share information, self-presentation is not a relevant determinant of that decision at all.

The seeming irrelevance of impression management-related benefits in triggering personal information disclosure could be attributed to respondents' low valuation of these benefits. This is evidenced by the low mean value of the aforementioned construct. An implication, hence, is that when adolescent Dutch Facebook users post information on their profiles, the action is motivated primarily by the need to maintain offline connections in an online environment and not by the need to be popular or be positively viewed by others.

The effect of trust on disclosure is also statistically insignificant. Trust, as a construct in this study, has a relatively complex nature. Initially it was surmised that Facebook users' trust could be measured in relation to two trust targets – Facebook and members of the user's network. Results of factor analysis, however, indicated that the items measuring 'trust in Facebook' and 'trust in network members' do not measure two different constructs but just one single construct. This suggests that respondents had difficulty distinguishing the two trust targets from each other.

Discussion of the impact of trust on information disclosure must be done in relation to the effect of risk perception. The negative effect of risk perception on information disclosure is not statistically supported. On the contrary, the negative relationship between trust and risk perception has been found to be statistically significant – a result very much similar to what previous studies [2, 4, 20] have indicated. While respondents expressed high trust in both FB and in their network members, the relevance of trust as a predictor of information disclosure might have been reduced by respondents' low levels of risk perception.

Respondents' high levels of trust and low levels of risk perception could be partly explained by how much control they believe to have over their personal information. When people are convinced of their ability to manage their information, their trust in the parties receiving the information might increase, which also reduces their perception of the risks of disclosing information.

The research described in this paper provides a starting point for understanding the relationship between habits and personal information disclosure, as the impact of the former on the latter is not yet fully understood. When looking at the possible relationship between these two constructs, one could focus on the interaction of habit with the individual's age as a determinant of disclosure. Furthermore, future research could also investigate the extent to which the habit of information disclosure might be determined by information type. It is highly likely that some people are habitual disclosers of photos but not of their views and thoughts on issues and things.

Research into the impact of online network size is something that has not yet received substantial research attention. A study by Young and Quan-Haase [48] reported that the amount of personal information disclosed on OSN sites depends on the sharer's network size. Despite this finding, however, it remains unknown whether or not the proportion of network members with whom OSN users share strong ties contributes to their decision to post certain types of personal information on Facebook.

While people share personal information on OSN sites for the many benefits that can be derived from disclosure, OSN researchers are still to understand the link between various types of disclosure benefits and the types of information to disclose. It is imaginable that entertainment- or enjoyment-related benefits could shape OSN site users decision to post photos on Facebook but not the decision to post their views on political matters. Further still, impression management-related benefits might prompt OSN site users to post their daily activities but not their frustration with the services of a certain telephone company.

References

1. Andrews, L.: I Know Who You Are and I Saw What You Did: Social Networks and the Death of Privacy. Free Press, New York (2012)
2. Belanger, F., Carter, L.: Trust and risk in e-government adoption. J. Strateg. Inf. Syst. **17**(2), 165–176 (2008)
3. Beldad, A., De Jong, M., Steehouder, M.: A comprehensive theoretical framework for personal information-related behaviors on the internet. Inf. Soc. **27**, 220–232 (2011)
4. Beldad, A., De Jong, M., Steehouder, M.: I trust not therefore it must be risky: determinants of the perceived risks of disclosing personal data for e-government transactions. Comput. Hum. Behav. **27**, 2233–2242 (2011)
5. Beldad, A., Van Der Geest, T., De Jong, M., Steehouder, M.: Shall I tell you where I live and who I am? Factors influencing the behavioral intention to disclose personal data for online government transactions. Int. J. Hum. Comput. Inter. **28**(3), 163–177 (2012)
6. Brandtzaeg, P.B., Lüdersa, M., Skjetnea, J.H.: Too many Facebook "friends"? Content sharing and sociability versus the need for privacy in social network sites. Int. J. Hum. Comput. Inter. **26**(11–12), 1006–1030 (2010)

7. Central Bureau voor Statistiek: Zeven op de tien gebruiken sociale media (Seven in ten internet users active on social media) (2013). http://www.cbs.nl/nl-NL/menu/themas/vrije-tijd-cultuur/publicaties/artikelen/archief/2013/2013–3907-wm.htm. Accessed 29 January 2015

8. Cheung, C.M.K., Lee, M.K.O.: A theoretical model of intentional social action in online social networks. Decis. Support Syst. **49**(1), 24–30 (2010)

9. Christofides, E., Muise, A., Desmarais, S.: Information disclosure and control on Facebook: are they two sides of the same coin or two different processes. CyberPsychology Behav. **12**(3), 341–345 (2009)

10. Christofides, E., Muise, A., Desmarais, S.: Hey mom, what's on your Facebook? Comparing Facebook disclosure and privacy in adolescents and adults. Soc. Psychol. and Pers. Sci. **3**(1), 48–54 (2012)

11. Culnan, M.J., Armstrong, P.K.: Information privacy concerns, procedural fairness, and impersonal trust: an empirical investigation. Organ. Sci. **10**(1), 104–115 (1999)

12. Davis, K., James, C.: Tween's conceptions of privacy online: implications for educators. Learn. Media Technol. **38**, 4–25 (2012)

13. Das, T.K., Teng, B.S.: The risk-based view of trust: a conceptual framework. J. Bus. Psychol. **19**(1), 85–116 (2004)

14. Dinev, T., Hart, P.: An extended privacy calculus model for ecommerce transactions. Inf. Syst. Res. **17**, 61–80 (2006)

15. Elliott, G.C.: Self-esteem and self-presentation among the young as a function of age and gender. J. Youth Adolesc. **11**(2), 135–153 (1982)

16. Ellison, N.B., Heino, R., Gibbs, J.: Managing impressions online: self-presentation processes in the online dating environment. J. Comput. Mediated Commun. **11**(2), 415–441 (2006)

17. Ellison, N.B., Steinfield, C., Lampe, C.: The benefits of Facebook 'friends': Social capital and college students' use of online social network sites. J. Comput. Mediated Commun. **12**(article1) (2007). http://jcmc.indiana.edu/vol12/issue4/ellison.html

18. Grazioli, S., Jarvenpaa, S.L.: Perils of internet fraud: an empirical investigation of deception and trust with experienced internet consumers. IEEE Trans. Syst. Man, Cybern. – Part A: Syst. Hum. **30**(4), 395–410 (2000)

19. Hu, L., Bentler, P.M.: Cutoff criteria for fit indexes in covariance structure analysis: conventional criteria versus new alternatives. Struct. Equ. Model. **6**, 1–55 (1999)

20. Kim, D.J., Ferrin, D.L., Rao, H.R.: A trust-based consumer decision-making model in electronic commerce: the role of trust, perceived risk, and their antecedents. Decis. Support Syst. **44**(2), 544–564 (2008)

21. Kline, R.B.: Principles and Practice of Structural Equation Modeling, 2nd edn. The Guilford Press, New York (2005)

22. Krasnova, H., Günther, O., Spiekermann, S., Koroleva, K.: Privacy concerns and identity in online social networks. IDIS **2**, 39–63 (2009)

23. Krasnova, H., Spiekermann, S., Koroleva, K., Hildebrand, T.: Online social networks: why we disclose. J. Inf. Tech. **25**, 109–125 (2010)

24. Lewis, J.D., Weigert, A.: Trust as a social reality. Soc. Forces **63**(4), 967–985 (1985)

25. Livingstone, S.: Taking risky opportunities in youthful content creation: teenagers' use of social networking sites for intimacy, privacy and self-expression. New Media Soc. **10**, 393–411 (2008)

26. Malhotra, N.K., Kim, S.S., Agarwal, J.: Internet users' information privacy concerns (IUIPC): the construct, the scale, and a causal model. Inf. Syst. Res. **15**, 336–355 (2004)

27. Mayer, R.C., Davis, J.H., Schoorman, F.D.: An integrative model of organization trust. Acad. Manag. Rev. **20**(3), 709–734 (1995)

28. Meztger, M.J.: Privacy, trust, and disclosure: Exploring barriers to electronic commerce. J. Comput. Mediated Commun. **9**(4) (2004). http://jcmc.indiana.edu/vol9/issue4/metzger.html
29. Moor, J.H.: Towards a theory of privacy in the information age. Comput. Soc. **27**(3), 27–32 (1997)
30. Norberg, P.A., Horne, D.R., Horne, D.A.: The privacy paradox: personal information disclosure intentions versus behaviors. J. Consum. Aff. **41**, 100–126 (2004)
31. Nosko, A., Wood, E., Molema, S.: All about me: disclosure in online social networking profiles: the case of Facebook. Comput. Hum. Behav. **26**, 406–418 (2010)
32. Pavlou, P.: Consumer acceptance of electronic commerce: integrating trust and risk with the technology acceptance model. Int. J. Electron. Commer. **17**(3), 101–134 (2003)
33. Petronio, S.: Boundaries of Privacy: Dialectics of Disclosure. State University of New York Press, Albany (2002)
34. Raacke, J., Raacke, J.B.: MySpace and Facebook: applying the uses and gratifications theory to exploring friend-networking sites. CyberPsychology Behav. **11**, 169–174 (2008)
35. Steiger, J.H.: Understanding the limitations of global fit assessment in structural equation modeling. Pers. Individ. Differ. **42**, 893–898 (2007)
36. Strandburg, K.J.: Social norms self-control, and privacy in the online world. In: Strandburg, K.J., Raicu, D.S. (eds.) Privacy and Technologies of Identity: A Cross-Disciplinary Conversation, pp. 31–53. Springer Science, New York (2006)
37. Strater, K., Richter, H.: Examining privacy and disclosure in a social networking community. In: ACM International Conference Proceeding Series – Proceedings of the 3rd Symposium on Usable Privacy and Security 229, pp. 157– 158 (2007)
38. Taddei, S., Contena, B.: Privacy, trust, and control: which relationships with online self-disclosure. Comput. Hum. Behav. **29**(3), 821–826 (2013)
39. Tavani, H.T.: Philosophical theories of privacy: implications for an adequate online privacy policy. Metaphilosophy **38**(1), 1–22 (2007)
40. Tavani, H.T.: Informational privacy: concepts, theories, and controversies. In: Himma, K.E., Tavani, H.T. (eds.) The Handbook of Information and Computer ethics, pp. 131–164. Wiley Interscience, Hoboken (2008)
41. Valenzuela, S., Park, N., Kee, K.F.: Is there social capital in a social network site? Facebook use an college students' life satisfaction, trust, and participation. J. Comput. Mediated Commun. **14**, 875–901 (2009)
42. Vandoninck, S., d'Haenens, L., De Cock, R., Donoso, V.: Social networking sites and contact risks among Flemish youth. Childhood **19**, 69–85 (2011)
43. Verplanken, B., Orbell, S.: Reflections on past behavior: a self-report index of habit strength. J. Appl. Soc. Psychol. **33**(6), 1313–1330 (2003)
44. Warkentin, M., Gefen, D., Pavlou, P.A., Rose, G.M.: Encouraging citizen adoption of e-government by building trust. Electron. Markets **12**(3), 157–162 (2002)
45. Waters, S., Ackerman, J.: Exploring privacy management on Facebook: motivations and perceived consequences of voluntary disclosure. J. Comput. Mediated Commun. **17**(1), 101–115 (2011)
46. Woollaston, V.: The meteoric rise of social networking in the UK: britons are the second most prolific Facebook and Twitter users in Europe with a fifth of over 65 s now using these sites (2013). http://www.dailymail.co.uk/sciencetech/article-2340893/Britons-second-prolific-Facebook-Twitter-users-EUROPE-fifth-aged-65.html
47. Young, A.L., Quan-Haase, A.: Information revelation and internet privacy concerns on social network sites: a case study of Facebook. In: Proceedings of the International Conference on Communities and Technologies, pp. 265–274 (2009)

Interaction Study of Shuriken: User Grouping and Data Transfer Based on Inter-device Relative Positioning

Jonathan Chung[1,2(✉)] and Adiyan Mujibiya[1]

[1] Rakuten Institute of Technology, Rakuten Inc, Tokyo, Japan
jono.chung@mail.utoronto.ca, adiyan@acm.org
[2] Department of Electrical and Computer Engineering, University of Toronto,
Toronto, Canada

Abstract. We present Shuriken, a method for user grouping and data transfer for smart devices that are in close proximity. Users point their devices towards each other to link them into a group (point to link). The relative positions are estimated between the grouped devices (link to group) with Bluetooth low energy received signal strength indication and the digital compass readings. The relative positions are then used for identifying the recipients for data transfer by swiping towards the physical direction (swipe to send). In this paper, we studied the possible operations to enable: point to link, link to group and swipe to send and compared Shuriken to existing techniques for user grouping and data transfer. We envision practical uses of Shuriken in collaborative shopping in a café, data transfer in business meetings and localisation of smart devices.

1 Introduction

The affordance of smart mobile devices has made it an essential method of group communication. Messaging applications, such as WhatsApp, Line and WeChat, provide group-messaging services through an Internet connection that is designed for remote users. These applications extend their messaging services to allow transferring other forms of data. However, in order to preserve the affordance of the application, there is generally no strong distinction between transferring data and transferring messages. Due to the practicalities of using these applications, users often use these methods to transfer data even when they are in close proximity.

In close proximity, users can communication verbally while their smart devices are used to transfer data that cannot be easily described in words (e.g., images, shopping catalogues). In a scenario where a group of friends are browsing shopping catalogues in close proximity, the users have many more options to share their catalogues with a group other than through messaging services.

Infrared was a method of data transfer between devices. In order to identify your target, the users to physically point the phones together throughout the course of data transfer. However, the iPhone 3 did not ship with inherit infrared transceivers that may have caused the phase out using infrared for data transfer in smart devices. Infrared requires the user of the sending device to consistent point towards the receiving device. This method of

© Springer International Publishing Switzerland 2015
G. Meiselwitz (Ed.): SCSM 2015, LNCS 9182, pp. 196–206, 2015.
DOI: 10.1007/978-3-319-20367-6_20

identification is simple and intuitive, however, this physically limits the possibilities for user grouping and is inconvenient especially when the data transfer rate is slow.

Bluetooth technology has experienced a significant growth in the last 20 years. Prior to Bluetooth v2.0, the device designated as "master" searches for "slave" device and a relationship is established only when both devices have entered the same PIN. After Bluetooth v2.1, many other methods of pairing, such as passkey entry (instead of a PIN) and out of band pairing methods emerged. A popular method for out of band pairing is NFC however, the physical constraints NFC also limits the capabilities of user grouping.

Similar to Bluetooth, WIFI direct allows data transfer in the absence of an Internet connection. AirDrop (developed by Apple Inc.) incorporates Bluetooth Low Energy (BLE, Bluetooth v4.0) to discover devices and WIFI direct to send the data.[1] AirDrop provides an ad hoc data transfer mechanism for users in close proximity. However, the interactions of using AirDrop do not differ from typical messaging services where users select recipients of data transfer through a list of usernames.

We present Shuriken, an intuitive method to create a group of devices in an ad hoc network and to identify recipients for data transfer. Users point their devices together to create a linkage between devices and linked devices are placed in the same group. The locations of the devices within a group are used to identify recipient of data (based upon methods of passing tangible media). Shuriken is built upon the BLE framework to create an ad hoc network and uses the BLE RSSI and digital compass readings to estimate the relative positions of the devices.

In this paper, we studied the operations for Shuriken to enable: point to link, link to group and swipe to send. In addition, the usage of Shuriken was compared to existing methods to group and transfer data between devices.

2 Related Work

Although Airdrop provides a simple medium to transfer data, the uses of usernames may be unintuitive for data transfer. In this section, we describe methods presented in the literature focusing on intuitive pairing solutions and intention based grouping.

2.1 Intuitive Pairing Solution

Intuitive pairing solution focuses on identifying recipients for data transfer in a simple yet secure manner.

Memory stones [1] describe a method where users imagine that they pick up a stone and place it to the device to be sent to. The central server records the touch positions during pick up and send it to the device that received the same touch positions. This method was designed for copy and pasting between devices in a network. For example, data can be copied from smart phones to tablets or from smart phones to printers. Memory stones provides an interesting and intuitive method to identify recipients of data. However, touch positions will be required in both the sending and receiving device, deeming Memory stones ineffective for multiple users.

---

[1] http://ipad.about.com/od/iPad_Guide/ss/What-Is-Airdrop-How-Does-It-Work.htm.

Bump [2] describes a method that requires two devices to be physically "bumped" together to share contact information. The time and positions are estimated and used to determine if two users are intending to share information. Specifically, to establish a connection, a "bump valid" signal from both devices must be received in the central server at approximately the same time from approximately the same location (e.g., from the same wireless network or within a predetermined distance estimated by RSSI). Bump provides a method to intuitively initiate and accept a connection for data transfer. However, Bump uses location to confirm connections that will be inaccurate when multiple users are in close proximity.

2.2   Intention Based Grouping

Intention based grouping systems extends intuitive pairing solutions to allow multiple devices to connect.

Point and Connect [3] describes a method where users physically point towards the recipient of the data. This system only uses ultrasound (i.e., speakers and microphone) therefore the system functions even in the absence of a central server. Ultrasound is used to determine the change in the relative positions of the devices while the user points their phone towards the target recipient of the data (causes a displacement towards the recipient). Point and Connect provides an intuitive method to group devices and to identify the recipients for data.

Airlink [4] uses in-air gestures to direct data transfer from sender to recipient. The Doppler-shifted reflections of ultrasound are measured to estimate the relative positions of the devices. Furthermore, the relative positions are used identify the sender and recipient of data.

3   Design Guidelines

Shuriken must be a pure software-based solution that does not require additional hardware and must not require any additional infrastructure support or modifications of the original operating system of the device. The implementation and the details of the operations that were studied were described in the subsections "point to link", "link to group" and "swipe to send".

3.1   Point to Link

Users link their devices by pointing them towards each other and a unique identifier and the digital compass reading are advertised using the BLE framework. Also Shuriken processes the incoming advertisements along with the received signal strength indication (RSSI). If the RSSI is within the "near" range (similar to the iBeacon protocol [5]) and the digital compass readings are approximately opposite, the users are required to confirm the linkage of the devices. We studied the accuracy of pointing a device towards another device with the three methods of confirming the link: (a) button, (b) timer (2 s) and (c) shaking (Fig. 1).

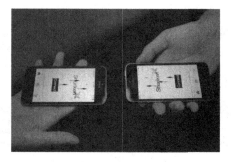

Fig. 1. An example showing the mechanism to point the devices together with the "button" method to confirm the device link.

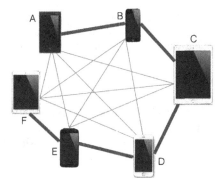

Fig. 2. The group created by Shuriken (bold edges represents BLE connections that were created between linked devices where relative positions are known. Non-bolded edges represent inferred connection between devices).

3.2 Link to Group

The confirmation of the linking acts as an acknowledgement to accept data transfer, estimates the relative positions and initiates a BLE connection between the linked devices. The devices also stop sending and processing incoming advertisements.

The relative positions between devices in a group that were not physically linked (e.g., device A and D in Fig. 2) are inferred through the linked devices (e.g., device A- > B- > C- > D). If the devices being were already in a group, information of all grouped devices will be sent and propagated to all devices. The information of the devices was displayed in a real-time map of devices.

3.3 Swipe to Send

The devices in a group can send information by swiping towards the physical direction of the intended recipient. As mentioned in Sect. 3.2, the data (which includes relative position information) is transferred using a multi-hop approach. The two methods of initiating swipe to send includes using: (a) two-finger-swipe and (b) hold-and-swipe.

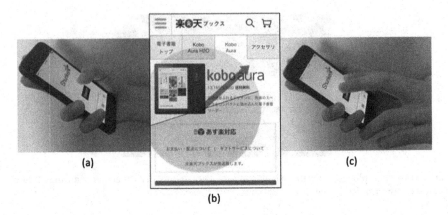

Fig. 3. (a) and (c) indicates the two possible operations to complete swipe to send, (b) shows an example of the guide presented after swipe to send has been initiated (where the arrow represents the direction of the swipe and the two semi-circles represent directions of the possible recipients).

4   User Study Design

An application was developed to evaluate the operations of Shuriken in a series of quantitative experiments. Furthermore, a qualitative study was conducted to compare Shuriken to no data transfer (i.e., physically showing the device) and using AirDrop in a collaborative shopping exercise. The following list summarises the user studies conducted:

Quantitative test

- Point to link operation accuracy (button, timer and shake)
- Swiping to send operation accuracy (2-finger-swipe, hold-and-swipe)

Qualitative tests for the collaborative shopping

- No data transfer
- AirDrop
- Shuriken

4.1   Subjects

Five participants (3 male, 2 female, age 24.6 ± 1.67) were assigned to perform the quantitative tests for operations. All the participants were familiar with the operations of the iPhone. To ensure that the users are novel to Shuriken, another three participants (2 male, 1 female, age 25.66 ± 0.577) were recruited to performing the qualitative tests for collaborative shopping.

4.2   Apparatus

An application of Shuriken was developed for devices running iOS 8.0. The devices used in the user study included: iPhone 5 (screen size: 4 in), iPhone 6 (screen size 4.7 in), iPhone 6 plus (screen size 5.5 in) and iPad mini 1 (screen size 7.9 in).

4.3 Quantitative Study

The quantitative study included testing the accuracy of point to link with three confirmation methods (button, timer and shaking) and swipe to send direction accuracy (two-finger-swiping, hold-and-swipe).

Three targets were securely fastened onto a stands that resulted in the targets being about 70 cm above the ground. The targets were pointing at the absolute north directions at 0, 90 and 270 degrees (Fig. 4).

Fig. 4. Quantitative study experiment setup

The participants were provided with an iPhone 6, an iPhone 5 s and an iPad Mini 1 and were instructed to hold the device about 30 cm away from the target. The following operations towards the targets were performed: (1) point and press a button, (2) two-finger-swipe, (3) point for 2 s, (4) hold-and-swipe and (5) point and shake. To ensure that the participants have to separately aim for each operation, they were asked to randomly move the device between operations. The steps were repeated ten times for each target and then repeated for each device.

The directional error is defined as the difference between the intended direction with the opposite of the actual direction (pointing directional error is shown in Fig. 5).

The directional error for swipe to send is calculated by finding the difference between the opposite of the actual target direction and the swipe direction with respect to the direction of the device.

The data was explored with descriptive statistics where the mean for every participant per device was calculated (i.e., mean for all trails for all targets). The differences between the point to link operations (button, timer and shake) was explored with repeated measures ANOVA with a within subject factor of device type (iPhone 6, iPad Mini 1 and iPhone 5 s). In addition, the difference between the swipe to send operations (2-finger-swipe and hold-and-swipe) was explored with the same repeated measures ANOVA. If significant differences were found, post hoc t-tests with Bonferroni corrections were preformed to find differences between the specific devices and operations.

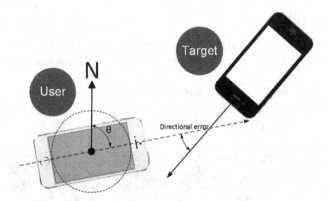

Fig. 5. The calculation of the directional error for point to link operations, that is, the difference in the estimated direction of the users' device compared to the actual device of the target.

4.4 Qualitative Study

The user satisfaction study was conducted to compare using Shuriken to existing techniques. The participants were engaged in a collaborative shopping exercise where the group was asked to purchase an outfit for a randomly chosen participant. The three participants were provided with a choice of using an iPhone 6, an iPad Mini 1 or an iPhone 6 preinstalled with Shuriken. The moderator provided brief instructions on how to use Shuriken and then the participants were asked to shop for an outfit with three grouping method: (1) without data transfer, (2) with AirDrop and (3) with Shuriken, for each participant in the group.

After the exercise, participants completed a questionnaire that discusses the perceived workload (based on NASA-TLX [6]) and satisfaction of each grouping method. Statements such as "the method requires a lot of physical effort" were asked and the participants provided a rating based on a 5-point Likert scale (2 = strongly agree -2 = strongly disagree). In addition, general comments and the overall preferences were recorded.

5   Results

In this section the qualitative and quantitative results are described separately.

5.1   Quantitative Results

The directional errors for the point to link operations are shown for each device in Fig. 6.

Repeated measures ANOVA suggest that the directional error in the point to link operations was not significant differences between the confirmation method $(F(2, 8) = 1.477, p = 0.284)$. However, significant differences were found between the devices types $(F(2, 8) = 7.349, p = 0.015)$. In addition, no significant interactions were found between the operations and the device type $(F(4, 16) = 2.386, p = 0.096)$. Post hoc

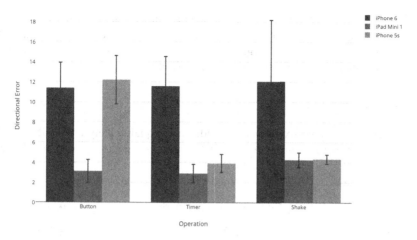

Fig. 6. Directional error in the point to link operations (Figure created by plot.ly)

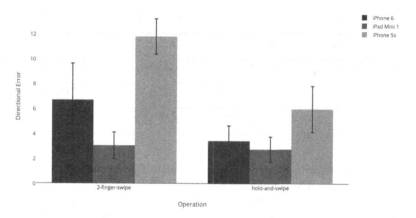

Fig. 7. Directional error in the swipe to send operations

t-tests showed that directional error was significantly different between the iPad Mini 1 and the iPhone 5 s (p = 0.045). Although no significant differences were found between the point to link operations, the results suggest that on average, the timer method was the most accurate (6.116 ± 0.834 degrees) followed by shaking (6.966 ± 2.396 degrees) then button (8.863 ± 1.278 degrees).

The directional error for the 2-finger-swipe and hold-and-swipe are shown in Fig. 7.

Repeated measures ANOVA showed that the directional error in the 2-finger-swipe and hold-and-swipe for swipe to send are significantly different (F(1, 4) = 12.592, p = 0.024) and significant differences were found in the directional error between the device types (F(2, 8) = 43.170, p < 0.001). In addition, significant swipe to send operation X device type interactions were found (F(2, 8) = 8.134, p = 0.012). Post hoc t-tests showed that the directional error of 2-finger-swipe and hold-and-swipe was significantly different (p = 0.024). Also, significant differences in the directional error were found between the devices (iPhone 6 vs iPhone 5 s: p = 0.018;

iPad Mini 1 vs iPhone 5 s: $p < 0.001$). The average directional error of the hold-and-swipe (4.026 ± 0.505 degrees) was found to be significantly smaller than the 2-finger-swipe (7.183 ± 0.487 degrees). The results obtained in quantitative study were incorporated into Shuriken prior to the qualitative study.

5.2 Qualitative Results

A collaborative shopping exercise was conducted to qualitatively test Shuriken. The results of the post-exercise questionnaire for each grouping method are shown in Table 1.

Table 1. Mean and standard deviation of the qualitative study

	No data transfer	AirDrop	Shuriken
Task easy	1.33 ± 0.57	-2.00 ± 0.00	1.33 ± 0.33
Task fast paced	2.00 ± 0.00	-2.00 ± 0.00	2.00 ± 0.00
Task demanding	-2.00 ± 0.00	1.66 ± 0.33	-2.00 ± 0.00
Task annoying	0.00 ± 1.00	2.00 ± 0.00	-1.66 ± 0.33
Small learning curve	2.00 ± 0.00	0.00 ± 0.00	2.00 ± 0.00
Task successful	2.00 ± 0.00	2.00 ± 0.00	2.00 ± 0.00
Task fun	1.33 ± 0.66	-2.00 ± 0.00	2.00 ± 0.00

The general comments made by the users were mainly comparing between no data transfer and Shuriken. The participants suggest that physically sharing the device is a natural method of collaborative shopping. However, as the distance between users and number of users increase, techniques with data transfer will become applicable. The participants felt that AirDrop was inappropriate for user grouping and data transfer in the context of collaborative shopping, as it does not support group interactions. Shuriken was positively received as a novel, smart and fun method for collaborative shopping.

6   Discussion

The user study indicated that the participants positively received Shuriken to create a group for collaborative shopping. Besides collaborative shopping, Shuriken could be used for business meetings, conferences and banquets. Also, Shuriken can be employed with mobile gaming, digital signage and gesture input.

The quantitative study suggested that the timer operation provided the least directional error for point to link. The timer operation allows user to carefully align their devices prior to linking the device however, the lack of manual input may cause erroneous relative position estimates. Also, the hold-and-swipe operation was found to have the least directional error. Hold-and-swipe allows the users to operate Shuriken with one hand (which is the preferred method according to Hoober [7]) however, the hold-and-swipe operation overrides the basic operations such as initiating copy and pasting.

The results of the qualitative study showed that the participants felt Shuriken was applicable for collaborative shopping. Table 1. Showed that Shuriken was similarly rated compared to collaborative shopping with no data transfer. However, the participants felt that Shuriken was more fun to use.

7   Conclusion and Future Work

In this paper we present Shuriken, a method for user grouping and data transferring based on inter-device relative positioning. Users intuitively link their devices by point their devices together. Linking the devices creates an ad hoc network using the BLE framework. Devices in the group can send data by swiping towards the physical direction of the intended recipient. Shuriken was developed on top of a shopping application for iOS enable collaborative shopping and a user study was conducted to test its feasibility. The users showed positive reviews of Shuriken felt that it improved collaborative shopping experience.

In the scenario where the users are grouped in a line, swipe to send will be insufficient to distinguish between the devices.

To mitigate these effects, the energy of the swipe can be inferred from the distance travelled during the swipe. Currently, when swipe to send has been initiated a guide with the possible recipients is shown (Fig. 3). This guide can be extended to include information about the energy of the swipe (left of Fig. 8).

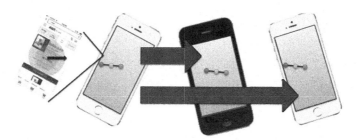

Fig. 8. Swipe to send is insufficient to distinguish between devices that were grouped in a line

References

1. Ikematsu, K., Siio, I.: Memory stones: an intuitive copy-and-paste method between multi-touch computers, pp. 1287–1292. ACM (2013)
2. Huibers, A. G.: Bump validation. (2011). at http://www.google.com/patents/US20110191823
3. Peng, C., Shen, G., Zhang, Y., Lu, S.: Point and Connect: intention-based device pairing for mobile phone users, pp. 137–150. ACM (2009)

4. Chen, K.-Y., Ashbrook, D., Goel, M., Lee, S.-H., Patel, S.: AirLink: sharing files between multiple devices using in-air gestures, pp. 565–569 ACM (2014)
5. Cavallini, A.: iBeacons Bible
6. Hart, S.G., Staveland, L.E.: Development of NASA-TLX (Task Load Index): results of empirical and theoretical research. Adv. Psychol. **52**, 139–183 (1988)
7. Hoober, S.: How People Really Hold and Touch (their phones). (2013)

Are Social Media Useful for Managing Reputation Online?: Comparing User Interactions Online with Reputation Indicators

Jasmine Yoo Jung Hong and Jang Hyun Kim[✉]

Department of Interaction Science, Sungkyunkwan University, Seoul, South Korea
{yjasmine,alohakim}@skku.edu

Abstract. Reputation is a growing concern to all organizations, regardless of their size or industry. Recently, social networking sites (SNS) such as Facebook have become effective and efficient channels for an organization to build relationships with various publics, which is fundamental for reputation management. Applying the dialogic communication theory and the halo effect, the present study seeks to explore whether there is a significant relationship between a company's reputation and the level of interaction on the respective company's Facebook page (measured by the number of page 'likes', number of wall comments and commented comments by both the companies and users). This study used a social network analysis tool called NodeXL to gather data on Facebook. Results from the present study provide practical implications regarding online reputation management for organizations.

Keywords: Reputation management · Social networking sites (SNS) · Facebook · Halo effect · Dialogic communication

1 Introduction

Reputation is a growing concern to all organizations, regardless of their size or industry, possibly due to its direct, positive relationship with revenue [1]. Doorley and Garcia [2] defined an organization's reputation as "the sum of how its stakeholders view it" [2, p. 381] and one that can and should be managed by organizations [2]. Moreover, it is the sum of images, composed of several elements: performance, behavior, communication and authenticity factor [2]; the present study examined the communication aspect, more specifically online communication.

Publics perceive a company's reputation based on the information provided by the company itself, media or from other sources [3]. And today, social media function as channels that allow organizations to communicate with different publics in novel ways that were impossible in the past [2]. Thus, social networking sites (SNS), such as Facebook, can be used as effective and efficient channels for an organization to build relationships with various publics, which is greatly important for reputation management. In fact, it is one of the most common ways that organizations reach their target audiences today. In 2014, of the Fortune 500 companies, 413 companies had Twitter accounts and

© Springer International Publishing Switzerland 2015
G. Meiselwitz (Ed.): SCSM 2015, LNCS 9182, pp. 207–215, 2015.
DOI: 10.1007/978-3-319-20367-6_21

401 companies had Facebook pages, which equal 83 % and 80 %, respectively [4]. Compared to the previous year findings, this was a 6 % and 10 % increase, respectively [4]. In addition, according to Facebook, 30 million small businesses had active Facebook pages in 2014 [5].

Therefore, the present study thoroughly examined the relationship between a company's reputation and the respective company's presence on social media, specifically Facebook.

2   Literature Review

2.1   Dialogic Communication

A dialogue is defined as "a product of an on going communication and relationships" [6, p. 24]. Subsequently, dialogic communication is a "negotiated exchange" of information [7, p. 325]. In addition, Kent and Taylor [7] argued that through the web, public relationships can be built and altered.

Applying the dialogic communication theory, Kim, Kim and Nam [8] conducted a study on how organizations used the four different social networking sites (SNSs) – Facebook, Twitter, YouTube and LinkedIn – for communicating online with their publics. The organizations were analyzed based on the industry type [8]. By examining various Facebook features, including, but not limited to, the number of page 'likes' (number of fans), the number of wall comments per posting by companies, the number of wall comments per posting made by fans, as well as the number of responses from both parties, researchers were able to measure the level of interaction between the organization and the public [8]. One of the key findings from the study is that Twitter and Facebook were the most widely used social networking sites, of which Facebook was the most used platform for dialogic interaction between the organization and the public [8].

2.2   Reputation Management and Social Media

There has been a plethora of studies on reputation management and social media, of which the majority focuses on online reputation management – how organizations and individuals should manage their reputation in an online environment (i.e. search engines, blogs, Facebook, Twitter, etc.). The emphasis is placed more on the privacy and how others search one's name, whether it be an individual or organization. On the other hand, Barnes, Cass, Getgood, Gillin and Goosieaux [9] studied how customer care on social media influences the brand reputation; however, the study did not analyze the different features of Facebook, such as the 'like' button and the number of comments on wall posts, to explain the connection with the organization's reputation.

In another study, Schultz, Utz, and Göritz [10] examined whether crisis communication strategies, both message and medium (traditional and social media), influenced the receiver's perception of organizational reputation, secondary crisis communication and secondary crisis reactions. Twitter and blog were used for online media [10]. One of the main findings of the study is that the medium was more important than the message itself [10]. For example, Twitter led to "the most positive effect on secondary crisis communication and reactions" [10, p. 26]. The results highlight the significance of social media effect on crisis communication, as well as on the perception of organizational reputation.

According to the ENGAGEMENTdb report [11], "the most valuable brands in the world are experiencing a direct correlation between top financial performance and deep social media engagement" [11, p. 1]. This finding implies that social media engagement can lead to improved reputation or vice versa, which is in line with Schultz et al.'s [10] research findings. Therefore, the following hypotheses have been formulated:

Hypothesis 1: A company's reputation is positively correlated with the frequency of dialogic communication.

Hypothesis 1a: A company's reputation is positively correlated with the number of wall comments by both companies and users.

Hypothesis 1b: A company's reputation is positively correlated with the number of commented comments (responses) by both companies and users. Hypothesis 1c: A company's reputation is positively correlated with the online interaction index.

2.3 Facebook 'Like' Button

On Facebook, there are various features used for engagement and interaction, one of which is the 'like' button; it has been utilized in copious studies for gauging various attributes. Researchers have scrutinized the motivation and implications of Facebook users' 'liking' a page.

Bushelow [12] explored Facebook fan pages and studied whether there is a causal relationship between the act of 'liking' a Facebook page and the users' brand loyalty and purchase intentions. The study's results showed that the 'likes' and activities on the Facebook page were not robust signs of the users' brand loyalty or purchase intentions [12].

In another study, Wallace, Buil and de Chernatony [13] examined whether social media has an effect on the interaction between the organization and consumers, as well as the relationship between Facebook features, such as the 'like' button, and consumers' brand advocacy. The researchers argued that "consumers who 'Like' brands on Facebook do so partly to express themselves" [13, p. 133]. In some sense, the 'liked' brand "becomes part of the consumers' online identity, as it is visible on their profile page" [13, p. 130]. One of the key findings of the study is that consumers with strong social ties tend to 'like' self-expressive brands [13].

Despite countless studies regarding the Facebook 'like' button, the direct association between Facebook page 'likes' and an organization's reputation has not been explored thoroughly. Furthermore, reputation is fairly difficult to quantify. As of February 2015, there are only a few rankings dealing with organizations, such as Reputation Institute's *Global RepTrak* and Fortune Magazine's *World's Most Admired Companies* list. Therefore, the following hypothesis was derived.

Hypothesis 2: A company's reputation is positively correlated with the number of Facebook page 'likes'.

2.4 Halo Effect

Another important aspect to consider when analyzing various Facebook features, such as the 'like' button and comments, is whether the public's preconception of an organization has a significant influence. This can be explained by the psychological phenomenon called the halo effect, which was first coined by Thorndike [14]. It is defined as "a problem that arises in data collection when there is carry-over from one judgment to another" [14, p. 25]. In other words, people make biased judgments about a subject based on their attitudes towards a few specific attributes [14]. This phenomenon can also come into effect in image building and reputation. As Reynolds [15] states, brand images are made by consumers. Thus, consumers can reach to a certain conclusion about a product or brand image from a limited amount of information that they are familiar with [15]. According to Reynolds [15], "an image produced by halo looks like a real image and may function like one" [15, p. 72].

2.5 Halo Effect and Reputation

The halo effect has been studied in a wide range of fields, even in an online setting. Several studies have examined the halo effect of customer satisfaction in e-commerce [16], as well as its presence relating to the level of attractiveness on online dating websites [17].

There has also been previous research on the relationship between reputation and the halo effect. Coombs and Holladay [18] conducted a study on the halo effect and its influence on the organization's reputation during crisis situations. According to the results, the halo effect of prior reputation protects organizations in the face of crisis [18]. However, the study did not cover the online environment.

As it can be implied from the aforementioned studies, there has been sufficient research on the relationship between reputation and social networking sites, as well as that of halo effect and reputation, yet there has not been a particular study on all three elements – the influence of the halo effect on organizational reputation on social media such as Facebook. Thus, the following research question has been derived:

Research Question 1: Is the halo effect of organizational reputation present on Facebook?

In an attempt to fill some of the aforementioned research gaps regarding the direct association between reputation and social networking sites, the purpose of the present study is to examine whether there is a significant relationship between an organization's reputation and the level of presence and interaction on the respective organization's Facebook page (measured by the number of page 'likes', number of company's wall comments, the number of users' wall comments, as well as the number of responses (commented comments) from both parties), based on the dialogic communication theory and the halo effect.

3   Method

The sample of the present study was collected from the 2014 rankings of Fortune Magazine's "World's Most Admired Companies" [19] and Reputation Institute's "Global RepTrak" [20]. Of the companies that were co-listed, their rankings were averaged to obtain the top 10 companies with best reputations. The sample of the study consists of the following companies in the respective ranking order: Google (#1), Apple (#2), Walt Disney (#2), BMW (#3), Amazon.com (#4), Samsung Electronics (#5), Nike (#6), Microsoft (#7), Johnson & Johnson (#8) and Nestle (#9).

The Facebook pages of the abovementioned ten companies were scrutinized. As outlined in Kim et al.'s [8] study, the number of page 'likes' (number of fans), the number of company's wall comments, the number of users' wall comments, the number of company's commented comments (responses) and the number of users' commented comments (responses) were measured to determine the level of interactivity.

Each organization's official Facebook page that has interaction with users was visited to record the number of page 'likes' on February 1, 2015. In order to collect data on other elements, social network analysis software NodeXL was used. The time period of the analysis was set to March 1 to March 31 of 2014, since "World's Most Admired Companies" list was released in February, and the Global RepTrak ranking in April. The number of wall comments and commented comments by both companies and users were recorded by sorting through 'commented post' and 'commented comment' relationships on NodeXL. Applying the equation employed by Kim et al. [8], the interaction index (the level of company's direct involvement in communication) was calculated by dividing the number of company's commented comments by the number of user's wall comments.

4   Results

Google. Google Google had a total of 19,357,176 Facebook page 'likes', 0 company's wall comments, 1,127 user's wall comments, 0 company's commented comments and 0 user's commented comments. Google's interaction index equaled 0.

Apple. Apple had a total of 605,623 Facebook page 'likes', 0 company's wall comments, 744 user's wall comments, 0 company's commented comments and 14 user's commented comments. Apple's interaction index equaled 0.

Walt Disney. Walt Disney had a total of 50,320,343 Facebook page 'likes', 0 company's wall comments, 2,624 user's wall comments, 0 company's commented comments and 0 user's commented comments. Walt Disney's interaction index equaled 0.

BMW. BMW had a total of 19,590,942 Facebook page 'likes', 6 company's wall comments, 1,144 user's wall comments, 0 company's commented comments and 268 user's commented comments. BMW's interaction index equaled 0.

Amazon.com. Amazon.com had a total of 26,186,147 Facebook page 'likes', 26 company's wall comments, 4,482 user's wall comments, 25 company's commented comments and 359 user's commented comments. Amazon.com's interaction index equaled 0.006.

Samsung Electronics. Samsung Electronics had a total of 789,383 Facebook page 'likes', 2 company's wall comments, 1,585 user's wall comments, 7 company's commented comments and 9 user's commented comments. Samsung Electronics' interaction index equaled 0.004.

Nike. Nike had a total of 22,834,501 Facebook page 'likes', 0 company's wall comments, 124 user's wall comments, 0 company's commented comments and 0 user's commented comments. Nike's interaction index equaled 0.

Microsoft. Microsoft had a total of 6,335,813 Facebook page 'likes', 59 company's wall comments, 1,398 user's wall comments, 64 company's commented comments and 290 user's commented comments. Microsoft's interaction index equaled 0.046.

Johnson & Johnson. Johnson & Johnson had a total of 663,232 Facebook page 'likes', 2 company's wall comments, 202 user's wall comments, 2 company's commented comments and 2 user's commented comments. Johnson & Johnson's interaction index equaled 0.010.

Nestle. Nestle had a total of 7,406,235 Facebook page 'likes', 1 company's wall comment, 38 user's wall comments, 1 company's commented comment and 3 user's commented comments. Nestle's interaction index equaled 0.026.

Table 1. Summary of Facebook Data. Key: CWC: company's wall comments; UWC: user's wall comments; CCC: company's commented comments; UCC: user's commented comments; CCC/UWC: company and user interaction index;

Ranking	Company	CWC	UWC	CCC	UCC	CCC/UWC
1	Google	0	1127	0	0	0.000
2	Apple	0	744	0	14	0.000
2	Walt Disney	0	2624	0	0	0.000
3	BMW	6	1144	0	268	0.000
4	Amazon.com	26	4482	25	359	0.006
5	Samsung Electronics	2	1585	7	9	0.004
6	Nike	0	124	0	0	0.000
7	Microsoft	59	1398	64	290	0.046
8	Johnson & Johnson	2	202	2	2	0.010
9	Nestle	1	38	1	3	0.026

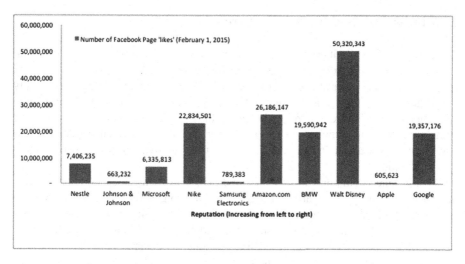

Fig. 1. Relationship between reputation and the number of Facebook page 'likes'

Please refer to Table 1 for the summary of Facebook data. Overall, hypothesis 1 was not supported, while hypothesis 2 was partially supported. Please refer to Fig. 1 for the summary of the Facebook page 'likes'.

5 Discussion

The present study examined whether social media is helpful for managing reputation online; in other words, it studied whether there is a significant relationship between a company's reputation and the level of company's direct interaction with users online, such as on its official Facebook page. The study's main findings have several implications.

First, the results suggest that the upper half of the top-tier reputation companies are engaged in less interaction than those in the lower half, since four out of five companies in the upper half of the reputation ranking did not engage in any dialogic communication with the users, whereas only one out of five companies in the lower half of the reputation ranking had an interaction index that equaled 0. In fact, the company with the highest interaction index was Microsoft, which was in the lower half. Second, the fact that the lower half of the top-tier has a higher interaction index indicates the efforts of the lower half of the top-tier reputation companies' to further improve their reputation by more actively engaging in conversations with their publics. At last, based on the present study's findings, there was no direct positive correlation between the number of Facebook page 'likes' and the company's reputation level, implying that the halo effect may not necessarily exist on social media.

6   Limitations and Future Research

There were several limitations to the present study. First, the organization's official Facebook pages were examined, thus leaving out other affiliated branches, which may result in a higher number of page 'likes'. Second, since the collected data represent only a 1-month period, it is just a snapshot of the company's overall online interaction with users on Facebook. Third, regarding the Facebook 'like' button feature, a survey on the motivation of 'liking' a company's Facebook page should be conducted in order to assess whether it is an adequate indicator of Facebook users' motivations towards the company's reputation.

At last, since communication is just one aspect of many other components that influence a company's reputation, it may be difficult to generalize the implications to the overall reputation. Furthermore, since dialogic communication is based on both frequency and content. The present study focused only on frequency. Thus, for future studies, it is recommended that researchers conduct a semantic network analysis to examine the content as well. Furthermore, other major social media platforms, such as Twitter and Instagram, should be analyzed concurrently to gather a more comprehensive data on online dialogic communication and its relations to the company's reputation.

Acknowledgements.   This research is supported by BK21 + project administered by Sungkyunkwan University and governed by Ministry of Education, Republic of Korea.

References

1. Kim, Y.: Measuring the economic value of public relations. J. Public Relat. Res. **13**(1), 3–26 (2001)
2. Doorley, J., Garcia, H.F.: Reputation Management: The key to Successful Public Relations and Corporate Communication. Routledge, New York (2011)
3. Fombrun, C., Shanley, M.: What's in a name? reputation building and corporate strategy. Acad. Manage. J. **33**(2), 233–258 (1990)
4. Barnes, N.G., Lescault, A.M.: The 2014 Fortune 500 and social media: LinkedIn dominates as use of newer tools explodes (2014). http://www.umassd.edu/cmr/socialmediaresearch/2014fortune500andsocialmedia/
5. Ha, A.: Facebook Says There Are Now 30 M Small Businesses With Active Pages, Including 19M On Mobile. TechCrunch, 3 June 2014. http://techcrunch.com/2014/06/03/facebook-30m-small-businesses/
6. Kent, M.L., Taylor, M.: Toward a dialogic theory of public relations. Public Relat. Rev. **28**(1), 21–37 (2002)
7. Kent, M.L., Taylor, M.: Building dialogic relationships through the World Wide Web. Public Relat. Rev. **24**(3), 321–334 (1998)
8. Kim, D., Kim, J.H., Nam, Y.: How does industry use social networking sites? An analysis of corporate dialogic uses of Facebook, Twitter, YouTube, and LinkedIn by industry type. Qual. Quant. **48**, 1–10 (2013)
9. Barnes, N.G., Cass, J., Getgood, S., Gillin, P., Goosieaux, F.: Exploring the link between customer care and brand reputation in the age of social media. S. f. NC Research (Ed.): Society for New Communication Research (2008)

10. Schultz, F., Utz, S., Göritz, A.: Is the medium the message? Perceptions of and reactions to crisis communication via twitter, blogs and traditional media. Public Relat. Rev. **37**(1), 20–27 (2011)
11. Wetpaint & Altimeter Group. The world's most valuable brands. Who's most engaged? ENGAGEMENTdb report (2009)
12. Bushelow, E.E.: Facebook pages and benefits (2012). Available on http://www.studentpulse.com/a?id=829
13. Wallace, E., Buil, I., De Chernatony, L.: Facebook 'friendship' and brand advocacy. J. Brand Manage. **20**(2), 128–146 (2012)
14. Thorndike, E.L.: A constant error in psychological ratings. J. Appl. Psychol. **4**(1), 25–29 (1920)
15. Reynolds, W.H.: The role of the consumer in image building. Calif. Manage. Rev. **7**(3), 69–76 (1965)
16. Chong, B., Wong, M.: Crafting an effective customer retention strategy: a review of halo effect on customer satisfaction in online auctions. Int. J. Manage. Enterp. Dev. **2**(1), 12–26 (2005)
17. Bak, P.M.: Sex differences in the attractiveness halo effect in the online dating environment. J. Bus. Media Psychol. **1**, 1–7 (2010)
18. Coombs, W.T., Holladay, S.J.: Unpacking the halo effect: reputation and crisis management. J. Commun. Manage. **10**(2), 123–137 (2006)
19. Fortune, http://fortune.com/worlds-most-admired-companies/
20. Reputation Institute, http://www.reputationinstitute.com/thought-leadership/global-reptrak-100

Investigating Usability and User Experience from the User Postings in Social Systems

Marília S. Mendes[1]([✉]), Elizabeth Furtado[2], Vasco Furtado[2],
and Miguel F. de Castro[3]

[1] Federal University of Ceará (UFC), Russas, CE, Brazil
marilia.mendes@ufc.br
[2] University of Fortaleza (Unifor), Fortaleza, CE, Brazil
elizabet@unifor.br, furtado.vasco@gmail.com
[3] Federal University of Ceará (UFC), Fortaleza, CE, Brazil
miguel@great.ufc.br

Abstract. Social Systems (SS) are dynamic systems, with features such as: frequent exchange of messages and expression of feelings spontaneously. The postings of users on SS reveal their opinions on various issues, including on what they think of the system. In this study, we classified postings of users from two SS of different contexts: a popular SS (entertainment) - Twitter and an academic SS of a university – forums, to investigate information related to usability and user experience (UX) of such systems. Results showed they are useful to (i) obtain user's sentiments about the system; (ii) to identify possible problems during their experience and (iii) to perceive from the set of classified postings the context of use of the system.

Keywords: Human computer interaction · User experience · Usability · Social systems · Postings related to the use (PRUs)

1 Introduction

With the explosive growth of social media on the Web (Social Systems, SS), e.g., reviews, forum discussions, blogs, micro-blogs, Twitter, comments, and postings in social network sites, individuals and organizations are increasingly using the content in these media for decision making [24]. In this sense, some authors have been devoted to collect such data in order to study people's feelings, their behaviors, collaboration, relationships etc. Wang et al. [41], for instance, investigated regrets from the messages of users on Facebook; Lim and Datta [23] studied communities that share common interests on Twitter; Mogadala and Varma [31] did a study about the humor mood transition of Twitter users. Other studies have focused on the analysis of postings from users in order to understand their views as for health [1, 11, 16, 17, 32], politics [7] etc.

In the area of Human Computer Interaction (HCI), the opinions of users are important in the evaluation of a system. Asking their opinion regarding a product, checking whether they enjoy it, checking whether the product is aesthetically appealing, how they accomplish what they want, and checking whether they face problems when using it are possible forms of evaluating a system [37]. The main techniques for

© Springer International Publishing Switzerland 2015
G. Meiselwitz (Ed.): SCSM 2015, LNCS 9182, pp. 216–228, 2015.
DOI: 10.1007/978-3-319-20367-6_22

collecting user opinion about the system are: field research, interviews and question-naires [2, 9, 37]. However, such techniques do not consider the spontaneity of the users at the moment when they are using the system [28, 34, 37]. We believe that the spontaneous way of the users in describing a problem with the system to their friends, while using it, may be different from a description they do to a specialist. Preece, Rogers and Sharp [37] raised the following thought: "What users say is not always what they do". People sometimes give answers which are not true, or they may just have forgotten what happened. Thus, can evaluators believe all the answers they receive? Are respondents saying "the truth", or are they simply providing the answers they presume the evaluator wants to hear? Moreover, in SS the interaction is mainly constituted of written texts. Why not to take advantage of this feature in SS commu-nication for obtaining relevant data on the use of the system?

In our previous work, we did studies with postings of users in SS [26, 27]. In [28], we did a systematic review of studies in the field of HCI and Natural Language Processing (NLP). In [26], we investigated whether SS users post messages about the system in use, for which we had a positive conclusion. Users praise the system, criticize it, make comparisons, clarify doubts and provide suggestions about the system. In [27] we conducted two experiments with postings of users on SS in order to investigate how users express their feelings regarding the use of the system, and how to assess the Users eXperience (UX) by using their postings during the system interaction. Results showed some characteristics of postings related to the use which may be useful for Usability and UX (UUX) evaluation in SS. Therefore, our goal in this work is to investigate UUX of a system from the users' postings when using it, specifically, we hope to get assessment results UUX from the posts of two SS of distinct contexts.

We collected users' postings from two SS: a popular SS (entertainment) - Twitter - and an academic SS of a university – forums. This investigation sought to answer the following research questions: (i) Is it possible to classify users' postings in dimensions of UUX? (ii) Is it possible to find out, from users' postings, which the main problems of the system are? (iii) Is it possible to realize, from users' postings, the context of use of a system?

In this study, 29 participants (students and specialists in HCI) classified 1,210 postings and discussed their impressions about this form of evaluation.

This paper is organized as follows: in the next section, we present some related works. In Sect. 3, we describe concepts about SS, postings related to the use and UUX. In Sects. 4 and 5, we describe the investigative studies, followed by final considerations and future work.

2 Related Work

Some studies that have focused on user narratives in order to study UUX or UX are: [13, 14, 22, 35, 40]. In [13], the authors, focusing on studying UX from positive experiences of users, collected 500 texts written by users of interactive products (cell phones, computers etc.) and presented studies about positive experiences with inter-active products. In [22], the authors collected 116 reports of users' experiences about their personal products (smartphones and MP3 players) in order to evaluate the UX of these products. Users had to report their personal feelings, values and interests related to the moment at which they used those. In [35], the authors collected 90 written reports of beginners in mobile applications of augmented reality. The focus was also evaluating the UX of these products, and the analysis consisted in determining the subject of each text and classifying them, by focusing attention on the most satisfactory and most unsatisfactory experiences. Following this line, in [40], the authors studied 691 narratives generated by users with positive and negative experiences in technologies in order to study the UX from them.

In the four studies mentioned above, the information was manually extracted from texts generated by users. The users were specifically asked to write texts or answer a questionnaire, unlike the spontaneous gathering of what they post on the system.

In [14], the authors extracted reviews of products from a reviews website and did a study in order to find relevant information regarding UUX in texts classified by specialists. However, they did not investigate SS, but other products used by users. In this case, the texts were written by products reviewers. It is believed that the posture of users in a product review website is different from that when they are using a system and face a problem, then deciding to report this problem just to unburden or even to suggest a solution.

In this work, we focused on considering the opinions of users about the system in use from their postings on the system being evaluated. We intend thereby to capture the user spontaneously at the moment they are using the system.

3 Background

3.1 Social Systems

Social Systems focus on enabling its users to communicate and interact with each other in different ways and for several purposes [1, 8, 19]. Complementing this concept, [6] specify SS as web-based services that allow individuals to (1) create a public or semi-public profile within a limited system, (2) articulate a list of other users with whom they share a connection, and (3) view and surf through their list of connections and through those made by others within the system.

For [36], SS are communication systems often used in the composition of collaborative systems such as: social networks, in which various types of communication systems are adapted to allow multiple forms of interaction between users; learning environments, in which multiple communication systems are available to be used and configured in each course; or in virtual environments, which often contain a chatting service and audio conferencing. This work considers the latter definition, by considering as the main interaction the text messages posted by users: their postings.

The SS used in this research were: Twitter[1] and SIGAA.[2] Twitter is one of the largest microblogging services on the Internet with over 600 million active users.[3]

---

[1] Available: <https://twitter.com/>. Access in: January 2015.

[2] Available: <www.si3.ufc.br/>. Access in: January 2015.

[3] Available: <http://www.statisticbrain.com/twitter-statistics/>. Access in: January 2015.

Microblogs are short text messages that users produce to share all kinds of information with the world. On Twitter, these microblogs are called "Tweets" and may contain news, announcements, personal affairs, jokes, opinions etc.

The SIGAA (Integrated System of Academic Activities Management) is the academic control system of the Federal Universities in Brazil, and, through such system, students can have access to various features such as: Enrollment receipt, academic history, enrollment procedure etc. The system allows the exchange of messages through a discussion forum. Its users are students and university staff.

3.2 Postings Related to the Use

The main form of interaction in social systems are their posted messages, whether they are public or private. In their postings, users deal with various issues. This work focuses on the public postings in natural language in which the users refer to the SS they are currently using (Postings Related to the Use, PRUs). For example, if the user is using Facebook, we are interested in Facebook PRUs; if the SS under evaluation is Twitter, the PRUs should be regarding Twitter.

Next to this field of text analysis, there are studies about reviews of products or services on the web. In recent years, the use of websites to evaluate products and services has become increasingly common. Websites such as Booking.com, Decolar. com, Tripadvisor etc. provide a space for clients to disclose their reviews on products and services.

A review is a small text written by a user of the product or service who used it for some time, detailing its positive and negative points and possibly providing an evaluation of it and a recommendation to other potential buyers [14].

It is worthy highlighting the reflection about these two concepts: reviews of products or services and user comments in SS. From studies and empirically, we come to the description of their differences in the following aspects:

1. Form: reviews are structured texts, presenting certain regularity in the format of the information, such as, for example, a completed form. There are fields to score, text input for evaluation and even a field of the aspect to be evaluated, whereas postings in SS are unstructured texts, presenting no regularity in its format. Postings of users may display images, various types of texts and characters and even links referencing pages;
2. Motivation: a series of online articles [10, 20, 30, 38] have been written in order to explain why people write reviews. Among the main reasons given, the authors generally agree that people write reviews because they care about their fellow consumers and want to help others in making a decision [10]. In [26], we conducted a research on characteristics of PRUs of SS and noted that users praise, criticize, make comparisons, clarify doubts and provide suggestions about the system, which leads us to believe that such comments contain users' reports about their experiences of use in the system; and
3. Context: at the time of review, the reviewer is not using the system being evaluated. The fact that the users make comments on the own SS they are using may be a way to request help to solve a problem at the time of use.

The postings used in this research were obtained from previous experiments. We extracted 295,797 Twitter postings using an extraction tool in six samples taken from October to December 2012 [29]. For the SIGAA system, we extracted 24,743 postings after system installation (2nd half of 2010) until January 2014 [25]. Of these, PRUs were selected for evaluation of both systems

3.3   Usability, User Experience and Their Goals

Usability, according to [37], is generally considered to be the factor which ensures that products are easy to use, efficient and pleasant - from the user's perspective. According to [15], usability is a measure in which a system, product or service can be used by specified users in order to achieve specified goals with efficacy, efficiency and satisfaction in a specified context of use.

UX, in turn, consists of perceptions and responses of people, resulting from the use and /or from the anticipated use of a product, service or system [15]. According to [15], it includes all emotions, beliefs, preferences, perceptions, physical and psychological responses, behaviors and user achievements that occur before, during and after use.

In [14], the authors investigated the main goals of UUX, based on studies [3, 5, 12, 21, 39] and came to the following goals (Table 1). We used these dimensions in this paper.

Table 1. Dimensions of UUX used for the studies in this paper

[12, 39]	[5]	[5, 21]	[3]
Dimension	*Dimension*	*Dimension*	*Dimension*
Learnability	Likeability	Anticipation	Affect and Emotion
Memorability	Pleasure	Overall Usability	Enjoyment, Fun
Efficiency	Comfort	Hedonic	Aesthetics, Appeal
Errors/effectiveness	Trust	Detailed usability	Engagement, Flow
Satisfaction		User differences	Motivation
		Support	Enchantment
		Impact	Frustration
			Hedonic

Fonte: Hedegaard and Simonsen [14]

4   First Investigation

4.1   Participants

This investigation was conducted in March 2014 with 17 students of a HCI discipline of the course of Computer Science, 14 men and 3 women aged 22–25 years old.

4.2   Procedure

As this investigation was applied with students of a discipline of HCI, the theoretical basics of UUX and its goals had been previously taught in previous classes, as well as UUX assessment methods.

The research consisted in: each student would classify 50 PRUs, arranged in a worksheet, according to the following categories: (1) type of PRUs; and (2) UUX goals. The types of PRUs are criticism, question, compliment, suggestion, help and comparison [26]. The UUX goals were those proposed by [14], arranged in Table 1. We also presented the examples arranged in Table 2. The deadline for classification was 2 weeks, and at the end, the student should deliver the worksheet with the 50 classified PRUs and a completed questionnaire. In addition to personal information such as name, age and the SS analyzed, the questionnaire contained only three questions: (1) what is the feeling os users you have noticed more frequently in postings? (2) what are the main complaints (problems faced in the system)? and (3) what are the main compliments (system benefits) perceived in the messages? Ten students worked with PRUs of Twitter and seven students worked with the PRUs of SIGAA.

Table 2. Examples of PRUs classified

PRUs	Dimensions of UUX
"Twitter is way slow today"	Efficiency
"I looooove Twitter"	Satisfaction
"It's been returning error when I send Tweets from my mobile"	Effectiveness
"I guess I'm loving Twitter more than Facebook, once there I don't express myself that much *-*"	Motivation
"I'm already in love with this website!!"	Satisfaction, Enchantment
"I HATE this new Twitter interface!!!"	Emotion, Aesthetics
"How can I remove this timeline?"	Support
"It took half a year to read the Tweets grrr damn bug"	Efficiency, Emotion, Frustration

4.3   Results

After two weeks, the students delivered us the PRUs classified by them, which were corrected by two HCI specialists, authors of this paper. We noted that 80 % of the postings were correctly classified. However, their main mistakes were:

1. Regarding the type of PRU: confusion between the types doubt and help (for SIGAA). Although some PRUs were actually doubts, the students classified them as help, for instance: *"Does anyone know how I can get a history of disciplines here?"* represents a doubt, whereas *"Go to "see previous courses" on your homepage.. then click the small blue arrow there is in each discipline, then on the left you will see "students" and then "see marks"."* is an example of help;

2. Concerning the classification by UUX goals: confusion between the goals effectiveness, efficiency and utility.

The classification of 50 postings enabled each student to have a perception of the system, providing an evaluation result through their questionnaires. In their responses, they identified the main feelings of users towards the system, their complaints and compliments. Figures 1, 2 and 3 illustrate the students' perception regarding the set of PRUs analyzed on SIGAA.

Fig. 1. Main feelings perceived on SIGA

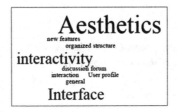

Fig. 2. Main causes/functionalities perceived on SIGAA

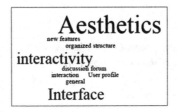

Fig. 3. Main compliments perceived on SIGAA

From the experiment with the students, we concluded that it is possible to obtain results of an evaluation from a set of PRUs. In this study, it was possible to create a relationship of categories of PRUs classified by the students. For example, 48 % of the criticisms were related to the effectiveness goal, and 86 % of them were related to the frustration goal. However, we did not request the students to indicate the functionality referred by the user when reading a PRU. Still, in order to answer the questionnaire, the student described the main features mentioned by users (Fig. 2). We note that the functionality is a required information to be collected. From this, we would be able to discover the main features presenting UUX problems in the SS. We could also carry out a correlation between the functionalities and the other features of classification suggested in this paper, for instance: "x% of the doubts were related to the functionality y" or "w% of the criticism was related to the functionality y and to the effectiveness goal".

5 Second Investigation

5.1 Participants

This research was carried out in November 2014 and had 12 specialists in HCI, 4 from academia and 8 from industry. We consider as academy specialists those who teach in universities and as industry specialists those who work with HCI in companies, following the profile shown in Table 2.

Table 3. Profile of specialists in HCI

Participants profile	
Gender	Women (8)
	Men (4)
Age	From 26 to 35 years old (7)
	From 36 to 45 years old (3)
	Above 45 years old (2)
Field	Academia (4)
	Industry (8)
Time of experience	From 4 to 8 years (7)
	From 9 to 13 years (3)
	Above 13 years (2)

5.2 Procedure

The 12 specialists in HCI were invited two weeks in advance, and the investigation occurred during a morning following the schedule below (Tables 3 and 4).

The specialists received the postings to be classified, the goals for UUX classification (Table 1) and examples of PRUs classified by UUX (Table 2). Each specialist received 30 PRUs to classify. Half of the specialists received PRUs from SIGAA, and the other half had PRUs from Twitter. In the validation step, the SS were exchanged; the specialist who had classified SIGAA validated Twitter, and vice versa. This was done so that each specialist could have a view of a different SS.

After the classification step, we provided a moment for brainstorm, at which the specialists discussed about: the user feelings, their intended uses, types and the importance of PRUs (conclusions, actions or how they would represent). Two authors of the research took notes on the whiteboard. After the brainstorm, participants should write on a blank sheet their main difficulties regarding the classification of PRUs.

5.3 Results

The results are presented in difficulty of classification and perceptions for evaluation using the PRUs of users in SS. The main difficulties of the specialists were: 1) great number of goals, leading to uncertainty at the time of classification; and 2) some goals

Table 4. Agenda of investigation with specialists in HCI

Time	Activity	Description
From 08:00 to 08:30	Welcoming the specialists	Cooffe break
From 08:30 to 09:00	Presenting the investigation	Short presentation explaining the main concepts of the work
From 09:00 to 09:30	Classification	Each specialist will classify the postings of users of a SS
From 09:30 to 10:00	Validation	Each specialist will validate the postings classified by another specialist colleague
From 10:00 to 10:55	Brainstorm	The participants will discuss about the experience
From 10:55 to 11:00	Closing and acknowledgment	Closing investigation

are intersections of others, such as: usability (effectiveness, efficiency, satisfaction, utility, learning, security, memorization) and emotion (satisfaction, frustration, affection, pleasure, enchantment).

During the analysis of PRUs classified by the specialists, we realized that some of them did not have the usability classification, only the UX, for example, the following PRU: "*Syndrome of screen exchange on Twitter. Whenever I refresh the screen, I place the cursor to the left and it goes to 'discover' tab Grrrr*". The feeling is so perceptive that they classified it regarding the UX goals frustration and emotion, but did not classify it as for the security goal.

In another example, "*I hate this feature of Twitter of favoriting a tweet by just laying the cursor on it, we cannot even stalk fearless anymore*", specialists classified the UX goals: frustration and emotion, but missed the goal usability, identifying a security issue.

Although the specialists had a short time for the analysis (30 min for classification + 30 min for validation, with two different SS), they were able to report some information about the evaluated SS and its users, such as: "*we can see that SIGAA users are beginners*"; "*SIGAA users are not yet used to the platform*"; "*Some features have not yet been implemented on SIGAA*"; "*Twitter users are satisfied, motivated and engaged! I had never imagined that...*". There were also other interesting discussions about the user: "*What is their purpose when posting?*", "*What do they want?*", "*What is their priority? Expressing feeling? Asking for help?*".

Regarding the feeling expressed by users in PRUs, a specialist noted that there are feelings in all cases; they only differ as for polarity and intensity, for example: very happy. On the other hand, other specialists noticed that the feeling was not always expressed, although system problems were reported. They commented that it would be interesting to also classify what caused that feeling.

We noted that, as the specialists become familiar with the method, they begin to classify the postings more easily, and also that analyzing only one posting is not enough, but from a set of PRUs it is possible to give some information about the context of use. The specialists discussed about what they would do with the result. We highlight the following answers: analysis of product acceptance, application development, interface improvement or correction of system bugs.

6 Final Considerations and Future Work

We conclude this research addressing the following issues raised in the study: (i) Is it possible to classify PRUs in dimensions of UUX? Yes, it is. The students and the specialists classified the PRUs in UUX goals. However, some measures should be taken in this regard in order to facilitate the classification process, such as: the classification of goals should be simplified, by removing intersections between them not to confuse the specialist. The goals should also be separated by quality of use, such as: usability goals and UX goals, preventing them from forgetting any of the criteria.

The second question raised: (ii) It is possible to discover, from a set of PRUs, which the major problems of the system used are? Yes, it is. In some PRUs, the problem is clearly presented. In these, a classification of the problem (or the cause of posting) could be made in order to establish a correlation with the other classifications made. The classification would be the cause or the functionality mentioned by the user, that is, referred in their PRU.

The third question was: (iii) Is it possible to perceive, from a set of PRUs, the context of use of the system? Yes, it is possible to perceive it from a simple set of classified PRUs, as well as in other evaluation methods such as heuristic evaluation, for example, in which certain items of the system have to be evaluated in order to reach a conclusion about it. For the evaluation from PRUs, it is necessary to have a number of items (PRUs) evaluated so we can reach any relevant conclusion.

We can therefore conclude that it is possible to achieve results of evaluation of UUX from the PRUs analysis. This investigation resulted in 1,210 PRUs analyzed, from which 850 were classified by students (350 from Twitter + 500 from SIGAA) and 360 were classified by HCI specialists (180 for each SS: Twitter and SIGAA).

Some studies have already been carried out from the PRUs of users in SS. In [25], we proposed an Evaluation Model of the User Textual Language. We intend to continue this work by studying characteristics of PRUs and how they can be useful in order to obtain user perceptions regarding the system.

References

1. Aramaki, E., Maskawa, S., Morita, M.: Twitter catches the flu: detecting influenza epidemics using Twitter. In: Proceedings of the 2011 Conference on Empirical Methods in Natural Language Processing, pp. 1568–1576, Edinburgh, Scotland, UK, 27–31 July 2011
2. Barbosa, S.D.J., Silva, B.S.: Interação Humano-Computador. Ed. Elsevier, Melbourne (2010)
3. Bargas-avila, J.A., Hornbæk, K.: Old wine in new bottles or novel challenges: a critical analysis of empirical studies of user experience. In: Proceedings of the 2011 annual conference on Human factors in computing systems, Vancouver, pp. 2689–2698 (2011)

4. Bevan, N.: Classifying and selecting UX and usability measures. In: International Workshop on Meaningful Measures: Valid Useful User Experience Measurement (2008)
5. Bevan, N.: What is the difference between the purpose of usability and user experience evaluation methods. In: Proceedings of the Workshop UXEM 2009, Uppsala, Sweden (2009)
6. Boyd, D.M., Ellison, N.B.: Social network sites: definition, history, and scholarship. J. Comput. Mediat. Commun. **13**(1), 210–230 (2007)
7. Cheek, G.P., Shehab, M.: Policy-by-example for online social networks. In: SACMATÕ12, Newark, USA (2012)
8. Chen, L., Achrekar, H., Liu, B., Lazarus, R.: Vision: Towards real time epidemic vigilance through online social networks. In: Workshop on Mobile Cloud Computing & Services: Social Networks and Beyond, San Francisco, USA (2010)
9. Cybis, W.A., Betiol, A.H., Faust, R.: Ergonomia e Usabilidade: Conhecimentos, Métodos e Aplicações, 1st edn. Novatec, São Paulo (2007)
10. Ditlev, J.: Review Motivation Part 1 – The Real Reason People Write Negative Reviews, http://blog.trustpilot.com/review-motivation
11. Dredze, M., Cheng, R., Paul, M. J., Broniatowski, D.: HealthTweets.org: a platform for public health surveillance using twitter. In: Association for the Advancement of Artificial Intelligence (2014)
12. Folmer, E., Van Gurp, J., Bosch, J.: A framework for capturing the relationship between usability and software architecture. Softw. Process Improv. Pract. **8**(2), 67–87 (2003)
13. Hassenzahl, M., Diefenbach, S., Göritz, A.: Needs, affect, and interactive products. Hum. Comput. Interact. **25**(3), 235–260 (2010)
14. Hedegaard, S., Simonsen, J.G.: Extracting usability and user experience information from online user reviews.In: ACM Conference on Human Factors in Computing Systems, pp. 2089–2098, Paris, France (2013)
15. ISO 9241–11. Geneve: International Organization For Standardization (1998)
16. Jamison-Powell, S., Linehan, C., Daley, L., Garbett, A., Lawson, S.: I can't get no sleep: discussing #insomnia on twitter. In: Proceedings of the SIGCHI Conference on Human Factors in Computing Systems (CHI 2012), pp. 1501–1510 (2012)
17. Kamal, N., Fels, S., Ho, K.: Online social networks for personal informatics to promote positive health behavior. In: Proceedings of second ACM SIGMM workshop on Social media (WSM 2010), pp. 47–52 (2010)
18. Kamal, N., Fels, S., McGrenere, J., Nance, K.: Helping me helping you: designing to influence health behaviour through social connections. In: Kolze, P., Marsden, G., Lindgaard, G., Wesson, J., Winckler, M. (eds.) Human-Computer Interaction. Lecture Notes in Computer Science, vol. 8119, pp. 708–725. Springer, Heidelberg (2012)
19. Karnik, M., Oakley, I., Venkatanathan, J., Spiliotopoulos, T., Nisi, V.: Uses & Gratifications of a Facebook Media Sharing Group. In: Proceedings of the 2013 conference on Computer supported cooperative work, pp. 821–826, San Antonio, Texas, USA (2013)
20. Karr, D.: Why Do People Write Online Reviews? Social media today. http://www.socialmediatoday.com/content/infographic-why-do-people-write-online-reviews
21. Ketola, P., Roto, V.: Exploring user experience measurement needs. In: 5th COST294-MAUSE Open Workshop on Valid Useful User Experience Measurement (2008)
22. Korhonen, H., Arrasvuori, J., Väänänen-Vainio-Mattila, K.: Let users tell the story.In: Proceedings of AMC CHI 2010 Extended Abstracts, pp. 4051–4056, Atlanta (2010)
23. Lim, K.W., Datta, A.: Finding Twitter Communities with Common Interests using Following Links of Celebrities. In: Proceedings of the 3rd international workshop on Modeling social media (MSM 2012), pp 25–32, Milwaukee, Wisconsin, USA (2012)

24. Liu, B.: Sentiment Analysis and Opinion Mining. Morgan & Claypool Publishers (2012)
25. Mendes, M. S.: MALTU - Model for evaluation of interaction in social systems from the Users Textual Language. 200 f. thesis (Ph.D in computer science) – Federal University of Ceará (UFC), Fortaleza, CE – Brazil (2015)
26. Mendes, M., Furtado, E., Castro, M. F.: Do users write about the system in use? an investigation from messages in Natural Language on Twitter. In: 7th Euro American Association on Telematics and Information Systems (2014)
27. Mendes, M.S., Furtado, E., Furtado, V., de Castro, M.F.: How do users express their emotions regarding the social system in use? a classification of their postings by using the emotional analysis of norman. In: Meiselwitz, G. (ed.) SCSM 2014. LNCS, vol. 8531, pp. 229–241. Springer, Heidelberg (2014)
28. Mendes, M.S., Sucupira Furtado, E., Theophilo, F., Franklin, M.: A Study about the usability evaluation of social systems from messages in natural language. In: Collazos, C., Liborio, A., Rusu, C. (eds.) CLIHC 2013. LNCS, vol. 8278, pp. 59–62. Springer, Heidelberg (2013)
29. Mendes, M., S., Furtado, E., Castro, M. F.: Uma investigação no apoio da avaliação da usabilidade em Sistemas Sociais usando Processamento da Linguagem Natural. In: IX Brazilian Symposium in Information and Human Language Technology, Brazil (2013)
30. Merritt, J.: Why Do People Write Reviews? Online Reputation Management. https://www.reputationmanagement.com/blog/why-do-people-write-reviews
31. Mogadala, A., Varma, V.: Twitter user behavior understanding with mood transition prediction. In: workshop on Data-driven user behavioral modelling and mining from social media (2012)
32. Newman, M.W., Lauterbach, D., Munson, S.A., Resnick, P., Morris, M.E.: It's not that I don't have problems, I'm just not putting them on Facebook: challenges and opportunities in using online social networks for health. In: Proceedings of the ACM 2011 Conference on Computer Supported Cooperative Work, pp. 341–350, (2012)
33. Norman, D. A., Miller, J., Henderson, A.: What you see, some of what's in the future, and how we go about doing it: HI at Apple Computer. In: Conference on Human Factors in Computing Systems, Denver, Colorado, USA (1995)
34. Obrist, M., Roto, V., Väänänen-Vainio-Mattila, K.: User experience evaluation – do you know which method to use? In: Conference on Human Factors in Computing Systems, Boston, Massachusetts (2009)
35. Olsson, T., Salo, M.: Narratives of satisfying and unsatisfying experiences of current mobile augmented reality applications. In: Proceedings of the SIGCHI Conference on Human Factors in Computing Systems (2012)
36. Pimentel, M.; Gerosa, M. A.; Fuks, H.: Sistemas de Comunicação para colaboração. In: PIMENTEL, Mariano; FUKS, Hugo (Orgs.). Sistemas Colaborativos, v. 1, pp. 65–93. Campus-Elsevier, Rio de Janeiro (2011)
37. Preece, J., Rogers, Y., Sharp, H.: Interaction Design: Beyond Human-Computer Interaction. J. Wiley & Sons, California (2002)
38. Rhodes, M.. Why do people write reviews? Freshminds. http://www.freshminds.net/2009/03/why-do-people-write-reviews/
39. Seffah, A., Donyaee, M., Kline, R.B., Padda, H.: Usability measurement and metrics: a consolidated model. Softw. Qual. J. **14**, 159–178 (2006)
40. Tuch, A.N., Trusell, R.N., Hornbæk, K.: Analyzing users' narratives to understand experience with interactive products. In: Conference on Human Factors in Computing Systems, Paris, France (2013)

41. Wang, Y., Leon, P.G., Chen, X.X., Komanduri, S., Norcie, G., Scott, K., Acquisti, A., Cranor, L.F., Sadeh, N.: From Facebook regrets to facebook privacy nudges. Ohio State Law Journal **74**(6), 1307–1334 (2013)
42. Zhao, X., Sosik, V.S. and Cosley, D.: It's complicated: how romantic partners use facebook. In: Conference on Human Factors in Computing Systems is the premier international conference on human-computer interaction, Austin, Texas (2012)

A Computational Study of How and Why reddit.com was an Effective Platform in the Campaign Against SOPA

Richard Mills[1(✉)] and Adam Fish[2]

[1] Department of Psychology, The Psychometrics Centre, University of Cambridge,
Cambridge, UK
rm747@cam.ac.uk
[2] Department of Sociology, Lancaster University, Lancaster, UK
a.fish2@lancaster.ac.uk

Abstract. In this paper, we analyze the posting and voting activities of reddit's users and show how these interact with the site's structure to create an environment where information activists could build a resource base to oppose the 2012 US House of Representatives bill, Stop Online Privacy Act (SOPA). The broadcasting function of the 'Front Page' was important in raising awareness of SOPA among reddit's users. Broadcasting the outcomes of collective voting back to the voters establishes an attentional feedback loop, and this imbued the collective action which followed with certain characteristics. Continuing a longitudinal investigation into changes in the ways that user attention and activity is distributed between the site's 240,000 'subreddits', we conclude by theorizing whether such collective action will be possible on the reddit of the present.

Keywords: Reddit · Social News · Public sphere · SOPA

1 Introduction

Reddit is a Social News site where users submit content and vote to dictate the prominence with which each item will be displayed. It was viewed by 174 million unique users in September 2014[1]. Reddit is divided into more than 240,000 "subreddits" or content categories (but 50 % of these are inactive and have received less than 5 posts in total). According to surveys conducted with reddit's users in 2010 and 2011, the site's users are predominantly male, white, young and living in the United States - a survey conducted in 2010 and completed by 25,000 reddit readers found that 40 % were white males aged 18–34 living in the United States [1].

Research on Social News platforms has tended to involve either a quantitative approach to describing the functioning of a particular platform as a whole [2–6] or users' behavior [7, 8] - or a more qualitative approach to a particular event or phenomenon which occurred on a Social News platform [9–11]. Published work tends to either focus on the platform itself (without making reference to the content) or on a particular case

---

[1] www.reddit.com/about.

© Springer International Publishing Switzerland 2015
G. Meiselwitz (Ed.): SCSM 2015, LNCS 9182, pp. 229–241, 2015.
DOI: 10.1007/978-3-319-20367-6_23

study (without making reference to how the platform works). This paper combines quantitative approaches to explore how reddit functions with a more qualitative approach to telling the story of reddit's involvement in the anti-SOPA movement and how this was shaped by the former. Reddit is recognized by [12] as playing an important role in this movement but their method, based on in-links, only captures reddit's role when it became part of the wider story (through the GoDaddy boycott). We consider how the 79 posts about SOPA which had previously appeared on reddit's Front page laid the foundations for the successful GoDaddy boycott, and the manner in which other attempts at collective action on reddit succeeded or failed.

2   Who Sees What on Reddit? Pages and Algorithms

Every post submitted to reddit is voted on through the ubiquitous up/down voting buttons. The posts which an individual user is shown are selected based on **subreddit** and **page** criteria. Users most commonly browse **aggregated** pages where they are presented with posts from the set of **subreddits** they subscribe to – for users who are not signed into an account the posts they see on aggregated pages are drawn from the 'default' subreddits. Users also have the option of seeing posts from 'all' subreddits or browsing posts from a specific subreddit.

The primary **page type** for browsing posts selects these based on the 'Hot' ranking algorithm. Reddit's **'Front page'** is the site's most viewed page and shows posts from the subreddits a user is subscribed to with the highest ranks as determined by this algorithm – users who aren't signed into an account see the **'default Front page'**. This 'Hot' algorithm uses only two variables to generate ranks – the post's score and time of submission [13]. Voting scores undergo a log10 transformation such that a score of 1000 bears only twice as much weight as a score of 100. Time of submission is used to penalize older posts, and coupled with the log10 transformation of voting scores the result is that even very popular posts cannot remain on the Front page for long.

To appear on pages which use the 'Hot' algorithm a post must have a high score – this requires users to browse (and vote) on pages which select posts on other criteria. The **'New'** page shows posts in reverse chronological order – every post appears on this page initially and is then pushed down the order by subsequent submissions. The **'Rising'** page shows posts which are relatively fresh and have already begun to accumulate up-votes. Before appearing on the default Front page, a post will always appear on the 'Hot' page for the subreddit it was submitted to (referred to here as the **'Main'** page for the subreddit) – votes cast here can help the post to out-score competitors from other subreddits and be shown on the Front page.

Each of these page types has been observed at 30-min intervals between August 20th and September 27th 2012. The subreddit-specific versions of the New, Rising, and Main pages have been recorded for a variety of subreddits. At each observation point, the posts' previous numbers of votes and comments have been subtracted to yield values which reflect the previous 30 min. These values have been modelled in R with a Negative Binomial regression using time since previous observation as an offset and the page(s) a post appeared on at a given observation point as explanatory variables. This allows us to estimate the levels of activity associated with appearance on each page. Table 1 shows details of the model fit for up-votes on the /r/funny[2] and /r/worldnews subreddits (both 'default' subreddits at the time).

Table 1. Model parameters for a negative binomial regression model of number of new up-votes by page- with an offset for the time since previous observation. In generating estimates for the number of up-votes per page, posts appearing on the Front page are assumed to appear simultaneously on the Main page.

Subreddit	Coefficient		Std. Error		p value		Estimated Up-votes per minute	
	Funny	Worldnews	Funny	Worldnews	Funny	Worldnews	Funny	Worldnews
Intercept	0.836	−4.7	0.03	0.01	<0.01	<0.01	2.3	0.01
New	−2.1	0	0.04	0.01	<0.01	<0.01	0.3	0.01
Rising	0.6	1.5	0.02	0.02	<0.01	<0.01	4.1	0.04
Main	1.7	3.8	0.03	0.01	<0.01	<0.01	12.2	0.5
Front – L1	1.8	3.8	0.02	0.02	<0.01	<0.01	75.7	20.2

The model for /r/funny posts shows that voting rates were lowest on the New page (0.3 vpm), with appearance on the Rising (4.1 vpm), Main (12.2 vpm) and Front (75.7 vpm) pages being associated with greatly increased voting rates. The /r/worldnews subreddit follows a similar pattern but with lower voting rates on every page – the New (0.01 vpm), Rising (0.04 vpm) and Main (0.5 vpm) pages are particularly disadvantaged as compared to /r/funny, while posts appearing on the Front page (20.2 vpm) suffer less of a deficit. Models of other activity types (down-votes, comments) are not presented here but follow the same pattern [1]. This suggests that /r/worldnews may be a subreddit which many users remain subscribed to but don't actively engage with – voting on posts only when they encounter them on the Front page.

These voting rates indicate that it is better to conceive of reddit's voting system as involving a number of stages or hurdles which a post must overcome if it is to earn a place on the Front page – rather than the singular process which the 'Hot' ranking algorithm intimates. The function served by the New page is to determine which posts will be displayed on the Rising page – while a post can appear on both pages simultaneously the voting rate on the Rising page is considerably higher. A similar relationship exists between the Rising page and the Hot pages (Main/Front). Posts which appear on the same page are in effect competitors, and only some of these will score well enough to earn a place on the next page in the sequence and the increased voting rate which comes with that territory – propelling them to much higher scores than rival posts which don't make the transition. The role of the New page as a gatekeeper for the Rising page, low

---

[2] The /r/ prefix denotes a subreddit name – e.g. the url reddit.com/r/funny loads the main page of the 'funny' subreddit.

levels of voting on this page, and log10 transformation of voting scores in the Hot algorithm – all combine to give early votes accentuated influence over reddit's collective decision-making.

3   Redditors' Submission and Voting Behavior

Reddit have provided access to post submission and voting data for the month of March 2009 – although this data relates to an earlier time in reddit's history it allows for analyses which are otherwise not possible with data collected through the API (as voting is anonymous). In March 2009 102,232 users cast 3,346,062 votes (of which 77 % upvotes) on 352,902 posts. Of these users 33,589 (33 %) only acted once (one vote or submission), whereas the most active user for the month registered 23,776 actions. The distribution of votes and submissions between users is highly skewed and similar to a power law distribution – with 80 % of votes being cast by 11.6 % of users. Users tend to specialize in either voting or submitting. Of the 68,643 users who acted more than once, 68 % only engaged in one form of activity (53 % voters, 47 % submitters). Users who submit posts are largely distinct from users who vote on these posts.

The most active voting users diverge from their less active peers by the frequency of their votes, but also by the nature of their votes – to the extent that they can be considered a class of voting 'superparticipants' [14]. These voting superparticipants are more likely to cast down-votes, are more likely to vote on fresh posts (first 20 votes cast on a post) and are more likely to vote quickly (voting within 10 s of their previous vote). Figure 1 shows the prevalence of these behaviors in user groups defined by activity level.

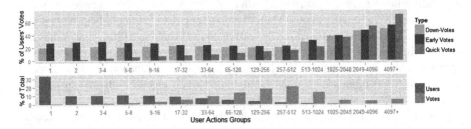

Fig. 1. Top: Percentage of a user's votes which correspond to the three 'expert' voting behaviors. Bottom: Percentage of total users and votes for each activity level group.

As noted above, early stage pages (New, Rising) see low voting rates but all posts must progress through these pages to reach higher visibility locations. If a user wished to try and censor reddit one approach would be to down-vote posts when they are fresh and thus prevent them from reaching areas where they will be seen and assessed by many more users. There may be strategic value to voting on the New and Rising pages, and some of the voting superparticipants who are active there may be aiming to maximize their impact on the site or to curb the capacity of certain perspectives to be heard – down-voting posts quickly based on their title alone.

There is however a more innocuous explanation which sees these users as pitching in on the New page and filtering out the many poor submissions so that other users don't have to sift through these. The argument against this explanation is the prevalence of quick votes (19.5 % of all votes in this month were cast within 10 s of the user's previous vote) – for most subreddits it is not possible to assess the quality of a post within 10 s and these votes are likely based on the title alone. The outcome is that many posts submitted to default subreddits are quickly discarded when early down-votes from a few users prevent them from progressing to the Rising page.

Digg, reddit's predecessor as the most active Social News site, was perceived to have problems related to censorship (e.g. the 'Digg Patriots', a group which coordinated to bury left-leaning content soon after submission [15]) and to be dominated by an elite of 'Power Users' whose submissions often occupied high-attention areas of the site [16].

The voting data for March 2009 allows us to assess whether 'voting superpartici-pants' on reddit fare well when they submit posts. The scores for a users' posts were first converted into an ordinal variable with 4 levels (<0, 0, 1–20, 21+) and then modelled in STATA's GLLAMM package using a multi-level ordinal logistic regression. Incorporating a random effect for users allows the model to estimate effects for the explanatory variables without being distorted by individual differences in users' ability to submit high-scoring posts. Details of the model fit are included in Table 2.

Table 2. Model parameters for a multi-level ordinal logistic regression model, with a random effect for Users and Post Score (ordinal) as the response variable (Deviance 552780.7).

	Coefficient	Std. Error	95 % Confidence	p-value
User's Post Submission Proportion	−0.0962	0.0167	−0.13, −0.06	<0.001
User's Total Post Submissions	−0.0007	0.0001	−0.001, −0.0005	<0.001
User's Account Age	0.0956	0.0069	0.08, 0.11	<0.001
Active on non-default subreddit	0.3193	0.0188	0.283, 0.356	<0.001
User's Total Votes	0.00116	<0.0001	0.001, 0.0013	<0.001
User's Quick Votes	−0.0012	0.0001	−0.0014, −0.001	<0.001
User's Early Votes	−0.0004	0.0001	−0.0006, −0.0002	<0.001
Cut-point 1 (Score < 0)	−1.008	0.0171	−1.18, −1.13	<0.001
Cut-point 2 (Score <= 0)	1.8	0.0175	1.76, 1.83	<0.001
Cut-point 3 (Score <= 20)	4.061	0.021	4.02, 4.1	<0.001

Users who submit a high number of posts, and have a high proportion of post submissions (relative to voting activity) tend to submit posts which don't score well. High levels of user voting are associated with successful post submissions – but this effect is more than offset by the effects of 'Quick' and 'Early' votes, with the result that users engaging in these behaviors don't tend to submit high-scoring posts. Users with older accounts, and those who had some activity on a non-default subreddit, tended to submit higher-scoring posts. These effects indicate that posts submitted by users who have more rounded involvement in reddit are more likely to score well. Through the lens of Common Pool Resources [17] – reddit appears resistant to free-riders (those who would consume the attentional resource through their submissions without contributing much of their own attention to the common pool by browsing and voting).

Longitudinal analysis of reddit's Front page over two years confirms that its content is not dominated by elite users to the same degree as Digg's was perceived to be at the peak of its popularity [16] – with 55 % of all posts observed on the Front page being submitted by a user who only achieved this once.

4   Reddit and the Stop Online Piracy Act (SOPA)

The above explorations of how reddit functions will now be used to provide context for a case study of reddit's involvement in the 'internet campaign' against SOPA. This case study considered the content, comments and timing of 258 posts about this subject observed on reddit's default Front page between October 27th 2011 and February 3rd 2012 [1][3].

Posts about SOPA appeared on reddit's default Front page before the legislation was being covered by Newspapers (television news channels didn't begin to cover the legislation until much later), being regularly mentioned on Twitter, or being regularly searched for on Google [1]. Early posts about SOPA on reddit linked to blog posts (redd.it/lq2b1[4]) and videos (redd.it/lrv38) about the legislation. It is telling that the 3rd, 4th and 5th posts about SOPA to appear on reddit's Front page were already moving towards collective action by asking users to sign petitions (redd.it/lvr2x & redd.it/lrux7) or recounting a user's own experience of writing to their elected representative to express their disapproval (redd.it/lvr2x). The appearance of two posts on the default Front page appears to have raised awareness of SOPA quite broadly among reddit's users, and the subsequent appearance here of posts calling for action suggests that a consensus quickly emerged that this legislation should be opposed.

From this point, many of the posts about SOPA observed on reddit's Front page were geared towards raising awareness and spreading opposition *beyond* the site's user-base. Two courses of action were particularly effective - a boycott of GoDaddy aiming to change their pro-SOPA stance which emerged from ordinary users in a grass-roots fashion, and reddit's involvement in the 'blackout' of January 18th which was implemented by administrators and moderators. The GoDaddy boycott will be described here.

On December 22nd /u/selfprodigy[5] submitted a post to the politics subreddit titled "GoDaddy supports SOPA, I'm transferring 51 domains & suggesting a move your domain day" (redd.it/nmnie). Once this post appeared on the reddit Front page it received

---

[3] Timeline and data-set available at: http://researchmills.com/sopa/index.html.

[4] This is a short-form URL linking directly to a reddit post.

[5] Prefix denoting a reddit user – www.reddit.com/u/selfprodigy shows their contributions.

considerable attention and ultimately more than 3,000 comments. Popular comment threads were supportive of the proposal, some criticizing GoDaddy on other grounds, some offering advice on how to avoid transferring to a GoDaddy subsidiary, some asking for and receiving evidence of GoDaddy's support for SOPA. Over the following eight days there were a further 24 posts about the GoDaddy boycott which appeared on reddit's Front page. The first of these was submitted to /r/technology and linked to the original boycott post on /r/politics (redd.it/nmsiu) – this post served to spread awareness of the boycott among redditors who were not /r/politics subscribers.

On the day after the original post was submitted two posts appeared on the Front page which linked to articles about the boycott published on the *Techdirt* blog and *Ars Technica* (redd.it/nn4j5). These articles were a sign that the boycott attempt was being noticed outside reddit, and this feedback was in turn broadcast through the Front page. Later in this eight day period posts appeared on the Front page which put numbers on the effectiveness of the boycott - a loss of 72,000 domains in a week (redd.it/npmav), 21,000 domains in a single day (redd.it/npj2q). Other posts appearing on the Front page during this period draw attention to the fact that certain organizations (e.g. Wikipedia) have domains registered with GoDaddy – the intention being to suggest that these organizations should transfer their domains. Subsequently there are posts announcing/ celebrating when organizations state that they will join the boycott.

On December 29th a post was submitted and up-voted to the Front page which reminded users that the designated 'transfer day' had arrived (redd.it/nuimq) - this post was not submitted by the same user who sparked the boycott. Later that day two posts appeared on the Front page through /r/politics (redd.it/nvdf4) and /r/technology (redd.it/ nvg18) which detailed a press release from GoDaddy stating that they now actively opposed SOPA – thus drawing the GoDaddy boycott episode to a close. In addition to meeting the aim of changing GoDaddy's stance, this boycott was also widely covered by the conventional news media[6] and online media [12], thus raising awareness of SOPA beyond reddit's users.

While the GoDaddy boycott was unfolding six posts also appeared on the Front page which proposed boycotting other organizations that supported SOPA, or questioned the emphasis on GoDaddy as the sole target of boycotting (redd.it/nq7cy). Suggested targets for boycotts included movie theatres (redd.it/nokhw), Time Warner (redd.it/nob8i), EA (redd.it/nqumv) and Nintendo (redd.it/nr2m3). These posts are interesting for two reasons. The first of these concerns the expression of dissenting opinions [18]. If one considers only posts about the GoDaddy boycott this idea seems to have emerged largely from a single post and quickly received widespread support from reddit users. The other posts considered here reveal that not all of reddit's users jumped on the 'GoDaddy boycott' bandwagon. These posts which question the strategy of only boycotting GoDaddy appeared on the Front page alongside posts which were supportive of the GoDaddy boycott.

Reddit users, through their use of the voting system, collectively 'decided' to broadcast opinions on the Front page which went against the perceived majority opinion. This could happen because redditors (excluding voting superparticipants)

---

[6] E.g. http://www.bbc.co.uk/news/technology-16320149.

generally cast more up-votes than down-votes. To appear on the Front page a post does not necessarily need the backing of a majority of reddit's users - it only needs to attract more up-votes than the posts which it is directly competing with (i.e. those which it appears alongside on the same page(s)).

The second point of interest here concerns the importance of comments. Although these posts reached the Front page their comments pages hosted discussions which tended to argue against the suggestion made by the post itself. Many popular comments on these posts explain why it is prudent to focus on GoDaddy or criticize the suggested target of the post. It is probably no coincidence that, despite appearing on the Front page, these posts failed to establish the momentum on reddit which was critical to the success of the GoDaddy boycott. This fits with the assertion in Sect. 3 that voting on posts tends to be quite 'shallow' and this in combination with the simplistic 'Hot' algorithm and low voting rates on early stage pages results in a degree of 'randomness' around the decision as to which posts appear on the Front page. The default 'best' comment sorting algorithm is more nuanced, using the proportion of up/down votes to generate a Wilson score confidence interval[7].

There are further examples from the SOPA case study of 'poor quality' posts which appeared on the Front page and had popular comments which were fiercely critical. For example, the post redd.it/mgw7f asks users to sign a Whitehouse.gov petition - popular comments are critical of the petition's grammar and the fact that it calls on the White-house to take action which is outside its power. Previous research indicated that once a post appeared on the Front page it was unlikely to receive more down-votes than up-votes - even when all of its high-scoring comments were very critical the level of up-voting at worst matched the level of down-voting [1]. This suggests a dichotomy of users who vote on Front page posts, those who read and contribute/vote on their comments pages and those who do not.

There are also examples which suggest that the 'Best' ranking algorithm on the comments pages may allow users to pick out and promote comments which are of high value (e.g. redd.it/lvr2x - a user details their letter to their member of congress and top-scoring comments include some from a 'former capitol hill staffer' explaining what happens to such letters and how to make this kind of appeal more effectively).

Reddit's success in raising awareness of SOPA and facilitating collective action against it can be largely attributed to its capacity to show a very large number of individuals the same set of items. The broadcasting of Front page posts sets the agenda on reddit, and among the many attending users there are often some with particular expertise – post and comment voting can allow contributions from these users to be widely seen, even where the user themselves is not a well-established redditor. In addition to insightful high-scoring comments, reddit's coverage of this story also incorporated a post by an individual attending a SOPA House Judiciary Committee hearing, providing a running commentary on proceedings and answering the questions of other users (redd.it/ne9zn) – a crowd-sourced on-location reporter.

During the SOPA case study reddit's users were also able to use the voting tools at their disposal to deal with a 'false dawn' in the GoDaddy boycott and to quickly adapt

---

[7] http://blog.reddit.com/2009/10/reddits-new-comment-sorting-system.html.

to a rapidly developing story (where the length of postponement of a vote on SOPA was initially over-estimated by a Front page post but quickly corrected by subsequent posts which displaced this on the Front page).

4.1 Collective Action on Reddit

The collective action against SOPA which was incubated on reddit called on a familiar set of repertoires to those employed by more conventional activism organizations (e.g. petitions, contact with representatives, boycotts). The major contrasts with activism organizations like *38degrees* and *Moveon* [19] are that (1) on reddit users were not dichotomized as 'leaders' or 'followers', proposals could come from any user and be circulated widely through the Front page, and (2) reddit set its own agenda for collective action in this case, rather than organizing around an issue which was already in the media spotlight.

In the absence of designated leaders, post and comment voting take on an organizational role. Instead of leaders who have the capacity to reach followers with messages – the messages which reach participants are merely those which score the most highly. This can result in mixed messages and chaotic action, but on the whole reddit's campaigns against SOPA show a surprising degree of strategy (quickly dropping campaigns which are seen as flawed, focusing on those which show early signs of impact through further Front page posts). The 258 posts about SOPA which appeared on reddit's default Front page were submitted by 223 different users. 16 users each submitted more than one post which appeared on the Front page, with 51 posts in total being submitted by these users. Aside from two administrator accounts with two posts each – all of the front page posts were submitted by 'ordinary' reddit users (i.e. not administrators or moderators). There is very little evidence of an oligarchy of power submitters who dominated reddit's coverage of this story or coordinated the community's attempts at collective action.

Reddit's capacity to set its own agenda for collective action stems from its function as an information broadcasting system – this could be likened to having an 'in-house' newspaper with a large readership. Although reddit is a 'Social News' site, collective action could emerge and thrive because of its loose specification of which items were eligible for submission. The latest article from *Ars Technica* could appear alongside a 23-page treatise from a Harvard law professor (redd.it/na3z8), a single-sentence summary by a reddit user (redd.it/nbepe), and the response received by another user from their member of congress (redd.it/lxrpk). All are merely 'posts', and have the capacity to appear on the Front page depending on how users vote.

Reddit has not been designed with collective action in mind, and its 'Social News' structure imbues attempts at collective action with certain qualities and limitations. Reddit posts are transitory in nature - for the hours they appear on the Front page they are highly visible, but when they slip from this page they become difficult to locate due to the site's notoriously poor search functionality. The post which proposes or ignites collective action is often edited to direct readers towards more lasting venues where that action can be pursued. These venues include newly created subreddits, websites, Facebook groups and IRC channels. Any user can provide these resources, and those who do so first, or whose resources are utilized, become *de facto* leaders within the ad hoc group that forms around the endeavor.

5 Reddit and the Fragmentation of Public Discourse

We posit that the speed with which awareness of SOPA could permeate reddit was dependent on the presence of 'default' subreddits with large readerships. For the first six weeks of the observation period high-visibility posts about SOPA were largely confined to the /r/technology subreddit – but through the default Front page these were also being shown to many readers with no particular interest in technology. By the end of the observation period posts about SOPA had appeared on the default Front page through 16 of the 20 default subreddits of that time – including humor-oriented subreddits like /r/funny and /r/AdviceAnimals. The variety of subreddits which 'covered' this story is evidence that awareness and opposition permeated reddit site-wide. Without this 'cross-fertilisation' of subreddits through the default Front page it is unlikely that SOPA opposition would have permeated the site's community.

Historically, reddit began in 2005 with just a single 'subreddit'. In 2008, the capacity to create a new subreddit was opened up to all users. This signaled the beginning of a slow but accelerating fragmentation of reddit's user-base: 240,000 subreddits have now been created by users, in February 2014 around 400 of these received more than 1,000 posts. This proliferation of subreddits, and the apparently increasing tendency for users to customize their subreddit subscriptions, is one of the most important developments on the site with regard to its broader social impact. In its early years reddit had a strong anti-fragmentation effect – users voted to select a small set of posts from the deluge of incoming submissions and these posts were shown to all users on the site's Front page. Now, with thousands of active subreddits to choose from, a reddit user can customize the site to generate their own personalized 'Daily Me' [18].

The site's administrators have been influential in this regard. For many years the number of default subreddits was fixed at 12, including /r/reddit.com which served as a 'miscellaneous' subreddit. In October 2011 the number of default subreddits was expanded to 25 and /r/reddit.com was decommissioned. In May 2014 the number of default subreddits was expanded again to 50. These changes served to expose reddit users to a much wider variety of subreddits, most likely including some they would have no interest in (therefore pushing users towards managing their subreddit subscriptions and viewing the site while signed into an account). Changes to the set of default subreddits are the primary means through which reddit's administrators have influenced the site's development and perceived identity. Reddit also began to display more messages which highlighted the subreddit system and prompted new users to begin managing their subscriptions.

The data which would allow us to quantify the level of fragmentation of reddit's readership is unavailable, but we can consider the levels of activity which occurs on default subreddits (and which can therefore appear on the uniform 'default Front page') as compared to non-default subreddits. Figure 2[8] shows the number of posts submitted to default and non-default subreddits by month. There is clearly an increasing proportion of posts being submitted to non-default subreddits, and these posts have no capacity to appear on the default Front page.

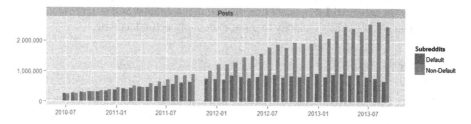

Fig. 2. Number of posts submitted to default and non-default subreddits by month, from July 2010 to September 2013.

While the trend may be towards users customizing their subreddit subscriptions and Front page, reddit has also added an '/r/all' option which shows the top-ranked posts from every subreddit (showing the same content to every user). Page view statistics for this page as compared to the 'default' and 'signed in' versions of the Front page would inform us about whether reddit users choose to embrace the 'Daily Me'.

6   Conclusions

The majority of posts submitted to reddit's bustling default subreddits are quickly jettisoned based on the votes of relatively few users – a small group of 'voting superparticipants' specialize in this role. There is however no evidence that this group systematically filters out certain types of content, or dominates the website with their own submissions. Taking the post voting system's structure and usage into account, it is no surprise that it does not result in reliable decisions about which posts to display on the 'Front page' [6]. These decisions are however controlled by reddit's users *en masse* and posts which appear on the Front page are broadcast to these users – their content and comments influences subsequent voting behavior in a feedback loop.

The reddit of late 2011 could be described as a more or less unified 'public sphere' [20] – albeit one which marginalized deliberation in favor of the rapid broadcasting of new information and ideas. In subsequent years this unified public sphere appears to be fragmenting as users increasingly choose a set of subreddits unique to their interests. Some of these subreddits exist for the purpose of criticizing other areas of the site (e.g. /r/ShitRedditSays, /r/SubredditDrama) and can be considered as 'subaltern counterpublics' [21].

Many of these newly populated subreddits have comprehensive rules about what can be submitted and moderators who enforce these rules through the deletion of submitted content – a departure from reddit's earlier history where the ideal of distributed

---

[8] Based on data fromhttp://redditanalytics.com.

moderation through voting dominated. In the campaign against SOPA, highly attended to default subreddits like /r/technology were instrumental in raising awareness and fomenting opposition broadly among reddit's users. The loose specification of what could be submitted to these subreddits was also important in allowing these users to transition seamlessly from raising awareness of the legislation to organizing against it. Writing now in early 2015 it appears that the campaign against SOPA represented the high water-mark of reddit's capacity to unite effectively behind a cause.

References

1. Mills, R.: Distributed Moderation systems - an exploration of their utility and the social implications of their widespread adoption. Ph.D. thesis, Lancaster University (2014). http://eprints.lancs.ac.uk/70128/1/R_Mills_PhD_Thesis_Final.pdf
2. Lampe, C., Resnick, P.: Slash (dot) and burn: distributed moderation in a large online conversation space. In: Proceedings of the SIGCHI Conference on Human Factors in Computing Systems, pp. 543–550. ACM (2004)
3. Lerman, K., Galstyan, A.: Analysis of social voting patterns on digg. In: Proceedings of the First Workshop on Online Social Networks, pp. 7–12. ACM (2008)
4. Lerman, K., Hogg, T.: Using a model of social dynamics to predict popularity of news. In: Proceedings of the 19th International Conference on World Wide Web, pp. 621–630. ACM (2010)
5. Wu, F., Wilkinson, D.M., Huberman, B.A.: Feedback Loops of Attention in Peer Production. Presented at CSE 2009 (2009)
6. Gilbert, E.: Widespread underprovision on reddit. In: Proceedings of the 2013 Conference on Computer Supported Cooperative Work, pp. 803–808. ACM (2013)
7. Halavais, A.: DO DUGG DIGGERS DIGG DILIGENTLY?: Feedback as motivation in collaborative moderation systems. Inform. Commun. Soc. 12, 444–459 (2009)
8. Lampe, C., Johnston, E.: Follow the (slash) dot: effects of feedback on new members in an online community. In: Proceedings of the 2005 International ACM SIGGROUP Conference on Supporting Group Work, pp. 11–20. ACM (2005)
9. Loudon, M.: "Research in the wild" in online communities: reddit's resistance to SOPA. First Monday 19 (2014)
10. Bergstrom, K.: "Don't feed the troll": shutting down debate about community expectations on Reddit. com. First Monday 16 (2011)
11. Halavais, A.: Home made big data? Challenges and opportunities for participatory social research. First Monday 18 (2013)
12. Benkler, Y., Roberts, H., Faris, R., Solow-Niederman, A., Etling, B.: 2013 - Social mobilization and the networked public sphere. Mapping the SOPA-PIPA debate. Berkman Cent. Res. Publ. (2013)
13. Dover, D.: How reddit ranking algorithms work (2008). http://www.seomoz.org/blog/reddit-stumbleupon-delicious-and-hacker-news-algorithms-exposed
14. Graham, T., Wright, S.: Discursive equality and everyday talk online: the impact of "superparticipants". J. Comput. Mediated Commun. 19, 625–642 (2014)
15. Halliday, J.: Digg investigates claims of conservative "censorship" (2010). http://www.theguardian.com/technology/2010/aug/06/digg-investigates-claims-conservative-censorship
16. Keen, A.: The Cult of the Amateur: How Today's Internet is Killing our Culture. Doubleday/Currency, New York (2007)

17. Ostrom, E.: Governing the Commons: The Evolution of Institutions for Collective Action. Cambridge University Press, Cambridge (1990)
18. Sunstein, C.R.: Republic.com. Princeton University Press, Princeton (2001)
19. Chadwick, A.: The Hybrid Media System: Politics and Power. Oxford University Press, Oxford (2013)
20. Habermas, J.: The Structural Transformation of the Public Sphere: An Inquiry into a Category of Bourgeois Society. MIT Press, Cambridge (1991)
21. Fraser, N.: Rethinking the public sphere: a contribution to the critique of actually existing democracy. Soc. Text **25**, 56–80 (1990)

Inter-Social-Networking: Accounting for Multiple Identities

Dominic Price[1]([⊠]), Derek McAuley[1], Richard Mortier[2],
Chris Greenhalgh[1], Michael Brown[1], and Spyros Angelopoulos[1]

[1] Horizon Digital Economy Research, University of Nottingham,
Nottingham, UK
{dominic.price,derek.mcauley,chris.greenhalgh,
michael.brown,spyros.angelopoulos}@nottingham.ac.uk
[2] Systems Research Group, Cambridge University Computer Laboratory,
Cambridge, UK
richard.mortier@cl.cam.ac.uk

Abstract. We argue that the current approaches to online social networking give rise to numerous challenges regarding the management of the multiple facets of people's digital identities within and around social networking sites (SNS). We propose an architecture for enabling people to better manage their SNS identities that is informed by the way the core Internet protocols developed to support interoperation of proprietary network protocols, and based on the idea of Separation of Concerns [1]. This does not require modification of existing services but is predicated on providing a connecting layer over them, both as a mechanism to address problems of privacy and identity, and to create opportunities to open up online social networking to a much richer set of possible interactions and applications.

Keywords: Social-networking · Privacy · Identity · Infrastructure · Architecture

1 Introduction

Online social network sites such as Twitter, Facebook and Google+ have become enormously popular over recent years, for example; Facebook now claims to have over 1 billion active accounts.[1] This popularity has been driven by many factors: the desire we have as people to communicate and to belong; the convenience that is provided by offloading contact management to external services; and the entertainment value of keeping up with our friends, family and acquaintances. Their popularity has led to these, and related, services becoming synonymous with social networking, but this popularity masks a number of problems with their implementation and structure.

In real life, social networking is far more broadly defined: as social beings we are well known to benefit from involvement and participation in groups [2]. We participate in multiple, often overlapping, social networks simultaneously rather than one

---

[1] http://news.cnet.com/8301-1023_3-57525797-93.

© Springer International Publishing Switzerland 2015
G. Meiselwitz (Ed.): SCSM 2015, LNCS 9182, pp. 242–252, 2015.
DOI: 10.1007/978-3-319-20367-6_24

all-encompassing social network as Facebook, Google+, etc. aspire to be. The tension between our many online identities and the desire of companies such as Facebook and Google to force us to present just a single identity through their 'real name' policies [3] is an example of the evidence that our lives are far more complex than that which is captured by these services.

Observing that at least part of the problem is the centralized nature of these commercial services, some have proposed decentralized equivalents, e.g., Diaspora.[2] Decentralization certainly mitigates many of the problems of the large centralized social networks, e.g., resilience, need for personal control, support for multiple identities, but it is not alone sufficient to address the problems raised in online social networking (discussed in Sect. 2).

Our position is informed by observation of the development of computer networking in the 1970 s and 1980 s: the industry moved from many different, mutually incompatible, proprietary networking standards towards a single common inter-operation protocol now recognize as the Internet Protocol (IP). We advocate a similar move in the world of online social networking, both to address problems of privacy and identity, but also to open up social networking to a much richer set of possible interactions and applications.

By analogy with the development of the Internet's TCP/IP protocol suite (discussed in Sect. 3), we argue that social networking requires a new architecture that is sufficiently flexible to encompass the very broad range of social network interactions in which we participate (discussed in Sect. 4). We present and discuss a proposal for such an architecture, alongside initial exploratory prototype development and experiments we are carrying out into its implementation (discussed in Sect. 5).

2 One Size Does Not Fit All

Notwithstanding the efforts of a handful of corporations to become pre-eminent in global social networking, notably Facebook and Google, it seems clear that need for a richer set of services will remain. Moving outside nations where English is commonly spoken, whether as first or second language, we find a rich set of social media services. For example, use of VK is widespread in Russian speaking countries; after having been created in the US, Orkut is now 59 % Brazilian; and in China, RenRen and Sina Weibo are used instead of Facebook and Twitter.

However, many other online communities also behave as social networks in terms of the interactions they support (commenting, following, sharing). For example, Amazon reviews, blog-specific commentator communities, personal and community YouTube channels, Github source code repositories, and even non-public Enterprise internal communications. Indeed, companies have been formed to support this broader definition of more specific communities. For example, Ning[3] supports over 2 million communities, ranging in size from just tens to over a million members, within which

---

[2] http://diasporaproject.org/.

[3] http://ning.com, acquired by Glam Media in 2011.

you can either reuse an existing identity (Facebook, Google+, Yahoo!) or create a fresh one. Examining the enterprise sector we find, for example, Yammer[4] and Jabber.[5]

As this plethora of social networks suggests, many (if not most) of us have multiple online identities through which we actively manage our social interactions. Often these identities are anonymous, and many of us would suffer embarrassment, loss or worse if all these identities were publicly linked. Many reasons why we choose to explicitly manage overlap among our social networks, even keeping some networks completely distinct from others, are completely normal and not in the least clandestine. For example, teenagers wishing to discuss sensitive health matters in online fora [4], employees complaining about treatment at work [5], or those engaged in political commentary in uncomfortable or dangerous situations [6].

Attempts by the major services to support this richness in our social networks via access control mechanisms, e.g., Facebook lists, Google+ Circles, have proved largely inadequate. Typically whilst users understand how these mechanisms work the cognitive effort required for creation and maintenance results in either their mis- or non-use. Furthermore, collating all of one's social interactions and data into a single service gives rise to serious risks such as identity theft.

Fully decentralized systems such as Diaspora have seen some success, but are still very much under construction and do not address the entire problem. Other decentralized versions of common services include status.net for microblogging (centralized equivalent: Twitter), wordpress.org for blogging (centralized equivalent: Wordpress. com), and use of the git repository management system and its built-in web-server for collaboration around code (centralized equivalent: Github). To take Diaspora as one of the more mature examples, it supports asymmetric sharing, and federation among Diaspora pods, whether community or individual, enabling much greater choice over who is trusted.

In all these cases, whether decentralized or not, the lack of proper boundaries between such groupings permits inappropriate linking and unexpected leakage of content and relationships between them and to the outside world [7–11]. Methods to detect and resolve privacy conflicts [12], and more generally, to limit and monitor information released online [13] are lacking.

The issues we note above are not completely new: some in the W3C have previously noted similar issues concerning uniformity of addressing and access around cloud storage,[6] for example. However, these and other Linked Data approaches to managing our online identities, tend to make presumptions of constituent data being public, and fail to properly address questions such as selective sharing of and delegation of access to data, and the need for an 'app ecosystem' rather than a focus on human consumption of data.[7]

---

[4] http://yammer.com/, acquired by Microsoft in 2012.

[5] http://www.cisco.com/web/products/voice/jabber.html, acquired by Cisco in 2008.

[6] http://www.w3.org/DesignIssues/CloudStorage.html.

[7] http://www.ted.com/talks/tim_berners_lee_on_the_next_web.html.

3   Your Grandfather's Internet

The essence of our argument is that current online social network platforms are ultimately limited, for one of two reasons. First, whether centralized or decentralized they are use-specific and to date have been designed with service specific APIs, limiting the scope of the applications that can be built[8] and requiring that any specific application be implemented afresh for each platform. Second, the terms and conditions commonly prohibit the use of multiple accounts: to express multiple identities we must use several services. Even for those services that permit – or at least, do not prohibit – multiple identities, the possibility of correlating accounts through means as simple as IP access address requires trusting (at least!) the provider to not do this, limiting privacy.

Our approach to this problem develops by analogy[9] to the development of the ARPANET into the CATENET and thus the Internet, and so we next sketch this historic development.

Proposed in the late 1960 and first implemented in 1969, the ARPANET was one of the first operational packet-switched networks.[10] A key part of the early ARPANET was the Host-to-Host protocol, known as the Network Control Protocol (NCP, 1970) [15], that provided connectivity and flow control between processes running on different ARPANET- connected hosts. In 1974 Kahn and Cerf presented a protocol for interconnecting distinct packet networks [16], separating the notions of host-host data transfer and inter-network communication via a sequence of gateways.

In 1977, Jon Postel introduced IEN 2 [17] as follows "The position taken here is that internetwork communication should be view as having two components: the hop by hop relaying of a message, and the end to end control of the conversation." and subsequently wrote "We are screwing up in our design of internet protocols by violating the principle of layering.". In IEN 2 he proposes the split of TCP into IP (known therein as "the Internet Hop Protocol") and TCP (known therein as "the Internet Host Protocol"), and subsequently as IP and TCP. Following the RFC process, the implementation of this split is described in RFC801 [18], with the final "flag day" (January 1st, 1983) when the ARPANET ceased to support NCP, switching over completely to IP/TCP.

Building on previous work by Pouzin [19], Cerf set out the "Catenet[11] strategy for internetworking" [20] in 1978. This, and other, elements were later elaborated into the Internet architecture by Clark [21]. Clearly a great deal of related work took place at the time, and things have developed enormously since then. However, the core of the Internet architecture is this separation between a network layer provided by IP and a transport layer provided by TCP. The former is responsible for addressing and transferring data between hosts (implicitly identified with network interfaces), and the latter for transferring data between processes.

---

[8] Never mind the limitations on use placed on many of the APIs.

[9] With awareness of the perils of this approach [14].

[10] http://www.internetsociety.org/internet/what-internet/history-internet/brief-history-internet.

[11] From 'concatenated networks'.

This architecture had, ultimately, enormous commercial impact. The simplicity of the IP layer meant that it could easily be ported to run over almost any underlying link layer technology [22]. Over the course of the 1970 s, 80 s and 90 s this led to the diminishing in importance of proprietary local area network technology from vendors such as IBM, DEC and Xerox in favor of support for IP. On the flip side, software developers could cease caring what particular flavor of network they were operating over, and simply assume that IP, and their choice of transport protocol (e.g., TCP, UDP), were available. The result was a steady explosion in the use of the network, reaching back to email in 1972, but continuing with other applications such as FTP, Gopher, the web, BitTorrent, YouTube, and on into the present day and foreseeable future.

4 Refactoring Social Networks

It is easy to see the inherent weakness of the dominant centralized social networks such as Facebook: by imposing a one-size-fits-all model on social interaction, while they (the social networks) may satisfy some of the needs of a large number of people, they will never be able to satisfy all the needs of all the people. In particular, their centralized cloud-hosted nature means that they very poorly, if at all, support our need for multiple online identities where we are in control of the linking of those identities [3]. Referring to our sketch of the Internet's evolution, we see commercial systems like Facebook as analogous to proprietary networking solutions: while initially successful and certainly satisfactory for many customers, they were too restrictive to enable the explosion of use that the Internet subsequently saw. Only by interposing a simple interconnection layer such as IP could the complexity of development for these proprietary networks be contained, and their utility accessed.

Decentralized approaches such as Diaspora address that weakness to some extent, but a more subtle – but still serious – problem remains. By baking the data types handled by the system into the data exchange protocols, users must either cast the data they wish to exchange into the formats supported, or install expensive, brittle and bug-prone gateways to interconnect different networks (cf. "Relay Service" [17]). Again, comparing to our sketch of the Internet' evolution, this is analogous to the mistake noted in the early development of the Internet protocols. Only by separating concerns between IP and TCP (and other transport protocols subsequently) could the combination of absolute flexibility and a simple, uniform protocol interface be pro- vided.

Finally, a key requirement for providing the levels of access control, communication privacy and (where desired) authenticated identity required by such disparate and personal interaction is the ability to securely and coherently generate, manage and distribute secrets. Only by providing consistent mechanisms for deriving and distributing appropriate public key material can we begin to meet the complex, multi-faceted identity needs of real life.

In short, without a simple way to interconnect and manage our identities on different social networks, we will not see the same explosion in creativity that the Internet gave rise to.

We close this discussion of the merits of refactoring currently popular social network services with a key observation concerning email. Since the early days of the ARPANET (ca. 1972), Internet users have commonly used several email addresses, e.g., to distinguish personal and university/corporate communication. Indeed, today's Internet users are often forced to have several email addresses, e.g., one in the cloud that provides some longevity, and one forced upon them by their ISP for ISP to consumer communication.

As a result, we have designed the tools – primarily email clients – to understand and manage this. Importantly, the only point at which these our many email identities must exist together is within those clients in the private context of our personal devices such as mobile phone, tablet and personal computer.[12]

5 An Inter-Social Network

We next elaborate on the technical implications of such a separation of concerns. We believe that the key features for an inter-SNS layer are: transport-independent addressing, format standardization for referring to data distributed through a particular social network, and flexible – but standardized – support for use of asymmetric encryption for per-service and per-recipient authentication and privacy. These features can be achieved through:

Loose Binding of Identities. Where a single person has multiple online identities, the linking of these identities will only be performed in client software based on out-of-band information; identities need not explicitly contain any information that can be used to link them together. Instead linking must rely on information provided by the person to whom the identities refer, or the knowledge of the person who has a social network connection to the first person. This will allow messages being produced by the same author to be identified whilst also protecting the identities of the author.

Semi-structured Data. By defining and making available schema details for messages, and providing enough information within the message (the semi-structure) to determine the scheme, the online social network service provider is at liberty to structure their messages as they see fit. In some cases a message might be nothing more than a string of specified length, or an image; in others, a message might have very rich structure, with extensive metadata in addition to the raw content.

Asymmetry and Authentication. Schema can be defined that support part or all of a message being encrypted, enabling privacy and authentication. Contacts would be required to associate trust relationships through out-of-band mechanisms such as OAuth or face-to-face interaction.

---

[12] Some folk may choose to configure a single cloud-hosted email service to fetch mail from all their accounts for simplicity, but this is a personal choice and by doing so they risk making confidential information available for data-mining by cloud-providers.

5.1 Discussion

Support for legacy social networks is straightforward to achieve, much as IP was provided over legacy proprietary networks. From a technical point-of-view, one could provide service shims[13] that implement the above abstraction over existing proprietary APIs. As noted above however the brittle nature of these APIs would necessitate constant updating of these shims to track the changes in the APIs, the technical challenge is therefore only one piece of the puzzle. From a regulatory point-of-view it looks increasingly likely that moves such as upcoming EU data protection regulation and the UK's midata[14] initiative will enshrine a right for each of us to extract all the data by and about us held by a social network, enabling us easily to move away from legacy services. Applications can then be written that make use of the simplicity and transparency of the new API (as specified by these regulations), enabling much smoother and richer social integration in our online interactions rather than the current state where we are limited to either using a social network identity with a third party service (and the privacy infringement that entails) or simple (re-)posting of data on pre-specified services.

5.2 Current Implementation

We are currently working towards the creation of a prototype social networking platform that will allow us to experiment with the key features of; *loose binding of identities, semi-structured data* and *asymmetry and authentication* as described above. Whilst there are many aspects to social networking, including identity and relationships (e.g., Twitter followers, Facebook friends), we have chosen messaging as our starting point and are developing prototypes in order to experiment and study with message structure and message transport; our initial goal being the development of a generic client for aggregating content across multiple social networks. Figure 1 shows a high-level diagram of the prototype architecture.

The *shim layer* is responsible for fetching messages (Facebook feed, Twitter timeline) and contacts from existing social networks (we have currently implemented shims for Facebook and Twitter) and posting messages to these networks. It is also responsible for conversion of messages and contacts from the network specific formats to the format used by the prototype (*semi-structured data*). The *storage* format we are experimenting with for storing messages in the Internet Message Format [23] (commonly referred to as email). Through MIME [24], an email body is able to store a wide variety of content, especially content typically associated with social network messages (text, images, video, etc.) making it an appropriate selection for message storage. Using this format also allows us to re-use existing email clients as *clients* for the prototype (e.g., we can use the Thunderbird[15] email client to read and write messages).

---

[13] http://en.wikipedia.org/wiki/Shim_%28computing%29.

[14] https://www.gov.uk/government/policies/providing-better-information-and-protection-for-consumers/supporting-pages/personal-data.

[15] https://www.mozilla.org/en-GB/thunderbird/.

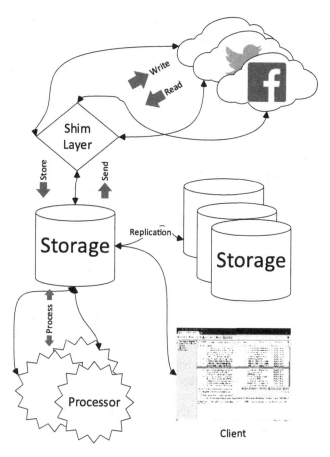

Fig. 1. Prototype platform architecture

Multiple social network accounts can be registered with the shim layer, where each account is treated as a separate identity. The platform is the only place where these identities are explicitly associated with each other (*loose binding of identities*). A user of the platform is able to aggregate content from their different accounts/identities but they are the only person who can view the aggregate, when sending messages they can explicitly control the account/identity (or multiples thereof) that is (are) used to transmit the message.

The *processor* layer is a queue through which incoming and outgoing messages are routed. Each processor is a small independent application that performs actions on each message as the message passes through the queue. One example processor that we are developing is to provide encryption for outgoing messages where the recipient is known to accept encrypted messages. Other suggested uses for the processor layer are to provide cross-social network search or integrated spam filtering.

Finally, *replication* of the storage layer across multiple locations allows redundancy and for clients to access messages from multiple independent locations, e.g., a mobile device could maintain a copy of the store so that messages can be accessed in periods of no-connectivity. In addition, replication will allow processors to run in the most appropriate environment, e.g., a processor intensive processor could run in the cloud on a high-performance device rather than a mobile device where computational power is at a premium.

5.3   Evaluation

At this present time, the prototype has not yet reached a point of development at which we can begin to experiment with it and evaluate it fully. We are able however to provide the following evaluation based on its current status. In particular we can begin to evaluate the implications of transferring the responsibility of message storage from social network providers to the individual. Taking the specific example of Twitter as a social network service provider, message storage is handled by Twitter and is thus of zero-cost to an individual user. Within our proposed system, storage for messages must be provided by the user the space requirements for which will only grow over time and thus incur a cost (options such as free online storage providers are an option there is however still an administrative cost involved in setting up and maintaining these). An analysis of the authors' Twitter streams when mapped to a MIME email message reveals an average size per message of 2 kilobytes (increasing significantly if the Tweet has an image attached). Whilst usage between users will vary greatly in terms of numbers of messages received we can begin to use this figure as a baseline to calculate storage costs. For example, a user receiving an average of 100 Tweets per day will require storage for approximately 71 megabytes within a year. Alone, a fairly trivial amount of storage but once we start factoring in other social networks, particularly media rich networks such as Flickr, this figure could increase significantly.

6   Conclusions

In this paper we have elaborated on three serious problems that we perceive with the current state of online social networking, from a systems/networking point-of-view. As a result, we believe it is necessary to revisit the ways that we have been architecting and building online social networking platforms, to provide a cleaner separation of layers. This will enable greater flexibility, creativity and utility in the exploitation of our social graphs, while also providing us with greater control over that exploitation. We believe that doing so will open social networking up to richer application development, and so will enable the same kind of explosion in use that the Internet caused with computer networking.

Acknowledgements. This work is supported by Horizon Digital Economy Research, RCUK grant EP/G065802/1; and by CREATe, the Centre for Copyright and New Business Models, RCUK grant AH/K000179/1. Packages and source are available under open source licenses at github.com/CREATe-centre/.

References

1. Hürsch, W.L., Lopes, C.V.: Separation of concerns. Technical report. North Eastern University (1995)
2. Portes, A.: Social capital: its origins and applications in modern sociology. Ann. Rev. Sociol. **24**(1), 1–24 (1998)
3. Edwards, L., McAuley, D.: What's in a name? Real name policies and social networks. In: Proceedings of 1st International Workshop on Internet Science and Web Science Synergies (INETWEBSCI), Paris, France, 1 May 2013
4. van der Velden, M., El Emam, K.: "Not all my friends need to know": a qualitative study of teenage patients, privacy, and social media. J. Am. Med. Inform. Assoc. **20**, 16–24 (2012)
5. O'Brien, C.N.: The top ten NLRB cases on Facebook firings and employer social media policies. Oregon Law Rev. **92**(2) (2014). http://ssrn.com/abstract=2277900
6. Attia, A.M., Aziz, N., Friedman, B., Elhusseiny, M.F.: Commentary: the impact of social networking tools on political change in Egypt's "revolution 2.0". Electron. Commer. Res. Appl. **10**(4), 369–374 (2011)
7. Madejski, M., Johnson, M.L., Bellovin, S.M.: The failure of online social network privacy settings. Technical Report CUCS-010-11, Columbia University Computer Science, Columbia University, New York, USA (2011)
8. Ozenc, F.K., Farnham, S.D.: Life "modes" in social media. In: Proceedings of the SIGCHI Conference on Human Factors in Computing Systems, CHI 2011, Vancouver, BC, Canada, pp. 561–570 (2011)
9. Zheleva, E., Getoor, L.: To join or not to join: the illusion of privacy in social networks with mixed public and private user profiles. In: Proceedings of the 18th International Conference on World Wide Web, WWW 2009, Madrid, Spain, pp. 531–540 (2009)
10. Le Blond, S., Zhang, C., Legout, A., Ross, K., Dabbous, W.: I know where you are and what you are sharing: exploiting p2p communications to invade users' privacy. In: Proceedings of the 2011 ACM SIGCOMM Conference on Internet Measurement Conference, IMC 2011, Berlin, Germany, pp. 45–60 (2011)
11. Pesce, J.P., Casas, D.L., Rauber, G., Almeida, V.: Privacy attacks in social media using photo tagging networks: a case study with Facebook. In: Proceedings of the 1st Workshop on Privacy and Security in Online Social Media, PSOSM 2012, Lyon, France, pp. 4:1–4:8 (2012)
12. Hu, H., Ahn, G.-J., Jorgensen, J.: Detecting and resolving privacy conflicts for collaborative data sharing in online social networks. In: Proceedings of the 27th Annual Computer Security Applications Conference, ACSAC 2011, Orlando, Florida, pp. 103–112. ACM (2011)
13. Gates, C.E.: Access control requirements for web 2.0 security and privacy. In: Proceedings of Workshop on Web 2.0 Security & Privacy (W2SP 2007) (2007). [15] Halasz, F., Moran, T.P.: Analogy considered
14. Halasz, F., Moran, T.P.: Analogy considered harmful. In: Proceedings of the 1982 Conference on Human Factors in Computing Systems, CHI 1982, Gaithersburg, Maryland, USA, pp. 383–386 (1982)
15. Crocker, S.: Protocol Notes. RFC 36, IETF, March 1970
16. Cerf, V.G., Kahn, R.E.: A protocol for packet network interconnection. IEEE Trans. Commun. **22**(5), 637–648 (1974)
17. Postel, J.: 2.3.3.2 Comments on Internet Protocol and TCP. IEN 2, ISI, 15 August 1977
18. Postel, J.: NCP/TCP transition plan. RFC 801, IETF, November 1981

19. Pouzin, L.: A proposal for interconnecting packet switching networks. In: Proceedings of EUROCOMP, Bronel University, pp. 1023–1036, May 1974
20. Cerf, V.: The catenet model for internetworking. IEN 48, DARPA/IPTO, July 1978
21. Clark, D.: The design philosophy of the DARPA Internet protocols. In: Proceedings of ACM SIGCOMM 1988, Stanford, California, USA, pp. 106–114 (1988)
22. Waitzman, D.: Standard for the transmission of IP datagrams on avian carriers. RFC 1149, IETF, April 1990
23. Resnick, P. (ed.): Internet Message Format. RFC 2822, IETF, April 2001
24. Freed, N., Borenstein, N.: Multipurpose Internet Mail Extensions (MIME) Part One: Format of Internet Message Bodies. RFC 2045, IETF, November 1996

Identifying Collaboration Strategies
in Scientific Collaboration Networks

Maria Lúcia Bento Villela[1,2(✉)], Simone Xavier[1],
and Raquel Oliveira Prates[1]

[1] DCC - ICEx, Universidade Federal de Minas Gerais,
Belo Horizonte, MG, Brazil
{mvillela,simone.xavier,rprates}@dcc.ufmg.br
[2] DECOM – FACET, UFVJM, Diamantina, MG, Brazil

Abstract. A number of virtual networks, called Scientific Collaboration Networks (SCNs) have been increasingly adopted as means to connect researchers around the world. In this article we have analyzed how the SCNs ResearchGate and Academia.edu support collaboration between researchers, through an analysis of their interface and contrast with the general purpose online social network (OSN) Facebook. The analysis of these systems allowed us to identify four categories through which network members collaborate: information sharing, interaction levels, communities and artifacts. Although the categories are the same for SCNs and OSNs, the strategies adopted in each context are different. We discussed how these strategies, which can be used to support design and evaluation of SCNs, are used to foster collaboration among researchers in these systems.

Keywords: Scientific Collaboration Networks · Social networks · Semiotic engineering · Semiotic Inspection Method · Communicability evaluation

1 Introduction

Applications and services that facilitate collective action and social interaction online between people with rich exchange of information, motivated by different interests, have come to dominate the Web [11]. Thus, a large number of online social networks (OSNs) have emerged, allowing for greater interaction between their users, based on exchanging and sharing of information. In the academic context, specifically, considering that scientific research is usually developed through collaboration between researchers and research groups, networks similar to OSNs can be used by researchers to share knowledge and find potential research partners, enabling collaboration on a global scale [9].

In this context, a number of virtual networks, called Scientific Collaboration Networks (SCNs) have been proposed. These systems support individual researchers' efforts to form and maintain collaborative relationships for conducting research within a specific context as well as expanding the scientific collaboration scope [13]. Thus, understanding collaboration strategies that are used in SCNs becomes important in order to ensure that they effectively meet scientific communities' needs.

© Springer International Publishing Switzerland 2015
G. Meiselwitz (Ed.): SCSM 2015, LNCS 9182, pp. 253–264, 2015.
DOI: 10.1007/978-3-319-20367-6_25

This article contributes to this line of research by identifying the collaboration strategies that are currently provided in SCNs. To do so, we analyzed the SCNs ResearchGate[1] and academia.edu[2], using the Semiotic Inspection Method (SIM) [5, 6]. In order to discuss the differences between these collaboration strategies and those adopted in OSNs, the results from the SCNs analysis were contrasted with the results from analysis of the OSN Facebook[3].

The results of this study contribute to researchers and developers of collaborative systems, specifically SCNs. To researchers, the identification of the types of collaboration provided in SCNs is a relevant step in understanding the context of collaboration and the proposed solutions in current SCNs. The results can also be useful in allowing for more effective design and evaluation of SCNs, and thus improving the quality of their interaction.

In the next section, we present the related works that investigate SCNs. We then present the underlying theoretical framework of our study and the method used in the analysis of the systems. Next we describe how SIM was applied in our study, followed by the results of the analysis. Finally we discuss our results and present the next steps in our research.

2   Related Work

SCNs are noteworthy for presenting a number of features designed specifically to meet the scientific community's needs [14]. Considering the importance these systems have acquired recently, due to their ability to enable collaboration and sharing of scientific knowledge, some studies have been conducted in order to encourage the SCNs projects to effectively reach their proposed goals [1, 2, 8, 13, 15].

Schleyer et al. [13] suggested a research agenda for SCNs that covers four areas that contribute to their success: foundations, presentation, architecture, and evaluation. "Foundations" addresses core principles and general factors that underlie the design of effective SCNs; "presentation" deals with issues concerning user interfaces, interaction design and system functionality; "architecture" is concerned with internal design of SCNs and how they interact with external information sources; and "evaluation" is concerned with how SCNs outcomes can be framed and measured.

Lackes et al. [8] presented a conceptual design model of an SCN that helps bridge the gap between researchers at universities and enterprises, improving collaboration within systems. Also regarding the conceptual modeling of SCNs, given that the turnover rate of users remains a great challenge for the viability of these systems, Cao et al. [2] explored the determinants that impact members' continued participation behavior in SCNs by attempting to address what factors would cultivate different forms of commitment of members to a virtual group. Besides, the authors explored how would these different forms of commitment impact members' continuance intention in

---

[1] www.researchgate.net.

[2] www.academia.edu.

[3] www.facebook.com.

SCNs and proposed a preliminary model for understanding continued knowledge sharing in SCNs.

However, we could not find studies that focus specifically on the analysis of types of collaboration provided by SCNs. In this article we analyze SCNs identifying and discussing the collaboration strategies used to support interaction among researchers through these systems.

3   Theoretical Framework

Semiotic Engineering [4] is an explanatory theory of HCI that perceives human–computer interaction as a special case of computer-mediated human communication. A system's interface is a message sent from designers to users about the designers' vision on who the users are and how their product meets the users' needs, and what benefits and value it can ultimately bring to the users' lives. Designers are not present at interaction time, so the message is conveyed to users as they interact with the system's interface. Thus the designer to user message is in fact a meta-message being conveyed by the interface.

In collaborative systems, such as SCNs, the message sent from designer, through the interface, is not to a single user, but to a group of people who will interact with each other through the system. In this case, the designers' message to uscrs also conveys their decisions with respect to the roles that each group member can take, the activities and tasks through which they can or should interact, and the protocols and languages that should be used by users to communicate [4].

The designer-to-user message is comprised of signs arranged at the interface. A sign, as defined by Peirce [12], is "anything that stands for something else, to somebody in some respect or capacity". Semiotic engineering classifies the signs in three classes [3, 5, 6]: static, dynamic and metalinguistic. Static signs are signs whose meaning is interpreted independently of temporal and causal relations and express the system's state. Dynamic signs represent the system's behavior. They are bounded to temporal and causal aspects of the interface and communicate the processing that leads to transitions between system states. Metalinguistic signs are explanations from designer to users about the system or other interface signs.

One of the methods that have been proposed to evaluate the quality of the system as a designer to user communication is the Semiotic Inspection Method (SIM) [3, 5, 6]. SIM is an inspection method that evaluates the intended message being sent by designers to users and identifies potential breakdowns users may have when interacting with the system. SIM is an interpretive and qualitative method and that can be used technically (to identify problems in a system's interface) or scientifically (to identify or explore research issues represented in the interface) [3, 6].

SIM is composed of one preparation step and five application steps. The preparation step is carried out in four sub-steps: (i) definition of the purpose of the inspection; (ii) informal inspection of the system in order to define the intended focus of the evaluation; (iii) identification of the intended users, main objectives and activities that the system supports; and (iv) preparation of inspection scenarios that provide the contextual structure necessary for the communication analysis.

The application steps of SIM are: (1) inspection of metalinguistic signs; (2) inspection of static signs; (3) inspection of dynamics signs; (4) compare and contrast the meta-message identified in steps (1), (2) and (3); and (5) carry out the appreciation of the meta-communication quality. Steps (1), (2) and (3) are done iteratively. In these steps the evaluator makes a segmented analysis of the system, one for each of the three classes of signs: metalinguistic, static and dynamic. As a result of each step the evaluator reconstructs the meta-message being conveyed by the designer through each type of sign and identifies the potential breakdowns (in the technical application) or evidences regarding the research issue of interest (in the scientific application). In step (4) the evaluator should contrast and compare the results generated in the first three steps. The evaluator should explore the possibility of the user assigning different meanings to the signs or even identify cases where the meta-message is incomplete due to the lack of signs that clarify the designer's intent. Finally, in step (5) the evaluator must reconstruct a complete/unified meta-communication message by comparing, integrating and interpreting the data collected in previous steps of the method. The evaluator is also expected to articulate his/her findings about the communication quality of the system based on the communicative strategies identified in previous steps.

When applied scientifically, the purpose of the evaluation is defined through the research question to be investigated. The system to be evaluated is only then chosen as an application instance that serves the purpose of research [3, 6]. Moreover, in this case, SIM requires a final triangulation step, in order to ensure the scientific validity of results, taking into account interpretations generated from other sources [3]. Figure 1 illustrates Semiotic Inspection Method steps for a scientific application.

In our study, SIM was applied to investigate whether SCNs offer collaboration strategies which are specific to the scientific collaboration context. To do so, firstly we applied SIM to ResearchGate and identified the collaboration strategies offered to users. Next, we applied SIM to academia.edu with the same focus and compared the results with the ones found through the inspection of ResearchGate. Finally, SIM was applied to Facebook to identify how the previously identified scientific collaboration

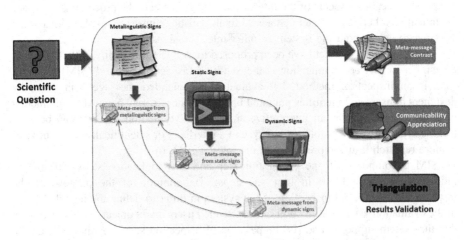

Fig. 1. Semiotic Inspection Method steps for a scientific application

strategies differed from social collaboration strategies. In the next section we briefly describe how SIM was applied in each case.

4 Methodology

In order to investigate whether there were collaboration strategies that were specific to Scientific Collaboration Networks, the first step in our study methodology was to identify which collaboration strategies were being used in SCNs. The next step was to contrast the strategies identified for SCNs with collaboration strategies being used in general OSNs. Figure 2 shows an overview of the methodology.

To perform the first step, two instances of SCN applications – namely, Research Gate and academia.edu were chosen. The two systems were chosen due to their high popularity[4]. Research Gate was initially inspected using SIM in November 2011 and the inspection was reviewed in July 2012, by two evaluators independently and their findings consolidated. As a result an initial set of the adopted collaboration strategies being used were identified.

Next, we proceeded with the application of SIM to academia.edu. The same inspection scenario used in Research Gate was used in academia.edu and the analysis was conducted by one evaluator in May 2012 and reviewed in September of the same year. The set of collaboration strategies identified for academia.edu were used to confirm and refine the initial findings for Research Gate. As a result, we identified what types of collaboration were being offered to researchers in SCNs and what was their focus.

The next aspect to be investigated was whether these collaboration types or their focus were specific to the scientific domain, as opposed to support needed in any online social network. Thus, we chose a general-purpose OSN – Facebook[5], in order to compare the results with those obtained for the SCNs. Facebook's inspection was conducted from September to October 2012 by two evaluators. The results[6] described in the next section show that although the categories of collaboration support are the same, the interaction strategies available are different in SCNs and OSNs.

It is worth noting that although the interface of all three systems have been modified since they were analyzed in our study, the results are still of interest to the community, since they do not focus on interface elements, but rather on the identification of scientific collaboration strategies in SCNs, as will be presented in the next section.

---

[4] At the time of the analysis Research Gate and academia.edu claimed to be used by over 1.5 and 2 million users, respectively. Currently (Feb. 2015) the number of users have increased to over 6 million users for Research Gate and over 18 million for academia.edu according to their websites - http://www.researchgate.net/ and http://www.academia.edu, respectively.

[5] At the time of the study (2012) Facebook had already reached over 1 billion users. In Feb. 2015 Facebook reports (http://newsroom.fb.com/company-info/) having over 1.39 billion active users.

[6] Due to the limited space available, we only present the final results of the analysis and not the individual analysis of each system.

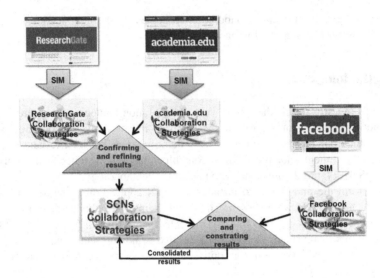

Fig. 2. Study methodology

5   Collaboration Strategies

The analysis of ResearchGate, academia.edu and Facebook allowed us to identify four categories through which members collaborate: information sharing, interaction levels, communities and artifacts. Although the categories are the same for SCNs and OSNs, the strategies adopted in each context are different.

5.1   Information Sharing

Users share information about themselves in ResearchGate, academia.edu and Facebook. However, the nature of the information of interest is different depending on the focus of the network system. In SCNs the focus is on aspects related to the person's research and expertise. Thus, these systems' information fields focus on users' background and research, such as their affiliation, their advisors, disciplines, skills and experience in research.

The **nature of the information shared** differs in SCNs and OSNs, since in the latter the information is more of a social focus. Thus, it usually includes general information about the person, such as birthday, civil status or sexual preferences. OSNs may also include some pieces of information related to professional aspects, such as workplace and professional skills, but these are superficial when compared to the researcher profile information in SCNs.

SCNs and OSNs also differ in relation to the **visibility of users' informabion**. In SCNs all information about a user is visible by all other users in the system, and there are no privacy settings available. This is suitable to the scientific context given that one of its main goals is to facilitate scientific knowledge dissemination and to provide visibility to one's work. Thus, it is interesting for researchers to know other researchers' background, as well as having access to their publications. OSNs, on their turn, consider that users may have different relationships with different people, and thus users may not want to share the same information with all other members of the network system. For instance, Facebook offers complex privacy settings to users, allowing them to define with whom they share the different pieces of information about themselves.

Another relevant aspect in SCNs is the researcher's scientific **reputation**, which refers to the reliability and significance of the information generated by each one. Therefore, SCNs present indicators regarding the relevance of each researcher's work. Some indicators are already associated to research (e.g. impact factor), whereas others are generated by the system itself and take into consideration data collected through the interaction of users, such as how many followers a researcher has, or how many of his/her publications were requested or downloaded. In this direction ResearchGate offers among other stats the RG Score for each researcher and academia.edu offers an analytical overview on the number of times that a researcher's profile, as well as his/her documents were visualized in the previous thirty days. OSNs do not always offer indicators associated to reputation, for instance in Facebook there is no such indicator. Nonetheless, when they do, indicators tend to point to users' popularity in the system. For instance, Orkut showed how many of a users' friends declared being their fan.

5.2   Interaction Levels

The analysis performed showed that SCNs offer researchers different levels of interaction with other researchers. The first interaction level identified is a weak tie relationship, which we have denominated **coexistence relationship**, and is available by default to all users of the system. This relationship allows any researcher to interact with any other researcher through asynchronous messages. These messages can either be of free content – user defines content of message; or of predefined content – the message is predefined by the system, and is sent by the system from one user to the other by request of the sender, for instance, requesting a copy of a publication. This type of relationship is also present in OSNs. However, the predefined messages are of a social nature, e.g. request to be a friend.

The second interaction level, called **unidirectional interest relationship**, represents relationships in which it is sufficient for one of the parties involved to be interested for a relationship to be established with another user. In SCNs they represent the possibility for a researcher to unilaterally state their interest in obtaining information on another network users' work. In the analyzed SCNs, instances of such a relationship were represented by the possibility of a researcher to "follow" other researchers within the system, being informed automatically about their updates or new content shared by them.

In OSNs unidirectional interest relationships may be available, but are not the main type of interaction between users. For instance, in Facebook, users may follow other users in order to receive information about them. However, this relationship is turned off by default and, if users wish to allow others to establish a unidirectional interest relationship to themselves, they must explicitly activate that possibility. Thus, we may conclude that it is expected that most users will not have an interest in such relationship.

The third interaction level identified is **bidirectional interest relationship**. This level consists of a situation in which two researchers establish a unidirectional interest to each other. For instance, researcher A decides to follow researcher B and researcher B also decides to follow researcher A. In this case, the system may treat them as two unidirectional interest relationships, or it may identify that the relationship is bidirectional and augment the relationship between the two by increasing the possibilities of interaction between them. For instance, in ResearchGate when two researchers follow each other they are allowed to suggest a publication to each other through the system. In academia.edu, on the other hand, this situation is treated as two independent unidirectional interest relationships.

Besides the previous levels of interaction, we have identified a stronger type of relationship, which we have denominated **trust relationship**. This relationship requires two users to agree upon establishing a relationship between themselves. For instance, in ResarchGate it is characterized by two researchers defining themselves as each other's "contact". To do so, a user adds another user as a contact and the latter has to accept the relationship. In ResearchGate[7] this level of interaction offered users a broader range of collaboration and communication between themselves, such as one being able to introduce another researcher to a trusted relation. In OSNs the friendship relationship is an instance of a trust relationship.

5.3   Communities

Communities in SCNs can be seen as a space for a group of people with common interests to communicate with each other and share content related to those interests. Specifically in this type of system, we can describe two types of communities: **communities of interest** and **working groups**. In the first one, the goal is to group content provided in these systems in specific areas of research, allowing for discussion on specific topics within these areas, besides involving a variable and unlimited number of people. These communities are open and users can join them without the need for approval, encouraging them to share their knowledge within such communities. In addition, users can create a community of interest at any moment, simply entering a name for it. However, a novel community name may require approval by system administrators to ensure that it is a research topic. The working group, on its turn, is a closed group, with a limited number of people. This community can be created by a user in order to allow for collaboration (not just discussion) between a specific group of researchers.

In ResearchGate, communities of interest are named "Topics" and their functioning is similar to forums devoted to discussing the scientific issues and sharing knowledge, in the form of questions, links, publications and archives. In academia.edu, these communities are named "Research Interests", which aim at bringing together people, questions, documents, journals and jobs within a specific area of research/knowledge.

---

[7] In the evaluated version of the ResearchGate all four interaction levels were available to users. However, an informal inspection of the current version indicates that these levels seem to have been simplified and reduced to only the first two levels.

Concerning the working groups, ResearchGate offered the resource known as "Workgroup"[8], which gave access to tools to facilitate collaborative work at a distance, such as collaborative document editing.

OSNs may offer users the possibility to create groups for (a subset of) their contacts on whatever topic they decide. For instance, Facebook works with the idea of groups, which can be open, closed or secret, and, within these, users can send messages, create events, share ideas, add photos, videos or files, or ask a question. It is interesting to notice that people have appropriated these groups and often use them for a virtual place for a workgroup. For instance, studies show that Facebook groups have been used in educational settings to support online or face-to-face courses [7, 10].

Once again both SCNs and OSNs may present the same categories of communities, however, the strategies of use of these communities are different. In SCNs communities of interest are public by definition and their topic must be recognized as a research topic. Working groups, on their turn, focus on offering more resources to researchers. In OSNs users can create their own groups or communities which are highly configurable and can be used for a wide range of purposes – from social purposes (sharing recipes with friends) or to work related purposes (supporting a course).

5.4 Artifacts

In SCNs, artifacts are related to scientific publications or material that can be referenced or made available through the system to disseminate research and allow users to collaborate with each other. In both SCNs analyzed researchers can include references to scientific articles and, if desired, also upload the associated text. However, the categories of **publications** and their organization are different. In ResearchGate the focus is on scientific articles. Users can view publication's content, suggest it to others or share it within the system. In academia.edu besides scientific articles, users can classify their publications as books, talks, teaching documents, drafts, book reviews, presentations or thesis chapters.

In the case of OSNs, artifacts are not categorized according to their publication type as in SCNs, they are just files that can be shared. The exceptions are photos and videos, which offer some specific actions that can be performed on them, e.g. tagging someone in a photo.

6 Discussion

Based on results obtained from the analysis of ResearchGate and academia.edu, and the contrast with the results of Facebook analysis, we can verify that the collaboration categories or types available are basically the same in SCNs and OSNs. However, the strategies provided and how they are emphasized characterizes the difference between these systems.

---

[8] Subsequently to our analysis, the name of this resource was changed to "Project" and this resource is not available anymore, in current version of ResearchGate (Feb. 2015).

Regarding user information available in the system, SCNs and OSNs focus on different information about a person. In SCNs, the focus is on professional and research related information. In these systems, such information is always visible, in order to stimulate scientific collaboration among its members. In OSNs, in turn, user information is more general and more interesting in social or informal contexts. Also, the f focus on information visibility is completely different. In SCNs reputation is built based on the number of people who have seen or are interested in the information shared. In OSNs the concern with privacy, being able to limit access to information.

Interaction levels have been classified in four different levels ranging from unidirectional to trust relationships. When comparing SCNs and OSNs, although both of them may include all four levels, their focus is different. In OSNs the most important relationship is friendship which is a trust relationship (strong tie). In SCNs, on their turn, the focus is on following another researcher's work, which is a unidirectional interest relationship (weak tie).

In SCNs communities play an important role, since they are one of the main places where scientific collaboration can occur within these systems. From the moment they become a user of an SCN, users are encouraged to join topics or research interests. Furthermore, in these systems, users' homepages always show the latest updates and discussions conducted within their topics of interest. In OSNs, community topics and rules are freely defined by users. Users may even choose to use communities for work purposes or scientific collaboration, but in this case they may limit the range of their reach to new collaborators.

As to artifacts, SCN's organize files according to their meaning to the community – so a draft and a published paper are distinguished in the system, whereas in OSN the distinction is related to medium of the file, there are different actions available depending on the file being a text or a photo.

7   Final Remarks

In this paper we have set out to investigate whether SCNs offered collaboration strategies that were specific to the scientific collaboration context. To do so, we applied the Semiotic Inspection Method to two SCNs – Research Gate and academia.edu, and contrasted their collaboration strategies to the one identified in an OSN – Facebook. Although all three systems analyzed had their interface modified after our study, the results are still interesting, given that they focus on the identification and discussion of scientific collaboration strategies in SCNs, rather than on interface elements.

The analysis indicated that both SCNs and OSNs offer users 4 types of collaboration opportunities, information sharing, interaction levels, communities and artifacts. Nonetheless, the strategies identified for SCNs and OSNs regarding each of these types are very different..

Our findings contribute to characterizing collaboration in SCNs and to the research regarding such systems. The strategies identified are directed to supporting scientific collaboration among users. As such they can be used by designers of SCNs to reflect upon the possible collaboration an SCN could support and which ones would be more relevant to prioritize in different contexts. They can also be used to evaluate the collaboration support of an SCS or compare different systems.

The next steps in our research involve using the identified categories and strategies to analyze other SCNs, allowing us to characterize the system, as well as consolidate them even further. Furthermore, we intend to analyze virtual networks aimed at other domains (e.g. education) to investigate whether the collaboration categories identified are the same (or not), and which strategies are used. A semiotic analysis of the results may allow us to identify which classes of signs are related to collaboration in general, and which are domain dependent.

Acknowledgments. The authors would like to thank FAPEMIG and INCT-Web (INWeb) (MCT/CNPq n° 57.3871/2008-6) for partially funding their research.

References

1. Arda, Z.: Academicians on online social networks: visibility of academic research and amplification of audience. Estudios Sobre el Mensaje Periodistico **18**, 67–75 (2012)
2. Cao, X., Cai, Z., Hua, Z., Zhang, X.: Understanding user's sustained participation in social research network sites. PACIS 2014 Proceedings. Paper 37 (2014). http://aisel.aisnet.org/pacis2014/37
3. de Souza, C.S., Leitão, C.F., Prates, R.O., Bim, S.A., da Silva, E.J.: Can inspection methods generate valid new knowledge in HCI? The case of semiotic inspection. Int. J. Hum. Comput. Stud. **68**, 22–40 (2010)
4. de Souza, C.S.: The Semiotic Engineering of Human Computer Interaction. MIT Press, Cambridge (2005)
5. de Souza, C.S., Leitão, C.F., Prates, R.O., da Silva, E.J.: The semiotic inspection method. In: Proceedings of VII Brazilian Symposium on Human Factors in Computing Systems (IHC 2006), pp. 148–157. ACM, New York (2006). http://doi.acm.org/10.1145/1298023.1298044
6. de Souza,C.S., Leitão, C.F.: Semiotic Engineering Methods for Scientific Research in HCI. Synthesis Lectures Series. Morgan & Claypool, San Francisco (2009)
7. Everson, M., Gundlach, E., Miller, J.: Social media and the introductory statistics course. Comput. Hum. Behav. **29**(5), A69–A81 (2013)
8. Lackes, R., Siepermann, M., Frank, M.: Social networks as an approach to the enhancement of collaboration among scientists. Int. J. Web Based Communities **5**(4), 577–592 (2009)
9. Lopes, G.R., Moro, M.M., Wives, L.K., de Oliveira, J.P.M.: Collaboration recommendation on academic social networks. In: Dobbie, G., et al. (eds.) ER 2010. LNCS, vol. 6413, pp. 190–199. Springer, Heidelberg (2010)
10. Munoz, C., Towner, T.: Opening facebook: how to use facebook in the college classroom. In: Proceedings of Society for Information Technology & Teacher Education International Conference 2009, pp. 2623–2627. AACE, VA (2009)
11. Parameswaran, M., Whinston, A.B.: Social computing: an overview. Commun. Assoc. Inform. Syst. **19**, 762–780 (2007)
12. Peirce, C.S.: In: Houser, N., Kloesel, C. (eds.) The Essential Peirce, vols. I and II. Indiana University Press, Bloomington (1992, 1998)
13. Schleyer, T., Butler, B.S., Song, M., Spallek, H.: Conceptualizing and advancing research networking systems. ACM TOCHI **19**(1), Article 2, 26 (2012). http://doi.acm.org/10.1145/2147783.2147785

14. Thelwall, M., Kousha, K.: ResearchGate: disseminating, communicating, and measuring Scholarship?. J. Assoc. Inform. Sci. Technol. **65**, 721–731 (2014)
15. Velden, T.: Explaining field differences in openness and sharing in scientific communities. In: Proceedings of the 2013 Conference on Computer Supported Cooperative Work (CSCW 2013), pp. 445–458. ACM (2013). http://doi.acm.org/10.1145/2441776.2441827

Author Index

Printed in the United States
By Bookmasters